Charles Darwin's *The Origin of Species*
New interdisciplinary essays

This volume marks a new approach to a seminal work of the modern scientific imagination: Charles Darwin's *The Origin of Species* (1859). Darwin's central theory of natural selection neither originated, nor could not be contained within the parameters of the natural sciences, but continues to shape and challenge our most basic assumptions about human social and political life.

Seven new readings, crossing the fields of history, literature, sociology, anthropology and history of science, demonstrate the complex position of the text within cultural debates past and present. Contributors examine the reception and rhetoric of the *Origin* and its influence on systems of classification, the nineteenth-century women's movement, literary culture (criticism and practice), and Hinduism in India. At the same time, a re-reading of Darwin and Malthus offers a constructive critique of our attempts to map the hybrid origins and influences of the text.

This volume will be the ideal companion to Darwin's work for all students of literature, social and cultural history and history of science.

David Amigoni is Senior Lecturer in English Studies at the University of Sunderland, and Jeff Wallace is Senior Lecturer in English at the University of Glamorgan.

D0495754

(TEXTS·IN·CULTURE

Series editors

Stephen Copley and Jeff Wallace

Advisory editors

David Aers, University of East Anglia
Lynda Nead,Birkbeck College, London
Gillian Beer, Girton College, Cambridge
Roy Porter, Wellcome Institute for the
History of Medicine
Anne Janowitz, Brandeis University, USA
Bernard Sharratt, University of Kent

This new series offers a set of specially commissioned, cross-disciplinary essays on a text of seminal importance to Western culture. Each text has had an impact on the way we think, write and live beyond the confines of its original discipline and it is only through an understanding of its multiple meanings that we can fully appreciate its importance.

Adam Smith's *Wealth of Nations*
Stephen Copley, Kathryn Sutherland (eds)

Charles Darwin's *The Origin of Species*
David Amigoni, Jeff Wallace (eds)

Sigmund Freud's *Interpretation of Dreams*
Laura Marcus (ed.)

Simone de Beauvoir's *The Second Sex*
Ruth Evans (ed.)

Niccolo Machiavelli's *The Prince*
Martin Coyle (ed.)

Charles Darwin's
THE ORIGIN
OF SPECIES

New interdisciplinary essays

DAVID AMIGONI
JEFF WALLACE

editors

Manchester University Press
Manchester and New York

distributed exclusively in the USA
and Canada by St Martin's Press

Published by Manchester University Press
Oxford Road, Manchester M13 9PL, UK
and Room 400, 175 Fifth Avenue, New York, NY 10010, USA

Distributed exclusively in the USA and Canada
by St. Martin's Press, Inc.,
175 Fifth Avenue, New York, NY 10010, USA

British Library Cataloguing-in-Publication Data
A catalogue record is available from the British Library

Library of Congress Cataloging-in-publication Data
Charles Darwin, the origin of species : new interdisciplinary essays /
    edited by David Amigoni and Jeff Wallace.
        p.   c.m. — (Texts in culture)
    Includes bibliographical references (p.   ) and index.
        ISBN 0-7190-4024-8 (hardback). — ISBN 0-7190-4025-6 (paperback)
        1. Darwin, Charles, 1809-1882. On the origin of species.
    2. Evolution (Biology). 3. Natural selection. I. Amigoni, David.
    II. Wallace, Jeff, 1958–   . III. Series.
    OH365.08C48 1995
    575.01'62—dc20   94-26485
                                                            CIP

ISBN 0-7190-4024 8 *hardback*
ISBN 0-7190-4025-6 *paperback*

Typeset in Apollo by Koinonia, Manchester
Printed in Great Britain by Biddles Limited, Guildford and King's Lynn

Contents

Series introduction

Texts are produced in particular cultures and in particular historical circumstances. In turn, they shape and are shaped by those cultures as they are read and re-read in changing circumstances by different groups with different commitments, engagements and interests. Such readings are themselves then re-absorbed into the ideological frameworks within which the cultures develop. The seminal works drawn on by cultures thus have multiple existences within them, exerting their influence in distinct and perhaps contradictory ways. As these texts have been 'claimed' by particular academic disciplines, however, their larger cultural significance has often been obscured.

Recent work in cultural history and textual theory has stimulated critical awareness of the complex relations between texts and cultures, highlighting the limits of current academic formations and opening the possibility of new approaches to interdisciplinarity. At the same time, however, the difficulties of interdisciplinary work have become increasingly apparent at all levels of research and teaching. On the one hand the abandonment of disciplinary specialisms may lead to amorphousness rather than challenging interdisciplinarity: on the other, interdisciplinary approaches may in the end simply create new specialisms or sub-specialisms, with their own well guarded boundaries. In these circumstances, yesterday's ground-breaking interdisciplinary study may become today's autonomous (and so potentially circumscribed) discipline, as has happened, it might be argued, in the case of some forms of History of Ideas.

The volumes in this series highlight the advantages of interdisciplinary work while at the same time encouraging a critical reflexiveness about its limits and possibilities; they seek to stimulate consideration both of the distinctiveness and integrity of individual disciplines, and of the transgressive potential of interdisciplinarity. Each volume offers a collection of new essays on a text of seminal intellectual and cultural importance, displaying the insights to be gained from the juxtaposition of disciplinary perspectives and from the negotiation of disciplinary boundaries. Our editorial stance is avowedly 'cultural', and in this sense the volumes represent a challenge to the conception of authorship which locates the significance of the text in the individual act of creation; but we assume that no issues (including those of disciplinarity and authorship) are foreclosed, and that individual volumes, drawing contributions from a broad range of disciplinary standpoints, will raise questions about the texts they examine more by the perceived disparities of approach that they encompass than by any interpretative consensus that they demonstrate.

All essays are specially commissioned for the series and are designed to be approachable to non-specialist as well as specialist readers: substantial editorial introductions provide a framework for the debates conducted in each volume, and highlight the issues involved.

Stephen Copley, University of York
Jeff Wallace, University of Glamorgan

A note on the text

All references to *The Origin of Species* in this volume, except where otherwise stated, are to the Penguin English Library (Harmondsworth, 1968) edition, edited by J. W. Burrow, of the 1859 text (first edition). Only the first
edition of the *Origin* is now available in print; a facsimile of this edition is
published by Harvard University Press. An invaluable aid to any close
study of the *Origin* and its textual history is Morse Peckham, *The Origin of
Species by Charles Darwin: A Variorum Text* (Philadelphia: University of
Pennsylvania Press, 1959), which clearly and systematically presents all
changes made by Darwin to the text across its six volumes. This edition is
unfortunately also out of print.

Chronology

This is a selective chronology which places the formation and reception of the *Origin* in a range of cultural and historical contexts. The entries refer mainly but not wholly to texts and events which feature significantly in the essays comprising the volume.

1794(–96) Erasmus Darwin, *Zoonomia*

1798 Thomas Malthus, *Essay on the Principle of Population*

1802 William Paley, *Natural Theology*

1809 Birth of Charles Darwin
J.B. Lamarck, *Philosophie Zoologique*

1830(–33) Charles Lyell, *Principles of Geology*

1831 British Association for the Advancement of Science

1832(–36) Voyage of HMS. *Beagle* (Darwin's researches published 1839–46)
First Reform Bill

1832(–34) Harriet Martineau, *Illustrations of Political Economy*

1833(–36) *Bridgewater Treatises*

1834 Abolition of slavery in British dominions
New Poor Law

1837 Darwin begins work on the Transmutation notebooks
William Whewell, *History of the Inductive Sciences*

1838 *The People's Charter*

1839(–49) Chartist agitation

1842 Preliminary sketch for *Origin*
The Structure and Distribution of Coral Reefs published

1844 Second Preliminary sketch for *Origin*
Robert Chambers, *The Vestiges of the Natural History of Creation*

1851 The Great Exhibition, Crystal Palace

1857 The Indian Mutiny; Britain founds Universities of Calcutta, Bombay and Madras

1858 Presentation of Darwin and Wallace papers at Linnaean Society

British Government assumes sole rule of India

1859
November *Origin*, First Edition published

John Stuart Mill, *On Liberty*; Samuel Smiles, *Self-Help*; Karl
Marx, *Critique of Political Economy*

1860
January *Origin*, Second Edition published
March/April   Adam Sedgwick, review of *Origin*, in *The Spectator*
April   Richard Owen, review of *Origin*, in *Edinburgh Review*
June–July   Articles on Darwin in *All the Year Round*
December   Serialisation of *Great Expectations* begins in *All the Year Round*

1861
April *Origin*, Third Edition published

1862 Herbert Spencer, *First Principles*

1862(–64) Max Müller, *Lectures on the Science of Language*

1863 James Hunt, foundation of The Anthropological Society of London
     T. H. Huxley, *Man's Place in Nature*; Charles Kingsley, *The Water Babies*

1864(–67) Herbert Spencer, *Principles of Biology*

1865(–66) Governor Eyre controversy

1866
December *Origin*, Fourth Edition published
     Women's Suffrage Committee

1867 Fleeming Jenkin critique, *North British Review*
     First Parliamentary debate on Women's Suffrage
     Second Reform Bill

1868
January *The Variation of Plants and Animals under Domestication* published

1869
August *Origin*, Fifth Edition published
     Francis Galton, *Hereditary Genius*; Matthew Arnold, *Culture and Anarchy*; John Stuart Mill, *The Subjection of Women*

1871
February *Descent of Man* published
     St. George Mivart, *Genesis of Species*

1871(–72) George Eliot, *Middlemarch*

1872
February *Origin*, Sixth Edition published
     The Expression of Emotions in Man and Animals published
     Samuel Butler, *Erewhon*

1873 Max Müller, 'Mr Darwin's Philosophy of Language', *Fraser's Magazine*

1875 Debate on the ethics of vivisection – Frances Power Cobbe's anti-vivisectionist Bill

1876 George Eliot, *Daniel Deronda*

1878 Thomas Hardy, *The Return of the Native*

1

Introduction: difficulty and defamiliarisation—language and process in *The Origin of Species*

JEFF WALLACE

Defamiliarisations

By the spring of 1838, Charles Darwin seemed well aware of the revolutionary potential of his developing materialist theories of nature, though expressing that awareness – even to himself – in characteristically hesitant fashion. 'Mention', he wrote in his transmutation notebook C, 'persecution of early Astronomers, – then add chief good of individual scientific men is to push their science a few years in advance only of their age...'[1] Over twenty years later, in the third edition of the *Origin*, this instruction came to fruition via an insertion made in one of the text's most memorable passages: that suggesting the possibility of the eye, in its complexity and apparent perfection, having been formed by the process of natural selection rather than by an act of Divine creation. Having freely confessed that this proposition would seem 'absurd in the highest possible degree', Darwin nevertheless interposed: 'When it was first said that the sun stood still and the world turned round, the common sense of mankind declared the doctrine false; but the old saying of *Vox populi, vox Dei*, as every philosopher knows, can never be trusted in science.'[2]

It is significant enough that in these instances Darwin chose to align himself with figures, such as Galileo, who had inititated irrevocable changes in cosmological thinking. This helps to complicate the long-received image of a man so overburdened with timidity and humility that the defence of his theories had largely to be conducted by others. But of equal significance is a particular representation of the nature of scientific revolutions and, by extension, of the manner in which scientific knowledges might exert their general influence. Cosmologies become transformed into a 'common sense', held by 'mankind', which can then only be shattered by a science willing to confront popular opinion with the 'absurd.'

In fact, as a mid-nineteenth-century natural scientist, Darwin's relation to notions of 'common sense' was a contradictory one, reflecting the complex transformations occurring within 'science' both as an ideology and as a set of practices and institutions in British culture. It has been argued, with particular reference to the founding of the British Association for the Advancement of Science in 1831, that the word 'science' took on new and narrower meanings in the 1830s and 1840s, ceasing to be a synonym for all knowledge and becoming instead the definition of a specific and allegedly more powerful mode of understanding.[3] This coincides with a process of professionalisation which gained momentum throughout the Victorian period. Yet it remained crucial for the ideological maintenance of that power for science to retain a kind of invisibility – to continue to appear not as the instrument of bourgeois hegemony it was becoming but, in the words of its most prominent practitioners and popularisers, as 'nothing but *trained and organized common sense*' (T. H. Huxley) or 'simply a higher development of common knowledge' (Herbert Spencer).[4]

The Origin of Species (1859) exhibits this tension between the familiar and the absurd, tradition and revolution, in its own form. Led by a mingled tone of painstaking honesty, caution and self-criticism, it is not impossible to read the *Origin* as a humble enquiry, paradoxically deriving its astonishing facts and conclusions from a method of empirical observation which the layman would adopt as a matter of course. At the same time, however, the text issues frequent reminders that its reception is dependent upon a decisive epistemological break or paradigm shift. Darwin's readers would need to be jolted out of their 'common-sense' complacencies, whether these took the form of that 'familiarity' which 'alone prevents our seeing how universally and largely the minds of our domestic animals have been modified by domestication' (p. 240), or of the 'load of prejudice' and 'blindness of preconceived opinion' which in the final 'Recapitulation and Conclusion' chapter are taken to characterise the widespread opposition to theories of the mutability of species. Such opposition, it should be noted, is here seen to reside within the established scientific community; Darwin's greatest hopes for the success of the *Origin* lay in the educated general public for whom it was orientated and in the generation of 'young and rising naturalists' whose minds were yet resistant to the hardening of creationist dogma (pp. 453–4). But the model of scientific world-pictures, assuming a notion of influence which pervades universalised entities such as 'mankind', can effectively subsume such specificities, and has certainly carried over into writing about the *Origin* itself. Thus, Ernst Mayr writes in the introduction to his 1966 edition of the text that 'every modern discussion of man's future, the population explosion, the struggle for existence, the purpose of man and the universe, and man's place in nature rests on Darwin'.[5] Mayr's important work lies firmly within a heroic mode which is familiar in Darwin criticism.

How appropriate are these models of influence for representing the enormous significance of a text like Darwin's *Origin*? How useful are they for exploring the complex and varied impacts of the text within a particular culture or cultures? Perhaps any fresh approach to the *Origin*, such as this volume of essays seeks to adopt, should start with the same kind of process of defamiliarisation, both of the text and of its cultural status, as Darwin himself hoped to achieve with his work. As the Russian Formalist critics of the early twentieth century maintained, habitualised perception prevents us from seeing things as they are. Faced with the most commonly abbreviated forms of the text's lengthy title, *The Origin of Species* or, more familiarly within intellectual life, the *Origin*, we may need to confront a process of linguistic naturalisation by reminding ourselves that Darwin's text is about the *origin* of *species*.

Or is it? One recent authority has suggested that, had

Darwin published his best-known book under its existing title
today, 'he would have been in trouble under the Trades
Descriptions Act', because, 'if there is one thing which the
Origin is not about, it is the origin of species. Darwin knew
nothing about genetics.'[6] This provocative observation reminds
us that we should not be completely misled by the second part
of the text's main title, 'by Means of Natural Selection'. While
the theory, or metaphor, of natural selection as a mechanism of
species-generation was clearly the central and most revolutionary proposal of the text, it was not the only form of species-
generation, as Darwin was all too ready to admit. Natural
selection was the 'steady accumulation' and preservation of
differences beneficial to individual organisms in the 'struggle
for life', eventually giving rise to the emergence of new species
– an external process working on internal variations across
countless generations. Such variations are rooted in 'the strong
principle of inheritance', but the laws governing inheritance
remained 'quite unknown' (p. 76). It has thus remained custom-
ary (though, as Robert Young has pointed out, somewhat 'crude
and anachronistic' in the light of Darwin's work as a whole) to
view the *Origin* as existing in a state of anticipation, awaiting
Gregor Mendel's discoveries of 1863, though yet having to wait
until the early twentieth century for the full revelation of those
discoveries, when a new synthesis of knowledge could be
produced to revive the by-now flagging fortunes of Darwinian
natural selection as a theory for explaining evolutionary change.[7]

To prise Darwin's title out of its self-evidence and look at
it afresh is thus to expose ambiguities. To the previous consid-
erations we can add two further, and apparently polarised,
senses in which the word 'origin' might signify within the text.
First, if the *Origin* is not about genetic origin, then neither is it
about the origin of life itself, upon which the development of
species is clearly predicated. While Darwin felt compelled to
challenge the principles of independent species-creationism
with a concept of 'the laws impressed upon matter by the
Creator', determining production and extinction through 'secondary causes', the issue of an ultimate beginning for species
inevitably impinged upon his project in the *Origin*. In the final
chapter of the first edition, the issue is approached with a

caution which verges on indecision and contradiction: the belief that 'animals have descended from at most only four or five progenitors, and plants from an equal or lesser number', is swiftly but hesitantly modified to allow the inference 'from analogy' that 'probably all the organic beings which have ever lived on this earth have descended from some one primordial form, into which life was first breathed' (pp. 454–5). Perhaps appropriately, the closing lines of the work refer to life, 'with its several powers, having been originally breathed into a few forms or into one...' (pp. 459–60). In subsequent editions there is some tinkering with these lines, including the attempt to suggest of the inference concerning one primordial originary form that 'it is immaterial whether or not it be accepted'.[8] Darwin was later to regret what he called the 'truckling to opinion' implicit in his reluctant broaching of such issues; yet it was perhaps disingenuous to claim that the text simply had 'nothing to do' with the origin of life itself (p. 234). Predictably enough, creationist critics exploited his hesitancy over the creation of one or several original forms; as Thomas Wollaston argued:

> To our mind, the wonder consists in the act *at all*, and not in the number of times that it may have been repeated: for a Being that *can create* may surely do so as often as he pleases; and we have no right therefore to limit that act, – at any rate on the question of its *probability*; for, if we admit that it has been exerted so much as once, there is no *a priori* reason why it should not have been a million times repeated, or why, if he had so willed it, it might not, at some period or other, have been in constant operation.[9]

Howard Gruber's view that 'by avoiding the issue of the origin of life, the *Origin of Species* gains in simplicity what it loses in scope' therefore needs some revising.[10] Wollaston's objection is not just a reasonable response to the logical frailty of this aspect of the text; it is also a useful indication that Darwin could not draw up his own interpretative parameters for the *Origin*.

In this light, there may be only one sense in which we can state unequivocally that the *Origin* is about the origin of species. According to this view, the 'origin' lies neither in the power of a Creator, nor in material genetic changes within organisms, but in the human systems of taxonomy, and there-

fore of language, which define 'species' — a concept of species
which is 'morphological' rather than 'biological', at the same
time expressing Darwin's distance from the practice of 'species-
ism' *per se*. The key to this lies in Darwin's admission that:

> I look at the term species, as one arbitrarily given for the sake of
> convenience to a set of individuals closely resembling each other,
> and that it does not essentially differ from the term variety, which
> is given to less distinct and more fluctuating forms. The term vari-
> ety, again, in comparison with mere individual differences, is also
> applied arbitrarily, and for mere convenience sake. (p. 108)

'Does not essentially differ' here embodies the radical challenge posed by the *Origin* to the possibility of defining species
in either of the two senses previously discussed. To assert as
much is, of course, to do a kind of hermeneutic violence to
Darwin's intentions: the *Origin* is not a work of linguistic
philosophy, and Darwin was not in any explicit sense committed to dissolving the question of the origin of species into
semantic relativity. For him, the effort was to make categorisa-
tion coincide with complex but actual existences and developments in nature.[11] Yet in noting his belief that 'species come to
be tolerably well-defined objects' (p. 210), we must register a
crucial element of vagueness. Increasingly, commentators have
cited various forms of textual ambiguity as a basis for claims of
a momentous revolutionary significance — for example, as the
precise means by which Darwin in the *Origin* effectively prob-
lematised the relationship between human knowledge and the
material world, and sought to deconstruct the essentialism
underpinning the metaphysics of Western culture.

These initial 'defamiliarisations' bring us to the limits of the
analogy with Formalist poetics: while helping us to see the
Origin anew, they also reveal that there no thing itself to which
defamiliarisation can give us access — no 'stone' to be seen in
its original 'stoniness'.[12] Even if it is true, as Loewenberg usefully
suggests, that in the *Origin* 'the word "origin" was never used
in its sense of "beginning"; it always implied changes in the
development of life-forms already in existence', neither
Darwin's text nor his culture could allow him to limit the word
thus.[13] Nor can Loewenberg deduce from his point the more
general thesis that 'Darwin was rarely inhibited by epistemo-

logical reservations'.[14] On the contrary, epistemological uncertainty was central to an already-fertile discourse of evolutionary debate into which the *Origin* inevitably stepped: the pervasive interpenetration of the philosophical, ideological and religious with the scientific in this discourse makes attempts to fix the *Origin* as a work unclouded by doubt, metaphysics or linguistic ambiguity look like the bizarre effect of a subsequent academic culture itself obsessed with disciplinary essences.

Darwin criticism has nevertheless been overburdened by variations on the search for a purified, essential thing-in-itself. In some studies, we look over Darwin's shoulder as he annotates the margins of his reading, in an attempt to deduce the processes actually taking place at that time.[15] Such analysis is, of course, an inevitable product of the vast stock of Darwin papers now collected in the Darwin Archive at Cambridge University, giving rise to an extensive literature enabling us to reconstruct in some detail the psychological and intellectual formation of Darwin's thought from his return from the *Beagle* voyage in 1837 to the first publication of the *Origin* and beyond. Re-entering the arena of Darwin studies in 1982 after a decade's absence, Robert M. Young observed: '[S]cholars are looking deeper and deeper and in greater and greater detail into the minutiae of Darwin's notes and thought processes. What is it that we wish to find there? Is it the key to genius? Why is a higher and higher power microscope applied to rethinking the thoughts of the "great"?'[16]

Young's questions are important. In an ideal world, such studies could co-exist happily alongside more 'externalist' studies of Darwin's texts and their varying cultural interpretations. But all too often, the tendency either in the studies themselves or in our reading of them has been to view the establishing of an accurate picture of Darwin's mental landscape as a corrective to the inherently precarious condition of a textuality which can somehow never quite transcribe the presence and plenitude of thought. In the next two sections of this chapter, I want to address two kinds of perceived threat to the purity or integrity of Darwin's *Origin*. First I will consider the way in which debates around 'Social Darwinism' highlight the methodological issues and anxieties surrounding the attribution of a political

position to Darwin and/or the *Origin*. Then I want to question
the tendency to isolate the text as a single and radically discon-
tinuous act, principally by surveying the history of its successive editions. Finally, in exploring particular aspects of the form
and reception of the *Origin*, I want to indicate how difficulty
and uncertainty – prerequisites of a defamiliarised perspective
– are built into the fabric of its language and are thus integral
to what David Amigoni calls its 'epistemology of representation'.

Cumulatively, I want to suggest a sense of the problems
posed for any understanding of the *Origin*'s cultural impact by
reducing the text to the hypostatised expression of Darwin's
scientific mind. Elsewhere in this volume, Fiona Erskine points
to the contradictory readings which emerge as the *Origin* is
disseminated across the late-nineteenth-century field of debate
over gender and emancipation. Dermot Killingley's survey of
Indian culture and Hindu theology in the same period reveals
an equally complex process of appropriation, within which the
specificity of texts matters less than the legitimating power of
Darwin's name in conjunction with a cultural encounter of great
indeterminacy. By contrast, Kate Flint examines mediation and
transformation in the more precise context of the encounter
between Darwinian science and Charles Dickens's writing of
Great Expectations. 'Defamiliarisation' in these senses leads us
to see the text as a cultural process, in which formation involves
complex patterns of influence, reception implies a constantly
shifting encounter between text and readers, and in which
textual form itself constitutes a provisional realisation perpetu-
ally dissolving under the gaze of historians, scientists, the
broader readership which the *Origin*, since its publication, has
always enjoyed – and of Darwin himself.

Political Darwin or Social Darwinism?

James Moore, one of the most important recent figures in a
tradition of articulating Darwin's work as a social and political
phenomenon, has been able to identify the power of the
impulse to 'purify' his subject by reflecting on his own attempt
to 'launder Darwin's language' in his earlier work, *The Post-
Darwinian Controversies* (1979). It is not coincidental that, in a

text which attempts to save Darwin from various misrepresentations and thus to exculpate him from the ideological taints of Social Darwinism (even in the nuanced form of declaring that 'Darwin was not a social Darwinist in any straightforward or unambiguous sense'), Moore should lay claim to having located 'at least one passage in the *Origin of Species* that remained substantially unaltered throughout the book's six editions (1859–72)', and which therefore – though Moore might now dispute this implied logic – 'distils the essence of Darwinism into less than five hundred words'.[17] Here, a welcome moment of textual stability is used to guarantee the very notion of an 'essence' of Darwinism which can affirm a stability in the real thought of Darwin the individual and protect both text and thought from subsequent misappropriations. This 'essence', then, simultaneously protects Darwin's thought from the vagaries of textual change and reception, and protects science from politics.

Moore's strategy differs somewhat from Valentino Gerratana's observation that in Darwin we encounter a 'mind ... virtually devoid of economics and philosophy'.[18] Yet they coincide, both in terms of the theoretical construct of the pure empirical scientist which haunts their accounts and in terms of that tradition, outlined earlier, of speculations on the contents of Darwin's mind. Since Gerratana's essay in 1973, and even before, research into Darwin's intellectual formation can be said to have discredited his view. But such knowledge does not fully account for a question which his comment continues to beg: what kind of relationship do we need to assume between the contents of Darwin's texts and the contents of his mind?

The language of the *Origin* suggests in fact that Darwin's mind was far from devoid of economics and philosophy. On the contrary, the theory of natural selection is consistently and explicitly cast as a theory of political economy in nature. The initial analogy between artificial and natural selection prepares the ground for this: discussions of breeding and cultivation are always closely related to the 'state of civilisation' of the society in question, and factors of human economic change such as land enclosure recur in Darwin's analysis of ecological balance. In the articulation of natural selection proper, the vocabulary becomes more explicit, with the predication of a field of intense competition for places within a 'polity' or an 'economy of nature', or a 'natural economy of the country'. Unmistakably, the imputation of willed activity which Darwin seemed to find impossible to expunge from his representation is that of thrifty capitalist enterprise, where bees are 'anxious ... to save time' and natural selection itself 'continually trying to economise in every part of the organisation' (pp. 141 and 186). There is an effort to acknowledge that this discourse, while in some sense borrowed, has a substantial basis and pre-history in natural science – 'no naturalist doubts the advantage of what has been called the "physiological division of labour"' – while the dictum 'in order to spend on one side, nature is forced to economise on the other side' is traced to Goethe but also to Geoffroy Saint-Hilaire (pp. 141 and 185).

The spatial implications of Darwin's theory in the *Origin* also produce a discourse of territoriality which gives a more expansive feel to the principles of competitive economy. In speculating upon the progess of natural selection in a country undergoing climatic change, he notes: 'If the country were open upon its borders, new forms' (subsequently, 'intruders') 'would certainly immigrate, and this would seriously disturb the relations of some of the former inhabitants'; the impossibility of perfect adaptation means that natural selection will always have its work of improvement to do, for 'in all countries, the natives have been so far conquered by naturalised productions, that they have allowed foreigners to take firm possession of the land. And as foreigners have thus everywhere beaten some of the natives, we may safely conclude that the natives might have been modified with advantage, so as to have better resisted such intruders' (pp. 131–2). Thus in 'the great and complex battle of life', thrift and competitiveness in the domestic economy combines with the need for strong defensive policies of immigration control and a policy of rational imperial expansion, the 'naturalisation of plants through man's agency in foreign lands' acting as an analogy for this process. This 'war' necessitates strength in alien conditions: geological history is figured as military campaign, whereby 'the arctic and temperate productions will at a very late period have marched a little further

north, and subsequently have retreated to their present homes';
they will have 'been exposed to nearly the same climate' and
will have 'kept in a body together' (pp. 361–2). Yet such strength
is founded upon stability at home: in his 'little' experiments on
a 'little' pond, Darwin's imagery is of the 'table-spoons' and the
'breakfast cup', in a section ending with nature characterised
as a 'careful gardener', distributing her seeds in appropriate
places. The discourses of war and domesticity may seem
contrastive: but they could be said to gell perfectly at the level
of Victorian bourgeois ideology.

/A reading of the *Origin* thus makes it difficult to assert that
Darwin's mind was 'devoid' of economics and philosophy. A
more sustainable conclusion is that it was permeated by principles of political economy and philosophy in the form of a
language which did not differentiate between the political and
the biological./ Here, in other words, we need a theory of
language which incorporates a concept of the political or ideological unconscious, missing from Gerratana's account. Yet this
remains problematic: if we describe the language of the *Origin*
as inherently political, how far can we assume that Darwin was
unaware of such a sub-text? And where does it leave the matter
of 'placing' Darwin or the *Origin* in political terms?

[In the light of his famous identification of a reading of
Malthus's *Essay on the Principle of Population* (1798) as the key
element in the precipitation of his theory of 'struggle for existence' – 'the doctrine of Malthus applied with manifold force
to the whole animal and vegetable kingdoms' (p. 117) – it has
been possible to relate Darwin quite explicitly to the dominant
capitalist ideology of Victorian *laissez-faire* liberalism/ Some
definitions encourage us to see Darwin as a bourgeois scientist
with either mildy conservative leanings – thus James Moore
again, in 1979: 'Clearly, Darwin's world-view may be variously
regarded as Christian, Victorian, Anglo-Saxon, capitalist, and
middle-class. It forms the setting apart from which the theory
of natural selection, and Darwin's theory of human evolution
in particular, can hardly be understood' – or, in the case of
Howard Gruber's gloss on Darwin's own definition of his position on the political spectrum as 'Liberal or Radical', as a 'radical' only in a strictly non-revolutionary sense:

[C]oncerned more with the preservation and extension of individual liberty than with the preservation of hallowed social institutions; concerned more with human rights than with property
rights; favourably yet cautiously disposed towards social change;
unattached to any organised group that would pursue the desired
aims in a manner disturbing to the comfort and tranquility of
upper-middle-class life.[19]

Yet, another glance at the trajectory of James Moore's work on
Darwin indicates a significant shift in conceptualising the 'great
man's' political identity. In Moore's 1985 essay, he presented a
'squarson-naturalist' Darwin poised between epochs, 'neither a
clergyman *manqué* nor a professional scientist in the manner of
his later-Victorian followers, but a sort of transformed "vicar"
in the root sense of the word, the mediator of a struggling,
improving, but law-bound nature to a struggling, improving
but law-abiding society'.[20] In the recent biography, however,
Moore and Adrian Desmond lay far greater emphasis on the
depth of a Dissenting tradition in Darwin's formation, the
prominence of radical materialist debate during the years of his
scientific apprenticeship, and a consciousness of the deeply
subversive implications of his own materialism which led to a
'double-life' symbolised in the secret transmutation notebook
he began in 1837. To peer into Darwin's mind at this point is,
for Moore and Desmond, to find a 'pandemonium', mirroring
the turmoil of a country deep in recession and Chartist agitation, but drawing its internal energy from a theory which
would transform the 'whole [of] metaphysics.'[21]

However much Darwin scholarship might strive to reconstruct the condition of his mind in the years before 1859, the
Origin itself reveals, as I hope to show, the schizoid, contradictory position of 'my theory' within its culture, and more particularly its political culture, more pointedly than any such
psychological speculations. As many commentators have noted
in different ways, Darwin's language in the *Origin* is not so
much his own as that of his culture: and again, not so much a
unitary thing as a tapestry of discourses, borrowed or inherited, with varying degrees of mindfulness, from the evolution-
ism already evident in much social theory, from the Natural
Theology the *Origin* is in other ways an answer to, from the

literature, perhaps of Shakespeare, and certainly of Milton, Dickens and Wordsworth, as well as from a common stock of rhetoric which he raided in order to make the text the object of popular consumption he wanted it to be.

In political terms, therefore, the language of the *Origin* acts out the struggle taking place within Darwin between the various contradictory impulses both feeding into and emanating from his theory of transmutation by natural selection. If the text voices the assumptions and sentiments of a bourgeois political economy founded on natural inequalities, it also embodies what Gillian Beer has called a 'levelling tendency', emphasising community and equality through the organic historical links between all life forms and their continuing ecological interdependence. If it gives biological validation to an individualist relativity, rooted in the critique of 'species' as Platonic abstraction and the crucial importance of individual differences in the struggle for life, it equally validates an overriding collectivity predicated upon the idea of the structured population as the basic functional unit of geographical space.

Such contradictions are not to be resolved in the imaginary space of Darwin's mind, or even in a consideration of his explicit political actions and positions (though these were complex and contradictory enough). They are, rather, the cultural material out of which his text was forged, and out of which a seemingly endless number of political or Social Darwinisms could be constructed. One reason for dissociating the *Origin* from its origin lies in Raymond Williams's suggestion that 'Darwin was much too humane a man to think in terms which were later to become possible – of the elimination of unfavourable variations, or of social policy in this conscious sense, to which he never fully applied himself' (and this despite the observation in the *Origin* that 'hardly anyone is so careless as to allow his worst animals to breed' (p. 91)).[22] Yet Williams himself belongs to that group of critics on the Left of Darwin studies, along with Robert M. Young and James Moore, who have insisted on the always-already social nature of Darwin's work, and thus to the problems inherent in a term, Social Darwinism, predicated upon an initially guiltless scientific theory which is not or was not Social but which is capable of being injected with the virus of ideology.

The work of these writers undeniably lays the foundations for our present volume. Yet there is a danger, perhaps most apparent in the polemical work of Young, of reinstating an unnecessarily strict dichotomy. Once the inescapably social and political nature of Darwinian theory is established, the function of that position need not be to discredit the value of 'Social Darwinism' in denoting a process of tailoring and appropriation which did undoubtedly occur. Spencer's synthetic philosophy and its enormous influence in late-nineteenth-century Britain and America, Galton's eugenics and the extension of this science into pre-war British policies and propaganda, or Thatcherite and Reaganite free-market liberalism in the 1980s, all benefited from naturalisations which could be derived from the theories, and even the name, of Darwin. In collapsing Social Darwinism into the formula 'Darwinism is Social', we risk losing the value of a formulation which identifies certain concrete and contentious uses of Darwin's work in the realms of policymaking and *realpolitik*, and which at the same time does not necessarily threaten the epistemological position that his work is inherently political. More precisely, the value of the term is perhaps to indicate how Darwin's work, with the *Origin* as its initial and most revolutionary public face, marked to an unprecedented extent the explicit incorporation of natural science into all kinds of value system within our cultures.

In, however, seeking to modify the force of Moore's assertion that 'The routine distinction between "Darwinism" and "Social Darwinism" would have been lost on the author of the *Descent of Man*, and probably on most of his defenders until the 1890s', we must acknowledge the innovatory importance of the essay from which it is taken. In 'Socialising Darwinism: Historiography and the Fortunes of a Phrase' (1986), Moore not only suggests that it is the pervasive presence of evolutionary discourse in contemporary Western life which constitutes the political force of Darwin's work; he also argues that Social Darwinism itself is an effect of discourse, 'invented as a problem for social theory in the 1890s, when it became a matter of urgency to pacify and contain the demands of labour in newly expanding and restructuring economies'.[23] Reified by academic professionalisation and the accompanying fragmentation of disciplines and knowledges, Social Darwinism is for Moore 'an artefact of bourgeois perception':

> The problem for radicals is ... to reconstruct the common context of language and assumptions in which biological and social theories once intermingled, in which Darwinism was Social (Young, 1985), and then to explain why this 'commons' was enclosed, how the language and assumptions were parcelled out among professional interests, and what impact this had on the masses of lay people who thereafter were barred from 'informed' debate on biological and social questions that affected their political destinies.[24]

In the next two sections of this chapter, I want to concentrate on aspects of the form and language of the *Origin*, adopting Moore's position that it is language which constitutes the rich yet 'common context' of an influence which is at once scientific and cultural.

Text in process

> The *Origin of Species* had, in the space of thirteen years, undergone a textual evolution. Variations, in the form of Darwin's changes, had appeared throughout the work in five successive editions. Despite the fact that each separate change was both a continuation of the general thesis, and consistent with it, it was nonetheless change. Consequently, just as in organic evolution, the cumulative result of a long, successive, and interrelated series of changes was a product no longer consistent with the original.
>
> Peter J. Vorzimmer, 1970.[25]

Only in one restricted sense could the *Origin* be said to constitute a distillation or essence of Darwin's work on transmutation theory up to 1859; namely, the literal sense in which the first edition of the text was an abstract of a larger abstract, written over a period of some eight months and precipitated by the necessity of declaring his findings alongside those of Alfred Wallace after the famous co-presentation of papers at the meeting of the Linnaean Society on 1 July 1858. Despite his often-noted struggle with linguistic expression, we should not be too quick to assume that the composition of the *Origin* placed

Darwin under unforseen and intolerable pressure: many of the
text's most significant polemical points and rhetorical structures
had already been outlined in the sketches of 1842 and 1844;
and if, as Desmond and Moore have recently stressed, the issue
of publication and its perils had been prominent in Darwin's
mind for some considerable time, it seems likely that a reser-
voir of potential devices and formulations would already be in
place. Nevertheless, the first edition bears the marks of an
author determined to convince his readership that distillation
in this case meant an unsatistactorily partial and even provisional demonstration of work either already completed on a
larger scale or yet to be undertaken. 'I have discussed the probable origin of domestic pigeons at some, yet quite insufficient,
length...' (p. 88); 'If I had space I could quote numerous
passages...' (p. 90); 'To treat this subject at all properly, a long
catalogue of dry facts should be given; but these I shall reserve
for my future work...' (p. 101) – such formulations periodically
resurface to remind us of the acknowledged insufficiency of the
argument as it stood.

This is not to underestimate the confidence with which the
original text makes its claims. The fact that, for some time now,
the first edition has been the only version in print, is seen as a
testimony to its qualities of freshness and directness: for the
Harvard editor, Ernst Mayr, it 'represents Darwin in his most
revolutionary spirit', while for the Penguin editor John Burrow
it is 'a more clear-cut and forceful' version of its five successors. Yet Gillian Beer introduced an intriguing modification to
this view when she suggested, in 1983, that the 'expressive'
qualities of the first edition are precisely the condition of a
linguistic indeterminacy and thus potential multivalency
which, in subsequent editions, it was Darwin's task to limit and
control.[26]

Beer's emphasis on the comparative openness of the first
edition, combined with the process of modification subsequently undertaken, invites us to question the sufficiency of
the received notion of the *Origin* of 1859 as a single act of
momentous significance, and directs our attention instead
towards the text as a process. The *Origin* might thus be viewed
not just as a culmination but also as an intervention, both in

Darwin's own trajectory (Vorzimmer has called it a 'stop-gap') and in a set of firmly-established debates around development hypotheses and their broader implications.[27] What made the *Origin* particularly susceptible to absorption into an arena of questioning and debate, and thus to the need for periodical textual response on Darwin's part, was its peculiar combination of scientific rigour and accessible structure and register, necessitating the urgent attention of the scientific community while issuing, in its own form, a challenge to the sole authority of that community to pronounce on its validity; Gillian Beer has elsewhere noted Darwin's Wordsworthian project in the *Origin*, 'to resolve scientific and common discourse as throughly as possible'.[28]

The process of revising the *Origin* fell into two clear stages. After its publication by John Murray and sell-out in late November 1859, work on a revised edition of the text was in hand almost immediately. While the second edition, which was on sale by the turn of the year, embodied mostly minor changes, Darwin did take the opportunity to make certain more significant revisions in response to a critical furore which was already mounting: he chose, for example, to delete a key sentence in his speculations concerning a race of bears growing more aquatic till a creature might be produced 'as monstrous as a whale', though not, as Ellegård has pointed out, before critical damage had been done;[29] and he also deleted the comparison of the 'face of Nature' with a 'yielding surface' of 'ten thousand sharp wedges', which was to prove prominent and ambiguously suggestive for subsequent commentators. When, almost a year later and with about 3,800 copies sold, Murray indicated the need for a third edition, Darwin promised many 'corrections, or additions, ... in hopes of making my many rather stupid reviewers at least understand what is meant'.[30] Published in April 1861, this edition contained one important structural innovation, the 'Historical Sketch of the Progress of Opinion on the Origin of Species', and saw Darwin beginning to revise his position on – and thus, his formulation of – certain key issues such as the nature of evolutionary change through saltation. Extended reflections on the terms 'natural selection', with particular regard to the attributions of conscious volition to

which they had given rise, were directed towards those reviewers whose 'stupidity' can perhaps be deduced from the role of
the exclamation mark here: 'Others have objected that the term
selection implies conscious choice in the animals which become
modified; and it has even been urged that as plants have no
volition, natural selection is not applicable to them!'.[31] Yet the
third edition contained only 14 per cent of the total amount of
variation to which the text was to be subjected.

It was thus in the second phase of revision, from 1866 to
1872, that the *Origin* underwent its most extensive transmutations, leading in Vorzimmer's words to a product 'no longer
consistent with the original' or, more pointedly, to a 'mass of
contradictions and incongruities' amounting to considerable
'structural weakness'. There is some critical concensus on this
view: for James Moore, Darwin's theory still stood in the sixth
edition, though 'neither so elegantly nor impressively as
before', while for Robert Young it is a 'useful exaggeration' to
say that the book should by then have been re-titled '*On the
Origin of Species by Means of Natural Selection and All Sorts of
Other Things*'.[32] In the intervening period, Darwin had of course
had time to reflect upon the accumulation of responses to the
text while continuing the work on the laws of variation which
was to lead to the publication of his *Variation of Animals and
Plants under Domestication* (1868); and the fourth edition,
published in December 1866, was the most thoroughly revised
yet. But it was in the last two editions that Darwin was obliged
to respond most fully to criticism in a way which led to the
expansion and, as critics imply, the mis-shaping of the text.

Two particular critiques are of note here: the Scottish engi-
neer Fleeming Jenkin's extensive review in the *North British
Review* of June 1867, and the Catholic biologist St George Mivart's
book *On the Genesis of Species* (1871). Arguing from what he
modestly decribed as 'mere mathematics' – notoriously, one of
Darwin's theoretical weak spots – Jenkin constructed a powerful case against the efficiency of natural selection to perpetuate
slight favourable differences. The careful statistical reasoning
behind his insistence on the 'swamping' effect in nature
exposed the weakness of Darwin's adherence to 'blending
inheritance' as the mechanism of genetic variation. Just before

completing work on the fifth edition of the *Origin* in February 1869, Darwin was expressing his debts to Jenkin – 'has given me much trouble, but has been of more real use to me than any other essay or review'[33] – and acknowledged the debt explicitly in the edition (August 1869) which, as Vorzimmer has noted, revealed the 'full extent' to which the theory of natural selection had changed since the first edition.

The major structural changes to the sixth and final edition of the text were largely the result of Darwin's response to Mivart, against whose distortions and misrepresentations he felt lasting bitterness. Mivart had attempted to reconcile evolutionary theory with Catholic theology by insisting that the theory applied to the material world only; yet this did not prevent him at the same time from challenging Darwin's evolutionary mechanisms, reinstating saltation as a metaphysically-charged principle of transmutation and undermining Darwin's position on the retention of useless organs. In a new chapter VII, 'Miscellaneous Objections to the Theory of Natural Selection', Darwin incorporated his critique of Mivart alongside responses garnered from earlier sections of the text; this final edition was some 20 per cent larger than the first. But the inclusion of a Glossary of necesary scientific terms points towards what was, for the cultural status and reception of the *Origin*, perhaps the most significant aspect of change: this was the first edition of the text to be aimed at a popular market, completely re-set in a much smaller typeface and, at 7s6d, selling at half the previous price. Ellegård's study of the reception of the *Origin* has clearly established that the momentous public debate occasioned by the text throughout the 1860s could in no sense be described as a 'popular' debate; yet the first run of 3,000 copies of the sixth edition had sold out within a year, sales rising from 60 copies a month to 250.[34] It is thus worth emphasising this important disjunction: while in 1872 Darwin, in a condition of nervous stress, felt that he had at last exhausted his role in that cultural process which was the revision of and debate surrounding the *Origin*, the process was barely beginning for a wider audience set to benefit from the 1870 Education Act. The text which reached this audience, the sixth edition, was a rather different animal from the first edition which we are obliged to read today; yet it was arguably this sixth edition which achieved the great popular impact now associated with the *Origin*.

To this sense of the text itself as a process, several contributors in this volume add a sense of the continuity of the *Origin* with its historical and discursive contexts. Harriet Ritvo maintains that the revolutionary 'discontinuity' of the *Origin* is a direct result of 'the inevitable selectivity of the historical gaze'; in contrast to the 'constructed isolation' framed by a retrospect which perhaps combines Kuhnian theory with heroic Darwinian narratives, she argues with a subtle irony that the text 'would have seemed to emerge *naturally* from contemporary scientific debates and preoccupations' (italics mine). Wilberforce's outrage at the suggestion of anthropoid connections pales in the popular cultural context of Victorian monkey shows, where such connections were taken for granted. David Amigoni notes the extent to which the *Origin* is 'never quite the intellectual dynamite that speculations about the "Darwinian revolution" have led us to expect', while Ted Benton's emphasis on the specificity of Darwin's explanatory purposes requires us to situate his thought in the context of a 'distinctive discourse of natural history'. Even on the question of that deafening silence in the *Origin*, the position of humankind in the evolutionary order, Peter Bowler has elsewhere noted the effect of Chambers's *Vestiges of the Natural History of Creation* (1844) in preparing the ground of debate, so that 'by the time Darwin published the *Origin of Species* in 1859, no one could be in any doubt as to the implications of applying the theory of evolution to mankind'.[35] If therefore the *Origin* can be defined as an ongoing process in Darwin's own work, these accounts equally place it within rather than outside a whole cultural and intellectual process: there is indeed a sense in which 'the world' was ready for the text.[36]

In identifying the denial of teleology as the true element of radical discontinuity in the *Origin*, Thomas Kuhn also highlights something of the contradictory nature of this discontinuity. 'Evolution' was well established as a development hypothesis when Darwin wrote, articulated in the work of Lamarck, Chambers, Spencer and the German *Naturphilosophen*, but it was clearly seen as a 'goal-directed process', with each new evolutionary development a step on the road towards 'the "idea" of man'. Natural selection was thus at its own historical juncture an *anti*-evolutionary theory, making terms such as 'evolution', 'development' and 'progress' 'suddenly seem[ed] self-contradictory'." The dialectic between continuity and discontinuity in the *Origin* is a complex one; but to appreciate the extent to which defamiliarisation, in the form of a certain self-contradictoriness, was integral to Darwin's project in the text, we need to look more closely at some specific aspects of its rhetoric and reception.

Difficulty and ingenuity: language and science

It is known that for a long time Darwin was worried by the difficulty which he saw in the absence of a long chain of intermediate forms between closely-allied species, and that he found the solution of this difficulty in the supposed extermination of intermediate forms. However, an attentive reading of the different chapters in which Darwin and Wallace speak of this subject soon brings one to the conclusion that the word 'extermination' does not mean real extermination; the same remark which Darwin made concerning his expression: 'struggle for existence', evidently applies to the word 'extermination' as well. It can by no means be understood in its direct sense, but must be taken 'in its metaphoric sense'.

Petr Kropotkin, 1902[38]

Let us turn, then, to the other hypothesis, and see how it would solve the problem. Adaptation, it says, is not merely elimination of the unadapted; it is due to the positive influence of outer conditions that have molded the organism on their own form. This time, similarity of effects will be explained by similarity of cause. We shall remain, apparently, in pure mechanism. But if we look closely, we shall see that the explanation is merely verbal, that we are again the dupes of words, and that the trick of the solution consists in taking the term 'adaptation' in two entirely different senses at the same time.

Henri Bergson, 1911.[39]

These extracts from early-twentieth-century critiques of Darwin, both taking the *Origin* as their point of engagement, seem to offer a marked contrast in orientation. Kropotkin's influential work of anarchist theory, *Mutual Aid,* took Darwinian evolutionary theory to task for its overweening emphasis on competitive struggle in nature, positing instead, and with particular reference to human life, the principle of co-operation as the fundamentally social means by which both individuals and species strive to maintain their existence and development. Bergson's *Creative Evolution,* which for Greta Jones had a considerable effect on evolutionary debate in Britain after its translation in 1911, helping to 'sharpen all the issues which had accompanied the original publication of the *Origin*', undertook a criticism of the explanatory logic of natural selection in the name of a vitalistic force or 'elan vital' driving transmutation in constantly unpredictable and non-teleological ways. Both, then, are libertarian texts, yet attributable to different ends of a spectrum of interest – Kropotkin's a basis for socio-political action, Bergson's an intervention in the realm of abstract philosophy or, as his critics might have it, of metaphysics.

It is thus important to note the common ground of analysis in these instances: to observe how the reader is enjoined to 'look closely' at, to 'an attentive reading of', Darwin's text, as the necessary basis of scientific and philosophical critique. For Kropotkin, Darwin's use of the word 'extermination', like the deployment of 'struggle for existence', is potentially misleading because of its metaphoric function, while for Bergson it is the term 'adaptation' in Darwin's lexicon which poses the crucial problem of ambivalence. Such examples indicate the centrality of linguistic analysis to the debate surrounding the *Origin.* Ted Benton's chapter in this volume makes a compelling case for the retention of a distinction between 'two interconnected but still analytically distinguishable struggles' in Darwin's work: 'to analyse Darwin's language', he notes, 'is not the same thing as to analyse his theory'. Nevertheless, Kropotkin and Bergson demonstrate the sense in which words inevitably constitute the ground upon which the scientific and philosophical veracity of Darwin's theory of natural selection is fought over; linguistic analysis appears inseparable from questions of scientific epistemology and procedure once we restore a text like the *Origin* to its earlier contexts of reception and debate. Thus,

David Amigoni finds Max Müller and Leslie Stephen simultaneously responding to the *Origin* as 'a form of dense, linguistic representation'. We glimpse here Moore's 'common context of language and assumptions', a relatively undifferentiated 'commons' which is subsequently enclosed by the same disciplinary formations that helped create the concept of Social Darwinism.

More surprising, perhaps, in the responses of Kropotkin and Bergson, is the sharing of a quite precise theoretical position on language itself. Kropotkin assumes a 'real' or 'direct' sense of 'extermination' which must be clearly distinguished from Darwin's 'metaphoric' use of the word. For Bergson, there is a realm of the 'merely verbal' from which Darwin's 'trick' of an ambivalent 'adaptation' must be rescued. Language in each case is an untrustworthy device, capable of achieving a pure referential fit with the world but equally capable of magical deception: we must guard against being 'the dupes of words'. Such attitudes to the waywardness of language, particularly in the form of metaphorical expression, are deeply inscribed in late-nineteenth- and early twentieth-century culture. The surprise lies only in the fact that inquisitive philosophical minds such as Kropotkin and Bergson, engaged in radical critiques of scientific orthodoxy, should reproduce a position on language which achieved its clearest theoretical expression in nineteenth-century positivist science. Herbert Spencer maintained an absolute distinction between 'real' and 'symbolic' conceptions, pointing out the 'perpetual danger' and 'error' of mistaking the latter for the former and grounding his positivist faith in the language of a civilisation evolving inexorably towards greater precision and definiteness.[40] T.H. Huxley, defending scientific knowledge against those 'extremely worthy, well-meaning persons' who might raise theological doubts, invoked the myth of Diogenes, who refuted the sophist's claim that all motion was an impossibility by 'simply getting up and walking round his tub'; the refusal of dialogue – 'the man of science says nothing to objections of this sort' – establishes a disdain of the verbal in the name of a mode of knowledge more practical and immanent.[41] And again, David Amigoni characterises metaphor for Max Müller as 'a principle of degeneracy inherent in the evolution of language'.

No less than his more voluble compatriots in scientific popularisation, Darwin can frequently seem to adhere to the existence of a fundamental divide between a language enclosed in its own world of narcissistic trickery and a language which realised truth. In a letter to Lyell in 1861, he arrives at a characteristic position:

> If you say that God ordained that at some time and place a dozen slight variations should arise, and that one of them alone should be preserved in the struggle for life and the other eleven should perish in the first or few generations, then the saying seems to me mere verbiage. It comes to merely saying that everything that is, is ordained.[42]

'Verbiage' and 'mere verbiage' reappear periodically as terms of denunciation in Darwin's private dialogues and responses to criticism. In the *Origin*, this emphasis emerges, with a scare-quoting to embody a specifically linguistic alertness, in the convicton that 'It is so easy to hide our ignorance under such expressions as "the plan of creation," "unity of design," &c., and to think that we give an explanation when we only restate a fact' (p. 453). However, the grounds upon which Darwin can deny heuristic value to such formulations and claim it for the language of science, by which he can distinguish between a language which signifies only itself and one which signifies some reality outside of itself, may, as Edward Manier's excellent study indicates, be more complex than we might expect.[43] Manier indicates how the Scottish enlightenment philosopher Dugald Stewart almost certainly provided Darwin with a 'realist theory of metaphor', through which human language could be seen as grounded in a lexicon of 'natural signs' out of which the use of a more sophisticated 'artificial' language develops. This natural/artificial polarity, together with the suggestion of an organic process of growth which binds them together, could create an alertness for points at which the 'artificial' use of language departed from its natural base; yet it equally facilitates a historicist view of language which undermines any simple idealist sense of linguistic essentialism.

Accordingly, the *Origin* reveals tensions in its assumed relationship between language and scientific knowledge which often hinge on the role of metaphor. In the concluding chap-

ter, and looking ahead confidently to the 'considerable revolution in natural history' he expects to follow, Darwin seems
unequivocally Spencerian: 'The terms used by naturalists of
affinity, relationship, community of type, paternity, morphology, adaptive characters, rudimentary and aborted organs, &c.,
will cease to be metaphorical, and will have a plain signification' (p. 456). Even in the first edition, he is frequently careful
to apologise for his 'convenient' uses of metaphor, for example
in the 'large and metaphorical' sense in which 'struggle for existence' also carries a sense of 'dependence', and to alert us to the
perhaps misleadingly anthropomorphic tendencies of his own
terms – 'But to use such an expression as trying to make a
fantail is, I have no doubt, in most cases, utterly incorrect' (p.
96). Yet a key passage in his thirteenth chapter, on Classification, indicates a more complex role for metaphor:

> Naturalists frequently speak of the skull as formed of metamor-
> phosed vertebrae: the jaws of crabs as metamorphosed legs; the
> stamens and pistils of flowers as metamorphosed leaves; but it
> would in these cases probably be more correct, as Professor
> Huxley has remarked, to speak of both skull and vertebrae, both
> jaws and legs, &c., – as having been metamorphosed, not one
> from the other, but from some common element. Naturalists,
> however, use such language only in a metaphorical sense: they
> are far from meaning that during a long course of descent, primor-
> dial organs of any kind – vertebrae in one case and legs in the
> other – have actually been modified into skulls or jaws. Yet so
> strong is the appearance of a modification of this nature having
> occurred, that naturalists can hardly avoid employing language
> having this plain signification. On my view these terms may be
> used literally; and the wonderful fact of the jaws, for instance, of
> a crab retaining numerous characters, which they would proba-
> bly have retained through inheritance, if they had really been
> metamorphosed during a long course of descent from true legs,
> or from some simple appendage, is explained. (pp. 418–19)

This is not one of the *Origin*'s most elegant passages, perhaps
because of the contradictions it is required to negotiate. First,
the language of metamorphosis is characterised as metaphorical
or, more to the point, 'only' metaphorical, in the tradition of
natural history. Yet we must note that metaphor in this context
is not opposed to 'plain signification'; on the contrary, the

metaphor of metamorphosed parts impresses itself upon the
naturalist precisely because it is a 'language' carrying 'plain
signification'. Darwin can thus see no inconsistency in re-defin-
ing or 'using' the metaphor in a 'literal' sense – neither does he
appear to see the extent to which his account has already prob-
lematised the divide between the literal and the metaphorical.
Here it is worth reflecting back on the irony of the common
root of 'metaphor' and 'metamorphosis': if Darwin affirms perpetual change or transformation as a law of the natural world, then
he must equally divest metaphor of its inferior connotations of
artifice and affirm it as a 'natural' law of language.

When, therefore, Darwin observes elsewhere that 'it is
scarcely possible to avoid comparing the eye to a telescope' –
that we 'naturally infer' that the eye has been formed by a
process analagous to the operation of the highest human intel-
lects – he crystallises some characteristic tensions produced by
a growing awareness of the role of language in nineteenth-
century scientific epistemology. In its context, the 'Difficulties
on Theory' chapter of the *Origin*, the observation prefigures an
extended reflection on the inadequacy of such anthropomorphic figurations to the complex material reality and development of the eye. Yet it also embodies an acknowledgement of
the inevitably or 'naturally' metamorphic functioning of human
knowledge, underpinned by a belief that this mode is not
simply a symptom of a humanity's fallen condition but does
have some necessary relationship to the order of nature. Darwin
may have exhibited some of the necessary positivist machismo
about the 'plain signification' of scientific language and its proud
distance from 'mere verbiage', but the fractures and tensions
we find in the *Origin* tell a different and more complex story.

When we turn to the immediate reception of the *Origin* from
within the scientific community, certain recurrent patterns of
response reinforce a sense of the singularity of the text as a
linguistic artefact. It seems clear that, in the words of the French
scientist Jules Pictet, Darwin was perceived to have represented
his evidence 'in a novel form, and in a way freed from the ordinary routine'.[44] The text elicits frequent observations on its
language and form, and central to such observations are the
terms 'ingenious' and 'ingenuity': 'thus', Pictet notes of the

transition from Lamarckian to Darwinian evolution, 'in an ingenious manner, he brings in a new agent which he calls *natural
selection*', ending his review with carefully-qualified praise for
Darwin's 'beautiful book' and 'seducing argument'. In different hands the same terms could appear to be a far less equivo-
cal indictment: Thomas Vernon Wollaston's damning yet
patronising review culminates in the sarcastic imputations that
the text was 'eloquently written' in a 'pleasant medium', finally
quoting Darwin's concluding 'entangled bank' passage as
'certainly very beautiful, though we can scarcely believe that
our author was in earnest when he wrote it'.[45] Earlier in the
review, Wollaston slurs Darwin's observation on descent from
one primordial form with 'This is plain language, at any rate!',
then immediately characterises it as an 'ingenious fancy'. Sir
William Armstrong, referring to the 'profound sensation' caused
by the *Origin* in his opening address to the British Association
for the Advancement of Science meeting at Newcastle in 1863,
noted that 'The novelty of this ingenious theory, the eminence
of its author, and his masterly treatment of the subject have
perhaps combined to excite more enthusiasm in its favour than
is consistent with that dispassionate spirit which it is so necessary to preserve in the pursuit of truth'.[46] Fleeming Jenkin, in
his powerful but even-handed critique, could observe:

> Some persons seem to have thought his theory dangerous to reli-
> gion, morality, and what not. Others have tried to laugh it out of
> court. We can share neither the fears of the former nor the merri-
> ment of the latter; and, on the contrary, own to feeling the great-
> est admiration both for the ingenuity of the doctrine and for the
> temper in which it was broached, although, from a consideration
> of the following arguments, our opinion is adverse to its truth.[47]

while in a similar spirit of hard-edged scepticism the American
philosopher C. S. Peirce maintained, in 1893, the following:

> What I mean is that his hypothesis, while without dispute one of
> the most ingenious and pretty ever devised, and while argued
> with a wealth of knowledge, a strength of logic, a charm of
> rhetoric, and above all with a certain magnetic genuineness that
> was almost irresistible, did not appear, at first, at all near to being
> proved; and to a sober mind its case looks less hopeful now than
> it did twenty tears ago.[48]

What did it mean to characterise the *Origin* as 'ingenious'? The term clearly embodies a varying faintness of praise, with the likes of Jenkin and Peirce at one end of the spectrum and Wollaston at the other. While Samuel Johnson's *Dictionary* of 1785 (sixth edition) gives 'witty, inventive; possessed of genius', with 'mental; intellectual' as secondary and anachronistic uses, it seems that in Darwin's context the term was mutating towards the present, somewhat diminished connotations of 'skilful contrivance'. Thus, in the context of scientific writing, it is not coincidental that Darwin's 'ingenuity' should lie in close association with his way with words in the production of an argument variously 'beautiful' and 'pretty', 'seductive' and 'charming'. This is clearly a skill – but what man of science would want it? The potentially wayward and magical qualities of language, and the manipulative skills of its practitioners in the realms of art and rhetoric, are a deeply feminised influence, embodying a mischievous intelligence which threatens to pull a man from the straight-and-narrow (to borrow Sedgwick's phrase) 'tram-road of all physical truth'.[49]

In the comparative anatomist Richard Owen's critique of the *Origin* in the *Edinburgh Review* of April 1860, these kinds of connotation are woven into a more complex example of the extent to which cultural values might surround and inform scientific criticism. The review was, in effect, the moment at which an uneasy build-up of professional and personal antagonisms, characteristic of the politics of evolutionary science within which Darwin was obliged to operate, could surface and become public.[50] The full extent of what it meant to be an 'ingenious writer' is revealed in Owen's explicit application of the terms to Robert Chambers, the anonymous author of the *Vestiges of the Natural History of Creation*, so important in preparing the cultural landscape for the entry of the *Origin* yet so heavily criticised for its speculative character and cavalier approach to scientific proof. Darwin is nevertheless linked by association, being accused by Owen of ungratefully ignoring his debts to Chambers and of speculating in a similarly 'rash' and 'unlawful' fashion. The review begins, however, with a set of biographical observations on Darwin which set an interpretative framework for the critique that follows. Here, Owen asserts, Darwin 'has long been favourably known, not merely to the Zoological but to the Literary World', thanks to the 'charming style' of his *Beagle* narrative. He then chooses to note that Darwin is of 'independent means', thus giving him 'full command of his time for the prosecution of original research': his 'tastes' have led him to Natural History and his 'favourite subject' has become the origin of species. In the *Origin* itself, 'the same pleasing style' which marked his earlier work and 'a certain artistic disposition' and structure of argument have led 'several, and perhaps the majority, of our younger naturalists' to be 'seduced into the acceptance' of the theory of transmutation by natural selection.

The explicit linking of a feminised linguistic ingenuity with the 'Literary World' – 'charming', 'pleasing', 'seductive' – is here supplemented by an unmistakeable discourse on class. 'Taste', an aesthetic category deriving from that 'artistic disposition' and polite culture of the Literary World to which his independent means gave access, led Darwin to science rather than – we assume – hard work or professional commitment. Owen suceeds in establishing a distance between the 'scientific world' and Darwin which at the same time separates the manly 'labourer' or 'fellow-labourer' – terms used by Owen to denote the scientific community – from an effeminate culture of privilege. Beneath the tone of sometimes-strained politeness in Owen's review is a barely-disguised insinuation that Darwin is not a proper scientist – just as Jenkin was able to become gradually more satirical in his own review about the ability of 'believers' to 'invent' any necessary set of circumstances, such as an unlimited amount of geological time, in order to make a theory work.[51] Such insinuations were a hazard always faced by Darwin because of his lack of formal education and training in science. Less obvious, but nevertheless manifest in them, was the suggestion that scientific integrity could be measured in inverse proportion to rhetorical skill and exertion.

There is, however, an irony in Darwin's association with the 'ingenious' which surfaces if we turn again to reflect upon the historical relationship of the adjective to 'ingenuity', whose primary definition in Johnson's *Dictionary* of 1785 affiliates it rather with 'ingenuous' – that is, to 'openness, fairness, candour,

freedom from dissimulation'. Only secondarily, 'from ingenious',
do we have 'wit, invention, genius, subtlety, acuteness' –
meanings which, according to the 1983 *Chambers*, are derived
from 'ingenious' 'by confusion'. It thus appears that 'ingenuity', in undergoing gradual change in use, has acted as a hinge
between virtually contradictory meanings: openness and freedom from dissimulation in its actual source, 'ingenuous', a
subtle and inventive wit or 'skilful contrivance' (1983 *Chambers* again) in its trajectory of change towards 'ingenious'.

We can only speculate on the degree of intermixture
inscribed in the deployment of these terms by Darwin's critics
from the 1860s onwards. What is arresting is the extent to
which the ambivalence of 'ingenuity' is appropriate to a central
ambivalence in representations of Darwin's scientific method.
Against the view of ingenuity we have been pursuing, perpet-
uated though turned to positive effect in James Moore's estimation of Darwin as 'the outstanding conjuror of all time', we
can set the claim that Darwin possessed 'an instinct for truth-
telling which had hardly ever been surpassed' and strove 'to
perfect himself as a fact-and-dust man'; against Gillian Beer's
uncovering of Darwin's deep youthful pleasure in 'the power
of lying, of invention, of telling and not-telling' – 'I recollect
when I was at Mr. Case's inventing a whole fabric to show how
fond I was of speaking the *truth*!' – we can set Emma Darwin's
belief that 'he is the most open, transparent man I ever saw,
and every word expresses his real thoughts'.[52]

The substantial and growing body of work on Darwin's
language and rhetorical strategies might be prefaced by Edward
Manier's observation that 'the *representation* of his theory is the
key to its scientific and its cultural interpretation'.[53] In the
remainder of this section of the chapter I want to offer a reading of the structure and some of the rhetorical features of the
Origin, exploring in particular some characteristics of the
linguistic ingenuity which has both troubled and impressed
Darwin's critics. My aim will be to move towards a precise
delineation of the kind of ambivalence identified, for example
by C. S. Peirce as 'a certain magnetic genuineness that was
almost irresistible', or more recently by David Hull as the desire
on Darwin's part to 'tell' in the *Origin* 'a totally consistent natu-

ralistic story or none at all'.[54]

The telling of this story, or alternatively the unravelling of its 'one long argument', spanned fourteen chapters in the original edition. The misgivings of Vorzimmer and others concerning the mis-shapen growth of the final sixth edition may in part be due to an overestimation of the perfected 'organic' form of the first: the *Origin* is neither a realist novel nor a romantic poem, though it does have affinities with each, and a fascinating organisational logic. Chapter I, 'Variation under Domestication', is an exercise in safety and tact: Darwin's appeal to what breeders and gardeners have long known is an appeal to practical, observed and common knowledge as the basis of the theory of natural selection, which terms are tentatively introduced towards the end of the chapter and only after the previous tentative introduction of the alternative 'Unconscious Selection'. 'Theoretical writers' are stigmatised, in the manner of Huxley's Sophists, as the only ones to have doubted the strong principle of inheritance; yet, Darwin's deference to the breeders is not total: his recollection of being 'laughed to scorn' by a celebrated raiser of Hereford cattle over the suggestion that his stock might have descended from long-horns is the pretext for a warning to naturalists not to adopt the same kind of narrowmindedness – breeders in general 'well know that each race varies slightly, for they win their prizes by selecting such slight differences, yet they ignore all general arguments, and refuse to sum up in their minds slight differences accumulated during many successive generations' (pp. 88–9). This is a brief glimpse, allowed to us in this otherwise cautious opening chapter, of the supreme confidence Darwin can show in his theory.

Chapter II, 'Variation under Nature', completes the famous analogy between natural selection and the practices of breeding and cultivation, whether conscious or unconscious, which constitutes the opening gambit of the *Origin*. Yet this short chapter does not press home the analogy with rhetorical force: the subject of variation in nature is instead approached as demonstrating the difficulty of distinguishing in any absolute sense between species and varieties. Some statistical analysis is used to demonstrate that 'species are only strongly marked and permanent varieties', prefiguring the necessary prominence of

this mode of analysis in the following chapter. It is in the next
two chapters, however, that the *Origin* reaches its dramatic and
argumentative core; here the twin arms of his theory, struggle
for existence and natural selection, are articulated together.
Chapter III marks a profound shift in tone and address appropriate to the active and emotive concept of Malthusian 'struggle' with which it is concerned. By contrast with the opening
pair, this is a piece of romantic writing, with an expressive
register (the early references to 'beautiful co-adaptations' such
as the woodpecker and the mistletoe mark a break from the
preceding text and set the tone for what follows), a more
personal note of address ('Nothing is easier than to admit in
words the truth of the universal struggle for life, or more difficult – at least I have found it so – than constantly to bear this
conclusion in mind' – pp. 115–16), and a gradually mounting
tone of Wordsworthian awe at the incessant process of struggle and its often incredible corollaries. The chapter is, for example, animated and given a cumulative rhythm by the increasing
use of exclamation in its later stages; like Wordsworth, Darwin
uses the exclamation mark to lift the denotation of a natural
process or phenomenon into a sense of wonder: 'Hence it is
quite credible that the presence of a feline animal in large
numbers in a district might determine, through the intervention first of mice and then of bees, the frequency of certain
flowers in that district!' (p. 125). While partly a response to the
colourful implications of 'struggle', such animation is also borne
out of the realisation that some mental energy and projection is
required on the part of his reader to envisage some of the practical effects of the abstract process of species 'striving to
increase at a geometrical ratio'; the final paragraph thus appropriately begins with the recommendation that it is good 'to try
in our imagination to give any form some advantage over
another' (p. 129 – my italics).

    If chapter III is dominated by the exclamatory mode, Chapter
IV, the key articulation of 'Natural Selection', is both more
interrogative and more strongly assertive of the legitimacy of
its own arguments. Rhetorical questions figure prominently, in
combination with a didactic insistence: 'Let it be borne in
mind...', 'let it be remembered...', 'let us now take...' This

mode, reinforced by the well-known branching diagram or 'great Tree of Life' simile (see Ritvo, p. 56–7), gives momentum to an argument growing in authority; Darwin has his own theory in the dock, but the apparent rigour of his cross-examination allows moments of almost unequivocal confidence: 'and as modern geology has almost banished such views as the excavation of a great valley by a single diluvial wave, so will natural selection, if it be a true principle, banish the belief of the continued creation of new organic beings, or of any great and sudden modification in their structure' (p. 142).

These first four chapters, establishing the basic proposals of the *Origin*, constitute the opening phase. From this point onwards, in both structural and linguistic terms, 'difficulty' becomes the dominant principle in Darwin's negotiation of the relationship in the text between self-criticism and assertion. Significantly, a chapter is immediately devoted to the 'Laws of Variation', before the sixth chapter 'Difficulties on Theory', reflecting the profound awareness on Darwin's part of the lack of a coherent genetic theory upon which to predicate the mechanism of natural selection. 'Difficulties on Theory' then initiates that process of extensive questioning which has led Fleming to speak of Darwin's unsurpassed 'instinct for truth-telling': 'has there ever been another scientist who included in his great book all the arguments against it that he could ever think of?'[55] Chapter VI outlines these main 'difficulties' and then proceeds to confront two of them, the absence of visible transitional forms in nature and the origin and development of common organs in creatures of widely different habit, reserving the following two chapters for a separate discussion of further major difficulties, the problem of the evolution of complex instincts through natural selection, and the questions of sterility, hybridism and the possibility of fluid transmuatation through intercrossing in nature. While the latter chapter constitutes a return to the deconstruction of the species–variety distinction initially undertaken in chapter II, it also marks the end of the discussion of what might be called the internal or organic difficulties confronting natural selection theory. In the four chapters which follow, Darwin turns his attention to problems inherent in the external dimensions of the theory: in the

adequacy or otherwise of geological evidence to account for the
gradual succession of organic beings, including the vexed issue
of extinction; and in the possibility of harmonising the actual
geographical distribution of the world's inhabitants with transmutation through natural selection. A thirteenth and penultimate chapter thus stands somewhat on its own, though its focus
on taxonomy via the 'Mutual Affinities of Organic Beings'
serves as an important reminder that the whole structure of the
Origin might be viewed as a debate around human systems of
classification as much as an attempt to give unmediated access
to the true principles of development in organic life.

'Difficulty' is, however, an ambivalent, and possibly therefore an ingenious, weapon in the rhetorical strategies of the
Origin. At times, the reader could be mistaken for thinking that
the function of the text is to convince her of the extent of our
ignorance on all of the issues that bear significantly on an
understanding of evolution: reiterations of the parlous state of
this knowledge are frequent, 'nor', Darwin maintains, 'do we
know how ignorant we are' (p. 440). Yet such admissions of
difficulty become, paradoxically, the precise condition of the
text's truth-claims. Darwin's rhetorical skill is to impress upon
his reader the extreme intricacy, precariousness and lack of
substance of his theory, yet simultaneously to give a sense that
the same reader already has, in their own observation of nature,
a fundamental insight into the basis of the theory: we know
hardly anything about this, and yet we know a lot, partly
because of our own common sense, and partly because knowing the true and vast extent of our ignorance clarifies and
enhances the basis of real knowledge we do possess.

There are a number of ways in which the *Origin* achieves
this effect. First, there is a recurrent tendency to counterbalance expressions of extreme difficulty with a cooly-rational
negation of them:

> Long before having arrived at this part of my work, a crowd of
> difficulties will have occurred to the reader. Some of them are so
> grave that to this day I can never reflect on them without being
> staggered; but, to the best of my judgement, the greater number
> are only apparent, and those that are real are not, I think, fatal
> to my theory. (p. 205.

The reader could be forgiven for admiring here the speed with which Darwin is able to recover from being 'staggered' by the gravity of his problems, courtesy of the deft use of the semi-colon and what follows it. Similarly, approaching the conclusion of chapter IX, on the imperfection of the geological record, Darwin declares the 'several difficulties here discussed' to be 'all undoubtedly of the gravest manner', to which the adherence of 'all the most eminent palaeontologists' to the theory of immutability of species seems eloquent testimony; yet this does not discourage him from invoking Lyell's doubts, and his metaphor of the geological record as 'a history of the world imperfectly kept, and written in a changing dialect', in order to arrive at a final striking sentence: 'On this view, the difficulties above discussed are greatly diminished, or even disappear' (pp. 315–16). Thus, radical scepticism and radical optimism co-exist *within* the concept of difficulty; by placing his theory on a knife-edge, Darwin is able to impress the reader both with his brutal honesty and with the resistance of his theory to a Popperian falsifiability: 'If it could be demonstrated that any complex organ existed, which could not possibly have been formed by numerous, successive, slight modifications, my theory would absolutely break down. But I can find no such case' (p. 219).

In a perhaps more ingenious sense, therefore, such as we find in the example of the electric organs of fishes – 'impossible to conceive by what steps these wondrous organs have been produced' – impossibility in the present is the very ground of possible proof in the future: if we cannot say definitively how these organs have originated, we cannot *not* say that a transitional development may have occurred:

> [A]s Owen and others have remarked, their intimate structure closely resembles that of common muscle; and as it has lately been shown that Rays have an organ closely analogous to the electric apparatus, and yet do not, as Matteuchi asserts, discharge any electricity, we must own that we are far too ignorant to argue that no transition of any kind is possible. (p. 222)

This instance points to the prominence of two further strategies. First, 'difficulty' in the *Origin* operates in two distinct

temporal senses: while it is often 'grave' and apparently almost
insuperable in the present, it is to be confidently eradicated in
the future. We should not therefore be misled by its frequent
recurrence in the text, because that recurrence is often in the
form of variants on the formula, 'I can see no difficulty', 'I can
see no great difficulty', 'I can see no very great difficulty', 'I
cannot see that it would be an insuperable difficulty'. The
formula is not selective, for it is used in negotiating the most
unlikely hypotheses and examples of transmutation, such as the
aquatic bear and the evolution of the eye. Second, Darwin is
adept and consistent in his deployment of the multiple negative form:

> [Y]et in the case of any organ, if we know of a long series of
> gradations in complexity, each good for its possessor, then, under
> changing conditions of life, there is no logical impossibility in the
> acquirement of any conceivable degree of perfection through
> natural selection. In the cases in which we know of no inter-
> mediate or transitional states, we should be very cautious in
> concluding that none could have existed, for the homologies of
> many organs and their intermediate states show that wonderful
> metamorphoses in function are at least possible ...We are far too
> ignorant, in almost every case, to be enabled to assert that any
> part or organ is so unimportant for the welfare of a species, that
> modifications in its structure could not have been slowly accu-
> mulated by means of natural selection. (pp. 231–2)

Here too, it is difficult to avoid linking the indirectness and
evasiveness associated with this linguistic form to a subtle
ingenuity in Darwin's procedure: what does the *Origin* have to
hide? The answer proposed for example by Desmond and Moore,
and confirming what is explicit in the notebooks from 1837
onwards, would seem to be, a great deal: Darwin had long been
preoccupied by the potentially incendiary materalism of his
theory, and the long years of reluctance and failure to publish
had produced a nervously-fraught, wary and defensive consciousness. Studies of Darwin's reading and intellectual influences have also suggested a depth and sophistication to modify
the image of the 'anaesthetic' scientific man.[56] The 'ingenious'
Darwin has thus re-emerged in recent Darwin criticism as an
important alternative to Darwin's own self-fashioned image as

a simple, honest but inarticulate toiler at the scientific chalk-face. Charles Kay Smith has proposed that Darwin cultivated 'rhetorical ambiguities' in order to avoid critical controversy, while Gillian Beer's seminal work has consistently stressed that the multivalent 'quagmire' of the metaphoric was necessary for the articulation of his theory: 'He needs its tendency to suggest more than you meant to say, to make the latent actual, to waken sleeping dogs, and equally its powers of persuasion through lassitude, through our inattention'.[57]

It is true that a certain guile becomes manifest at times: accounting for the absence of frogs, toads and newts on the 'peculiarly well-fitted' oceanic islands in the Pacific with the explanation that they could not be transported across the seawater which kills them, Darwin cannot resist a final gibe: 'But why, on the theory of creation, they should not have been created there, it would be very difficult to explain' (p. 382). Yet this is an instance of the broader and paradoxical fact that as the *Origin* moves through its substantial investigation of 'difficulties', so it becomes stronger and more self-assured in its argument: scepticism and confidence nourish each other. The vision of the 'revolution in natural history', the opening of 'a grand and almost untrodden field of enquiry' anticipated in the glowing utopian prose of the final 'Recapitulation and Conclusion' chapter are difficult to recognise as parts of the same work as the cautious opening 'Variation under Domestication'.

The 'ingenious' Darwin, subtly aware of the linguistic balancing acts necessary for the representation of a highly speculative theory in the terms of empirical method and observation, is an important aid to our understanding of the particular form of the *Origin*. Yet the image is inadequate if it leads to a wrenching of form from theory – that is, if it creates a sense of dichotomy between clever rhetorical contrivance and the scientific, epistemological and philosophical orientations of the work. This dichotomy, initially constructed by contemporary reviewers of the *Origin* who were often also professional opponents of Darwin, can be read as an attempt to discredit and defuse what *was* radically new not simply in the language of the text but in its wide-ranging and subversive cultural implications. If, on the contrary, 'difficulty' performs such a prominent role in the

shaping of the text, this may be because it is a central consti-
tutive aspect of Darwin's innovatory and challenging vision. In
concluding this chapter, I want to suggest that 'difficulty' in
the *Origin* is an inherent factor in the text's relation to the
linked concepts of relativity and modernity, and that Darwin's
relationship to Romantic discourse and representation is a
necessary starting-point for such a reading.

In his 1981 essay 'Darwin and Landscape', James Paradis
presents a Darwin who anticipates and prepares the ground for
the development of Cubist art. In the *Origin*, Paradis asserts,
Darwin had arrived at a way of seeing nature, of organising the
visual field, in terms of a 'repetitiousness of form, geometrics
of organisation', which represented a radical break from the
Romantic tradition: 'beyond the impression of the moment,
which is likely to fill one with a feeling of the beauty, the spon-
taneity and harmony of life in the natural landscape, there is
an unsuspected geometry of great preciseness and definition'.
Through this radical defamiliarisation, nature is re-thought – or
re-visualised – as a spatial economy of incredible density, a 'perpetual disequilibrium' of contending forces; and, for Paradis, 'it
would take art fully half a century to follow him into the
labyrinth of lines and patterns he had discovered in the familiar landscape'.[58]

Romanticism had, however, exerted a powerful influence
on Darwin's earlier vision, exemplified for Paradis by the *Beagle*
narrative and its 'celebration' of 'transcendent moments of
timelessness in the wilderness', and it clearly survives in, for
example, the 'Struggle for Existence' chapter of the *Origin*
briefly considered above. We would be quite wrong, as Paradis
himself acknowledges, to see Romanticism totally displaced in
the *Origin*; but we can say that the Romantic sense of the
grandeur and sublimity of nature which pervades the text is
shifted to a new object – no longer an inscrutable workman-
ship evident in things themselves and their harmoniousness with
human subjectivity, but the unthinkably slow and complex
processes of transformation in nature. Thus, in the revealing
conclusion to the chapter on 'Instinct', Darwin could declare
that while it might not be a 'logical deduction', it was far more
satisfactory to his 'imagination' to see complex instincts as

'small consequences of one general law'; or in reflecting on the possible denudation of some 12,000 feet of rock in Merioneth-shire, he could exclaim: 'The consideration of these facts impresses my mind almost in the same manner as does the vain endeavour to grapple with the idea of eternity' (pp. 263 and 296).

Wordsworthian parallels are inevitably brought forth by an examination of the *Origin*'s rhetoric. But Darwin's esteemed Wordsworth could also apostrophise Coleridge thus:

> Thou, my Friend! art one
> More deeply read in thy own thoughts; to thee
> Science appears but what in truth she is,
> Not as our glory and our absolute boast,
> But as a succedaneum, and a prop
> To our infirmity. No officious slave
> Art thou of that false secondary power
> By which we multiply distinctions, then
> Deem that our puny boundaries are things
> That we perceive, and not that we have made.
> To thee, unblinded by these formal arts,
> The unity of all hath been revealed.[59]

It is worth reflecting upon the contradictory relationship between this passage and Darwin's science in the *Origin*, in order to signal something of the complexity of Darwin's inheritance and appropriation of Romantic epistemology. A science which both multiplied and then reified its own distinctions is, of course, precisely what Darwin was conscious of in his deconstruction of the species–variety distinction – to him also, in this sense, 'the unity of all' had been revealed. Yet nature in the *Origin* is no less systematic, and therefore amenable to description and classification, for being unified; Darwin could accept Wordsworth's critique of the inherently anthropomorphic nature of all representation – indeed, it was a problem with which he continually wrestled, as the work of Robert M. Young and Gillian Beer has shown – while refusing the characterisation of representation as 'secondary'.[60] Rather, the 'officious slavery' against which the *Origin* was sent to do battle lay in the 'false distinctions' multiplied by Creationists or 'species-mongers' in the name of a specious 'unity of all' with which Wordsworth, in his critique of science, perhaps unconsciously colluded.

Two 'unities' therefore emerge: one guaranteed by an Absolute, spiritualised nature, the other guaranteed by the complex and specific interrelatedness of a physical system of disequilibrium in nature. As Paradis notes, the *Origin* of 1859 showed how Darwin had arrived at a new, naturalistic and physical understanding of the landscapes he had first seen and interpreted on the *Beagle* voyage, eclipsing spiritual law by acknowledging the 'conditions of existence' rather than the end of existence as the highest law of development. But 'naturalistic' must here be grasped in its full, paradoxical sense: a theoretical understanding of the physical or ecological interrelatedness of things brings with it a realisation of the impossibility of any stable, absolute knowledge of that condition.

Thus, half a century before an illustrious succesor whose new physics became synonymous with the moment of cultural modernism, Darwin produced in the *Origin* a general theory of relativity. 'By the experiment itself', he notes in his discussion of experimentation in domestic breeding, 'the conditions of life are changed' (p. 77) – a recognition of the relativity of knowledge to the observation process which constituted his basic understanding of the relation between theory and practice: 'without the making of theories I am convinced there would be no observation...'; 'How odd it is that anyone should not see that all observation must be for or against some view if it is to be of any service!'[61] If, however, results are relative to the frameworks in which they are interpreted, theoretical frameworks must also be relative to results: 'systematists', he reminds us, 'are far from pleased at finding variability in important characters, and ... there are not many men who will laboriously examine internal and important organs, and compare them in many specimens of the same species'; the result of such empirical rigour is that 'parts which must be called important, whether viewed under a physiological or a classificatory point of view, sometimes vary in the individuals of the same species' (p. 102). What constitutes 'importance' or 'fitness' is entirely relative even to individuals, almost always possessing a 'plasticity' of organisation, within a species – a key statement of the anti-essentialism which has been seen as the *Origin*'s fundamental challenge to Western metaphysics. When applied to the human and moral sphere, fascinating tensions result: underlining the conviction that savages must practise unconscious if not conscious selection processes in the breeding of their animals, the word 'even' in the following sentence condenses a perhaps unseen moral ambiguity: 'We see the value set on animals even by the barbarians of Tierra del Fuego, by their killing and devouring their old women, in times of dearth, as of less value than their dogs' (p. 94). The challenge, which the work of James Rachels has recently explored, of Darwin's moral individualism to the traditional morality by which humans and non-humans occupied separate moral categories, could clearly produce ambivalent results: a principled opposition to the practice of vivisection on the one hand, while on the other, as Ellegård observed of the 'relativistic view of human morality' implicit in Darwinian theory,

> There was no reason to expect the systems of values, whether ethical or aesthetical, which were actually to be found in human societies, to have any sort of universal and absolute validity. They had been developed in response to the particular conditions under which the different communities had found themselves. Communities adopting a moral code which made them prosperous and strong would tend to proliferate. To the extent that they succeeded in inculcating their beneficial code in their descendants, or in others who came under their influence, such a moral system would tend to gain ground. But the fact that a certain moral code had established itself did not prove that it was a perfect one, even for the society which had developed it.[62]

Finally, as Stanley Hyman has suggested, even death can be seen as an implicitly relative term in the *Origin*: 'death is not inherent in the properties of the protoplasm (the simplest organisms do not die), but is a trait evolved by natural selection, permitting a speedier improvement of the higher organisms, and thus an advantage for competition and a good for life'.[63]

Given this pervasive relativism, it is entirely appropriate that Darwin should have chosen for the *Origin* a mode of systematic uncertainty, inconsistency and contradiction. An irresistible and magnetic 'genuineness' is of course integral to this mode: the fact that Darwin can sustain the illusion of naturalism, guaranteed by a narrative voice of complete integrity, in the face of so much difficulty, and of such a radical assault on the common sense of the implied reader, is precisely the condition of his story's contradictoriness. In a recent essay, Phillip Barrish finds in the *Origin*'s 'oxymoronic' laws of variation a 'family resemblance' with deconstructive, psychoanalytic and Marxist models of theory, in all of which we find the 'intellectual necessity of theorising the agency of anonymous effects'.[64] The invisible or inaccessible origins of material effects can be formulated in laws only retrospectively, 'once the "natural order" they contribute to is in place'; Darwin's characterisation of natural selection, like Foucault's problem of having to name Power, bespeaks that 'snare of language (of the arch-fallacies of reason petrified in language)' which for Nietzsche obliged the scientist to present all activity as 'conditioned by an agent – the "subject"': 'for all its detachment and freedom from emotion, our science is still the dupe of linguistic habits; it has never got rid of those changelings called "subjects".'[65] Darwin may have been trapped in this snare, but his struggles in the *Origin* produced a dialectic – the refusal of law, yet the necessity to formulate law; the scientific verification of the absence of law – which identifies him precisely with the anxieties surrounding knowledge and expression so characteristic of the conditions of modernity. We might note that the origins of these conditions can be traced in the Romanticism which was such a formative influence on Darwin. While perhaps bearing himself the physical and psychological scars of an 'irritable reaching after fact and reason' for much of his mature life, Darwin's work is positively impelled by a 'negative capability' which produced, in the *Origin*, a critical and creative state of doubt and uncertainty.

Notes

1 Quoted in Howard E. Gruber and Paul H. Barrett, *Darwin on Man: A Psychological Study of Scientific Creativity, together with Darwin's Early and Unpublished Notebooks* (London: Wildwood House, 1974), p. 40; see chapter 2, 'The Threat of Persecution'.

2 Morse Peckham (ed.), *The Origin of Species by Charles Darwin: A Variorum Text* (Philadelphia: University of Pennsylvania Press, 1959), p. 337.

3 J. Morrell and A. Thackray, *Gentlemen of Science: The Early Years of the British Association for the Advancement of Science* (1981; Oxford: Oxford

University Press, 1983).

4 T. H. Huxley, 'On the Educational Value of the Natural History Sciences' (1854), in Huxley, *Man's Place in Nature and Other Essays* (London: J .M. Dent, 1906), p. 268; Herbert Spencer, *First Principles* (1862; London: Watts & Co., 1937), p. 14.

5 Charles Darwin, *On the Origin of Species by Means of Natural Selection*, edited by Ernst Mayr (Cambridge, MA: Harvard University Press, 1966), p. vii.

6 Steve Jones, *London Review of Books*, 22 April 1993.

7 Robert M. Young, 'Darwin's Metaphor: Does Nature Select?,' in *Darwin's Metaphor: Nature's Place in Victorian culture* (Cambridge: Cambridge University Press, 1985), p. 113.

8 Peckham, *Variorum*, p. 753.

9 Thomes Vernon Wollaston, 'Review of the *Origin of Species*', from *Annals and Magazine of Natural History* (1860) 5: in David L. Hull, *Darwin and His Critics: The Reception of Darwin's Theory of Evolution by the Scientific Community* (Cambridge, MA: Harvard University Press, 1973), p. 139.

10 Gruber and Barrett, *Darwin on Man*, p. 152.

11 See Michael T. Ghiselin, *The Triumph of the Darwinian Method* (1969; Chicago and London: University of Chicago Press, 1984), pp. 89–102.

12 Victor Shlovsky, 'Art as Technique', in K. M. Newton, ed., *Twentieth Century Literary Theory: A Reader* (Basingstoke: Macmillan, 1988), p. 24.

13 For alternative observations on the title of the text, see Gillian Beer, *Darwin's Plots: Evolutionary Narrative in Darwin, George Eliot and Nineteenth-Century Fiction* (1983; London: Ark, 1985), pp. 64–65.

14 Bert James Loewenberg, 'The Mosaic of Darwinian Thought', *Victorian Studies* III: 1 (1959), p. 13.

15 See for example John Greene, 'Darwin as a Social Evolutionist', *Journal of the History of Biology* 10 (1977), pp. 1–27.

16 Robert M. Young, 'Darwinism is Social', in David Kohn, ed., *The Darwinian Heritage* (Princeton: Princeton University Press, 1985), p. 633.

17 James Moore, *The Post-Darwinian Controversies: A study of the Protestant struggle to come to terms with Darwin in Great Britain and America 1870–1900* (Cambridge: Cambridge University Press, 1979), p. 125. Moore's reflections are contained in the essay 'Socializing Darwinism: Historiography and the Fortunes of a Phrase', in *Science as Politics*, ed. Les Levidow (London: Free Association Books, 1986).

18 Valentino Gerratana, 'Marx and Darwin', *New Left Review* 82 (1973), p. 79.

19 Moore, *The Post-Darwinian Controversies*, p. 159; Gruber and Barrett, *Darwin on Man*, p. 69.

20 James Moore, 'Darwin of Down: The Evolutionist as Squarson-Naturalist,' in *The Darwinian Heritage*, ed. David Kohn, p. 474.

21 Adrian Desmond and James Moore, *Darwin* (London: Michael Joseph, 1991), p. 237; see especially chapter 16, 'Tearing Down the Barriers'.

22 Raymond Williams, 'Social Darwinism', in *Problems in Materialism and Culture: Selected Essays* (London: Verso, 1980), p. 89.

23 Moore, 'Socializing Darwinism', in *Science as Politics*, ed. Levidow, p. 62.

24 Ibid., p. 63.

25 Peter J. Vorzimmer, *Charles Darwin: The Years of Controversy:* The Origin of Species *and its Critics 1859–1882* (Philadelphia: Temple University Press, 1970), p. 270.
26 Beer, *Darwin's Plots*, p. 38.
27 Ibid., p. 71.
28 Gillian Beer, 'Darwin's Reading and the Fictions of Development', in *The Darwinian Heritage*, ed. David Kohn, p. 561.
29 *Origin*, p. 215; Peckham, p. 333; Alvar Ellegård, *Darwin and the General Reader: The Reception of Darwin's Theory of Evolution in the British Periodical Press 1859–1872* (Gothenburg: Elanders Boktryckeri Aktiebolag, 1958), on 'The Bear becoming a Whale', pp. 238–41.
30 Quoted in Peckham, *Variorum*, p. 20.
31 Peckham, *Variorum*, p. 165.
32 James Moore, *The Post-Darwinian Controversies*, p. 127; Robert M. Young, *Darwin's Metaphor*, p. 119.
33 Letter to J. D. Hooker, 16 January 1869. Quoted in Hull, *Darwin and His Critics*, p. 302.
34 Desmond and Moore point out that the cheaper edition was at the insistence of Darwin himself; at a time when 'working men in Lancashire were clubbing together to buy the fifth at fifteen shillings', Darwin 'wanted them all to have copies' (*Darwin*, p. 582).
35 Peter J. Bowler, *Theories of Human Evolution: A Century of Debate, 1844–1944* (Baltimore and London: Johns Hopkins University Press, 1986), p. 2.
36 Mayr (ed.), *Origin*, p. ix.
37 Thomas Kuhn, *The Structure of Scientific Revolutions* 2nd edition (Chicago: University of Chicago Press, 1970), p. 172.
38 Petr Kropotkin, *Mutual Aid: A Factor of Evolution* (1902; Boston: Extending Horizons Books, date unknown), pp. 63–4.
39 Henri Bergson, *Creative Evolution* (1911; Trans. Arthur Mitchell. Lanham, MD: University Press of America, 1983), p. 57.
40 'Strike out from our sentences everything but nouns and verbs, and there stands displayed the vagueness characterizing undeveloped tongues. Each inflection of a verb, or addition by which the case of a noun is marked, by limiting the conditions of action or of existence, enables men to express their thoughts more precisely ... Again, in the course of its evolution, each tongue acquires a further accuracy through processes which fix the meaning of each word. Intellectual intercourse slowly diminishes laxity of expression. By-and-by dictionaries give definitions. And eventually, among the most cultivated, indefiniteness is not tolerated, either in the terms used or in their grammatical combinations'. Spencer, *First Principles*, pp. 337–8.
41 Huxley, 'The Method by which the Causes of the Present and Past Condition of Organic Nature are to be Discovered. - The Origination of Living Beings', in *Man's Place in Nature*, pp. 186-7.
42 Darwin to Lyell, 21 August 1861; quoted in Hull, *Darwin and His Critics*, p. 63.
43 Edward Manier, *The Young Darwin and his Cultural Circle: A Study of Influences which helped Shape the Language and Logic of the first Drafts of*

the Theory of Natural Selection (Dordrecht and Boston: Reidel, 1978). On Dugald Stewart, see especially pp. 37-40.

44 'On the *Origin of Species* by Charles Darwin', *Archives des Sciences de la Bibliothèque Universelle* 3 (1860) pp. 231–255 (translated by David. L. Hull), in Hull, *Darwin and His Critics*, p. 142.

45 Wollaston, in Hull, *Darwin and His Critics*, pp. 139-140.

46 Quoted in Ellegård, *Darwin and the General Reader*, p. 73.

47 Jenkin, quoted in Hull, *Darwin and His Critics*, p. 305.

48 C.S. Peirce, *Scientific Metaphysics*, vol. VI of *Collected Papers of Charles Sanders Peirce*, eds Charles Hartshorne and Paul Weiss (Cambridge, MA: Belknap Press of Harvard University, 1935). Quoted in Hull, *Darwin and His Critics*, pp. 33–4.

49 The phrase used by Adam Sedgwick in accusing Darwin in the *Origin* of deserting the established Baconian methodology of induction; see Hull, *Darwin and His Critics*, pp. 159–66.

50 See in particular the work of Adrian Desmond for this specific political context in relation to Darwin and Owen: e.g. *Archetypes and Ancestors: Palaeontology in Victorian London 1850–1875* (Chicago: University of Chicago Press, 1984) and *The Politics of Evolution: Morphology, Medicine and Reform in Radical London* (Chicago: University of Chicago Press, 1989).

51 Of Darwin's estimation of the process of the denudation of the Weald at some 300,000,000 years, Jenkin noted: 'The whole calculation savours a good deal of that known among engineers as "guess at the half and multiply by two."' This may be less of a comment on Darwin as a genuine scientist than it is the condescension of the physical sciences to the relatively-nascent biological sciences.

52 Moore, 'Socializing Darwinism', in *Science as Politics*, ed. Les Levidow, p. 74 – Moore's phrase follows Engels's emphasis on a language which becomes widely popularised and therefore integrated into the basic ways of seeing of a culture; Donald Fleming, 'Charles Darwin, The Anaesthetic Man', Victorian Studies 4 (March 1961), pp. 219–36; Beer, *Darwin's Plots*, pp. 29-30; quoted in Moore and Desmond, *Darwin*, p. 259.

53 Manier, *The Young Darwin and His Cultural Circle*, p. 16.

54 Hull, *Darwin and His Critics*, p. 54.

55 Donald Fleming, 'Charles Darwin, The Anaesthetic Man', p. 233.

56 See e.g. L. Robert Stevens, 'Darwin's Humane Reading: The Anaesthetic Man Reconsidered,' *Victorian Studies* 26:1 (autumn 1982), pp. 51–63.

57 Charles Kay Smith, 'Logical and Persuasive Structures in Charles Darwin's Prose Style', *Language and Style*, III:4 (1970), pp. 243–73; Gillian Beer, '"The Face of Nature": Anthropomorphic Elements in the Language of *The Origin of Species*', in *Languages of Nature: Critical Essays in Science and Literature*, ed. Ludmilla Jordanova (London: Free Association Books, 1986), p. 238.

58 James Paradis, 'Darwin and Landscape', in *Victorian Science and Victorian Values: Literary Perspectives*, eds James Paradis and Thomas Postlewait (1981; New Brunswick: Rutgers University Press, 1985).

59 William Wordsworth, *The Prelude*, Book II, lines 210-221.

60 See e.g. Young, 'Darwin's Metaphor: Does Nature Select?', in *Darwin's*

Metaphor, and Beer, *Darwin's Plots*.
61 Letter to Charles Lyell, 1 June 1860; letter to Henry Fawcett, September
    1861. Quoted in Hull, *Darwin and His Critics*, pages 229 and 277.
62 Ellegård, *Darwin and the General Reader*, pp. 321–2.
63 Stanley Edgar Hyman, *The Tangled Bank: Darwin, Marx, Frazer and
    Freud as Imaginative Writers* (New York: Atheneum, 1962), p. 41.
64 Phillip Barrish, 'Accumulating Variation: Darwin's *Origin* and Contem-
    porary Literary and Cultural Theory', in *Victorian Studies* 34 (summer
    1991), p. 443.
65 Friedrich Nietzsche, *The Genealogy of Morals* (1887), reprinted in *The
    Birth of Tragedy and the Genealogy of Morals* (New York: Doubleday
    Anchor, 1956), pp. 178–9.

2

Classification and continuity in *The Origin of Species*

HARRIET RITVO

Most modern biologists would find it difficult to separate the practice of classification from Darwinian evolutionary theory. They interpret the observable similarities – whether morphological, physiological or genetic – on the basis of which they assign organisms to species, genera and higher taxa, as indications of common ancestry. Thus the elaborate trees and bushes created by taxonomists are generally understood as the visible embodiment of evolutionary principles; as Mark Ridley has put it, 'phylogenetic classification aims to represent the branching hierarchy of evolution'.[1] When biologists contemplate the development of their discipline, which, like other scientists, they are inclined to do only infrequently, they attribute this congruence of evolutionary theory and taxonomic practice to Charles Darwin. In his survey of the history of biology, for example, Ernst Mayr began the chapter on 'Grouping according to Common Ancestry' with the statement that 'Darwin was the founder of the whole field of evolutionary taxonomy'. With this assertion of novelty, Mayr implicitly defined classification as one of the components of what he, along with many other historians and scientists, has termed 'the Darwinian revolution ... the greatest of all scientific revolutions'.[2]

Darwin would certainly have agreed with modern biologists about the connection between taxonomic theory and his theory of descent with modification. Classification was a recurrent theme in *The Origin of Species*. In the 'Introduction', Darwin suggested that 'the mutual affinities of organic beings, ... their embryological relations, their geographical distribution, geological succession, and other such facts' – that is, the raw material of taxonomy – might lead 'to the conclusion that each species had not been independently created, but had descended, like varieties, from other species'.[3] And if, in conscience, he had to admit that these affinities were merely suggestive, and not a sufficiently firm foundation for the evolutionary argument he was about to construct, at the conclusion of that argument he could confidently offer a new explanation of this suggestiveness, based on his theory. Darwin began the penultimate chapter of the *Origin*, entitled 'Mutual Affinities of Organic Beings', with a ringing assertion: 'From the first dawn of life, all organic beings are found to resemble each other in descending degrees, so that they can be classed in groups under groups. This classification is evidently not arbitrary like the grouping of stars in constellations.'[4] Nor, in Darwin's view, did it reflect mere superficial resemblance, whether imposed by a divine plan or by some other agent. He propounded his contrary conviction, that taxonomy expressed the genealogical relationships required by his theory, with the force of a credo: 'I believe ... that propinquity of descent – the only known cause of the similarity of organic beings, – is the bond, hidden as it is by various degrees of modification, which is partially revealed to us by our classifications.'[5]

This formulation implied a paradigm shift of Kuhnian proportions, since it offered to replace the existing theoretical frameworks that explained and supported the work of classifiers. Nevertheless, Darwin might not have been as ready as modern analysts to parlay the linkage between evolution and taxonomy into a new beginning or a sub-disciplinary revolution. After all, he did not necessarily make such a claim even for his evolutionary theory as a whole, although he was well aware of its wide-ranging implications for all the life sciences. Sometimes, indeed, he seemed to undersell the novelty of his argument, perhaps attempting to mute an anticipated recoil. He suggested, for example, that the germ of his theory was implicit in the common vocabulary of naturalists, who 'frequently speak of the skull as formed of metamorphosed vertebrae ...; the stamens and pistils of flowers as metamorphosed leaves'. He acknowledged that 'naturalists ... use such language only in a metaphorical sense: they are far from meaning that during a long course of descent, primordial organs ... have actually been modified', but then asserted that 'so strong is the appearance of a modification ... having occurred, that naturalists can hardly avoid employing language having this plain signification'.[6]

In any case, Darwin was less inclined than many subsequent commentators to discuss his work exclusively in the language of 'revolutions' and 'turning points', terms that simultaneously assume and emphasise discontinuity. As a result of this tendency, both the year of the first publication of the *Origin* and the name of its author have become metonymies for the changed understanding of the natural world associated with his theory of evolution, and can be invoked by themselves to indicate an intellectual watershed.[7] From the perspective of 1859, however, the disjunction was much less obvious. The *Origin* would have seemed to emerge naturally from contemporary scientific debates and preoccupations, no matter how controversial it was in some respects, and Darwin's explication of his theory carefully specified both its novelty and the ways in which it reflected existing understandings.

In fact, in its simultaneous appeal to innovation and tradition, the work resembled its author. Darwin was a well integrated member of his society and his profession: a country gentleman and a longtime member of the British scientific establishment, with a reputation based on collections and monographs, not on theories. He recalled the passing age of independently wealthy amateur naturalists of independent means, although he flourished in a period of newly professional scientists. Thus, in the early 1840s, he enthusiastically applauded the efforts of some prominent members of the British Association for the Advancement of Science to reform zoological taxonomy so as to exclude or diminish the contributions of naturalists who numbered vulgarity, lack of taste and patchy acquaintance with Latin and Greek among their scientific sins.[8] Indeed, according to his biographers Adrian Desmond and James Moore, the very spirit of the *Origin* could appear dated rather than radical, 'its bleak, uncharitable survivalism ... more suited to the poor-law 1830s than the optimistic 1860s'.[9] The theory of descent with modification itself might similarly suggest (although Darwin was not eager to make this connection) the discredited past – for example, the Lamarckian evolutionary debates of the 1830s and 1840s – as easily as the enlightened and progressive future.[10]

The inevitable selectivity of the historical gaze has, however, not only emphasised but also produced discontinuity. As the lapse of a century and more has tended to minimise Darwin's scientific context, thus transforming the *Origin* into the solitary, if lofty, survivor of a once dense forest, so it has tended to highlight the most abstract and theoretical aspects of his writings. As a result, Darwin's work has been retroactively isolated not only from that of his fellow theorists but also from the wider network of scientific and nonscientific practice of which he was unusually aware and to which he was notably open.[11] Again, the consequence of this constructed isolation has been to make even the most provocative of Darwin's assertions seem more startling in retrospect than they may have been in his own time. For example, the most notorious episode in the debate that followed the publication of the *Origin*, the confrontation between Bishop Samuel Wilberforce and several of Darwin's allies at the 1860 meeting of the British Association for the Advancement of Science, focused on the assertion that human beings were descended from non-human primates. (Although pious scientific mythmaking has retroactively exaggerated the drama and definitiveness of Bishop Samuel Wilberforce's discomfiture by Darwin's defenders, there is no question that the incident was triggered by a reference to apes in the family.)[12] Then as now, this connection seemed particularly disturbing to those with Creationist religious commitments.

But if Wilberforce found the suggestion of anthropoid kinship abhorrent, he should not have found it surprising. Darwin was hardly the first scientist to suggest a close connection. Eighteenth-century naturalists had been fascinated by the resemblances between great apes and human beings. Both orang-utans and chimpanzees (not clearly distinguished from each other at that period) were occasionally classified within the genus *Homo*; the term 'pygmy' was applied indifferently to apes and to people. Reports of the behaviour of wild apes corroboratively emphasised their ability to use tools and feel emotions; they were often reported to evince a particular fondness for human beings, a kind of acknowledgement of kinship. Nor was this fascination the exclusive prerogative of naturalists; members of the general public were equally delighted with evidence of their anthropoid affinities. Captive chimpanzees and orang-utans routinely attracted large crowds, who came, at least in the shrewd marketing judgement of the animals' proprietors, to admire similarity rather than to be assured of difference: the closer the apparent connection, the larger the gate. Thus such unfortunate apes routinely appeared fully clothed; depending on their talents and inclinations, they ate with table utensils, sipped tea from cups, leafed through the pages of books and slept under blankets.[13]

To those already persuaded by such evidence, the inclusion of human beings within the larger genealogical system described in the *Origin* should not have been particularly troublesome. Indeed, from this perspective, the human–ape connection might have made Darwin's powerful but often abstract arguments more palatable and familiar, anchoring them in traditional wisdom and common-sense observation. The revolution that Darwin proposed in taxonomic theory, in any case a less immediately sensitive topic than the descent of humankind, had a similarly dual, even paradoxical effect, extending and validating conventional practice at the same time that it completely revised its underlying explanatory framework. Indeed, as in his discussion of the more general effect of his theory on naturalists, Darwin hinted that taxonomists had already foreshadowed his ostensibly startling assertions – that 'community of descent', rather than 'some unknown plan of creation, or the enunciation of general propositions, and the mere putting together and separating objects more or less alike' was 'the hidden bond' that they had been 'unconsciously seeking'.[14] In the conclusion of the *Origin*, Darwin re-emphasised this paradox, simultaneously evoking images of upheaval and continuity. While advising fellow naturalists that 'when the views entertained in this ... volume are generally admitted, ...

there will be a considerable revolution in natural history', he
also reassured them that 'systematists will be able to pursue
their labours as at present'.[15] That is to say, the evolutionary
theory of the *Origin* did not threaten to revise the established
methods and arrangements of botanical and zoological taxonomy, although it did hint at a further diminution of significance
for an enterprise that had not been on the cutting edge of
science since the eighteenth century, with such statements as
'it is immaterial ... whether a multitude of doubtful forms be
called species or sub-species or varieties; what rank, for
instance, the two or three hundred doubtful forms of British
plants are entitled to hold'.[16]

What Darwin offered were plausible and dynamic explanations for the long-recognised affinities already enshrined in
taxonomic categories. The sometimes puzzling groupings that
had been identified by Enlightenment systematisers like Linnaeus
and John Ray, and even much further back by Aristotle, could
now be accounted for on the basis of shared ancestry, rather
than divine caprice. For example, the mammalian anatomy and
physiology of the superficially fishlike whales and dolphins
thus emerged as evidence of their furry terrestrial progenitors.
And, as a further corollary, Darwin offered solutions for some
persistent theoretical problems. Indeed, he predicted not only
that taxonomists would be able to pursue their researches without disruption but that they would be able to pursue them with
greater peace of mind, and hence, implicitly, greater vigour.
Once they accepted his theory of descent with modification,
'they will not be incessantly haunted by the shadowy doubt
whether this or that form be in essence a species. This, I feel
sure, and I speak from experience, will be no slight relief.'[17]

Here Darwin referred to an issue that had troubled scientific classification since its Enlightenment beginnings: how was
the species, which was widely, although not universally,
considered as the basic unit of classification, to be defined (on
the level of theory) and to be recognised (on the level of practice)? Although most species were, as Darwin put it, 'tolerably
well-defined objects', it could nevertheless be difficult to
discern where one left off and the next began, as well as to
judge whether a group of organisms displayed sufficient

distinctiveness to be ranked as an independent species rather than a mere variety.[18] By the middle of the nineteenth century, most naturalists acknowledged that divisions below the species (called varieties, races or breeds, depending on context and commentator) were mutable and therefore (on the implicit assumption that species were not mutable) taxonomically insignificant. Indeed, the general attribution of such alternative sub-specific forms to environmental influence can be seen as further evidence that Darwin's theory elaborated understandings that were already implicit in the literature of taxonomy, especially, as he pointed out, since 'no clear line has as yet been drawn between species and sub-species ... or ... between sub-species and well-marked varieties ... These differences blend into each other in an insensible series; and a series impresses the mind with the idea of an actual passage.'[19] There was also widespread recognition that divisions above the species (genus, family, order and class, in reverse order of inclusiveness) were, as Darwin said, 'merely artificial combinations made for convenience'.[20] But the notion that species were somehow real – that, in labelling a group of organisms with a latinate binomial, taxonomists were acknowledging it as an entity that had existence independent of that naming process – still persisted, in spite of a striking absence of consensus about the nature of the entity in question.[21]

There was certainly no single touchstone or characteristic that signalled when a group of organisms should be accorded species status. The inability to hybridise, or to produce fertile offspring when mated with non-group members, was most often proposed as a possibility, but as often rejected. Darwin himself admitted as one of the 'Difficulties on Theory' that constituted the subject of chapter VI of the *Origin*, the awkwardness of 'species, when crossed, being sterile and producing sterile offspring, whereas when varieties are crossed, their fertility is unimpaired'.[22] His rather regretful generalisation, however, was undermined by counterexamples as effectively as those of naturalists who would have been better pleased with confirmation; thus he cited crosses between common and Chinese geese ('species which are so different that they are generally ranked in distinct genera'), and between European and Brahmin cattle.[23] In the absence of a single distinguishing marker for species, most taxonomists pragmatically identified and delimited them by taking into account a range of information, including anatomy, physiology, embryological development, habits of living and geographical distribution. This method worked well enough most of the time, but occasionally, usually in the case of plants or animals about which a great deal was known, it could be counterproductive, generating further confusion rather than clarity. Indeed, beyond a certain point, the attention of naturalists tended to be counterproductive. The more scrutiny a group of organisms received, the less likely it was to remain a 'good and distinct species';[24] almost inevitably, firm boundaries would dissolve and problematic varieties would be discovered. In the light of 'the species question' it was particularly troubling that such information overload tended to reflect the social or cultural appeal, rather than the botanical or zoological interest, of the target organisms. Darwin noted that 'it is in the best-known countries that we find the greatest number of forms of doubtful value' and that 'if any animal or plant ... be highly useful to man ... varieties of it will almost universally be found recorded'.[25]

Darwin approached the species problem in much the same way that Alexander the Great approached the Gordian knot: he cut through its complexities instead of bothering to disentangle them. If his theory of descent with modification was correct, then the species was no more real than any other taxon. Adding the temporal dimension emphasised the point that difficulties with synchronic classification had only hinted. If species changed slowly but markedly through time – if no precise boundaries separated living species from their extinct forebears – then the lines between similar contemporary species similarly paled in significance. As he summarised this argument in the final chapter of the *Origin*:

> On the view that species are only strongly marked and permanent varieties, and that each species first existed as a variety, we can see why ... no line of demarcation can be drawn between species, commonly supposed to have been produced by special acts of creation, and varieties which are acknowledged to have been produced by secondary laws. On the same view we can

understand how it is that in each region where many species of
a genus have been produced ... these same species should present
many varieties; for where the manufactory of species has been
active, we might expect ... find it still in action; and this is the
case if varieties be incipient species.[26]

It may seem that such a sweeping and radical solution of
long-cherished problems would have been more unsettling than
reassuring to conventional taxonomists – unsteady ground
beneath their feet may have seemed better than no ground (or
even no feet) at all. But Darwin did not deny the value of their
work or the practical utility of the species as they habitually
deployed it, any more than he suggested that the higher taxa
should be abandoned. He merely insisted that the species was
a tool of science rather than a fact of nature. And if Darwin's
acknowledgement of the importance of this traditional classificatory concern may have seemed double-edged, at once
connecting the *Origin* to existing practice and undermining the
basis of that practice – in other ways the taxonomical discussions of the *Origin* integrated his insights more firmly into the
dense context of accumulated natural history.

For example, Darwin chose to illustrate the relationship
among organisms prescribed by his theory of evolution with a
diagram long familiar to naturalists. The elaborately branching
tree (pp. 56–7) that formed the centrepiece of the chapter on
'Natural Selection' embedded this most novel part of Darwin's
argument within a systematic tradition dating from the previous century. Although the chain of being, or the *scala naturae*,
an ancient metaphor that organised nature as a linked, one-
dimensional progression from the meanest animal (or vegetable
or mineral, depending on the perspective of the systematist) all
the way to humans, had been the dominant metaphor of system
throughout the eighteenth century, its limitations became
increasingly apparent towards the end of that period.[27] The
structure it provided was literally too strait and narrow to accommodate the burgeoning number of species and the increasingly complex relationships perceived to exist among them.

Systematists suggested a variety of alternatives to replace
this outmoded metaphor or image of the natural system. In his
old age, Linnaeus likened the living world to a map, and Oliver

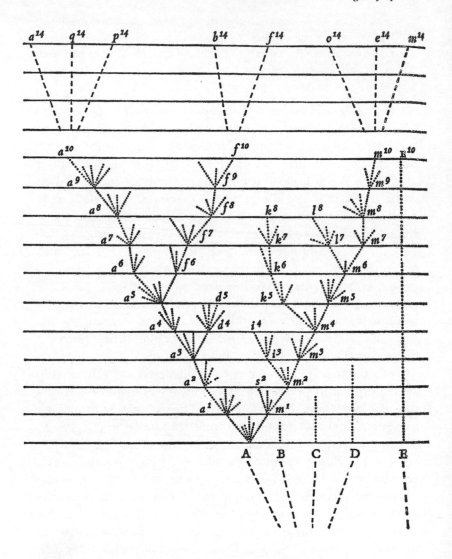

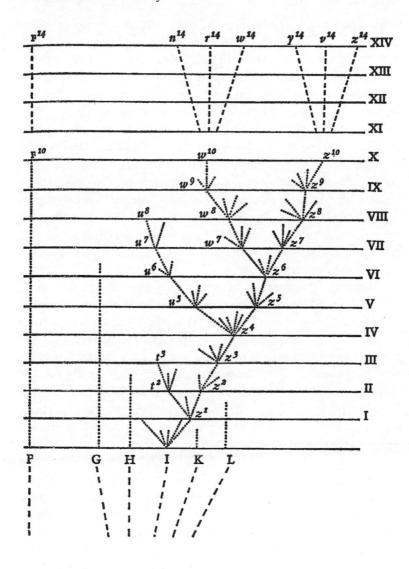

Goldsmith compared the class of mammals to a complex poly-
gon.[28] In the 1820s and 1830s the 'quinary system', an eccen-
tric attempt to represent the complex, overlapping sets of
resemblances among animals and plants through a series of
embedded circles, attracted both interest and scorn.[29] But the
metaphor that emerged as dominant was arboreal. Long before
the publication of the *Origin,* naturalists could refer to the tree
without any need for comment or explanation; twigs and
branches were as thoroughly embedded in their discourse as
links and scales had been earlier. For example, in 1841 Hugh
Strickland, a correspondent of Darwin's, urged his colleagues
'to study Nature simply as she exists – to follow her through
the wild luxuriance of her ramifications, instead of pruning and
distorting the tree of organic affinities into the formal symme-
try of a clipped yew tree'.[30]

Darwin's diagram was of course, severely abstracted, lack-
ing the woody shape and foliage featured by some other graphic
representations of this metaphor. And the straight dotted lines
of his version, along with the superscripted letters and the
Roman numerals that divided the y-axis into periods of time,
reminded readers of its unusually chronological and theoretical
character, as did Darwin's verbal explication (for example, 'Let
A to L represent the species of a genus large in its own country ...').[31] But at the end of his discussion of natural selection
he was at pains to connect his metaphorical tree with the less
strenuously argumentative trees widely current among
botanists and zoologists. First, he made this point by direct
assertion: 'The affinities of all the beings of the same class have
sometimes been represented by a great tree. I believe this simile
largely speaks the truth.'[32] He then went on to apply this
metaphor – or describe his tree – in terms continuous with
those employed by Strickland and a host of other naturalists,
unusual only in that they referred to death and decay as well
as life and growth: 'As buds give rise by growth to fresh buds,
and these, if vigorous, branch out and overtop on all sides with
many a feebler branch, so by generation I believe it has been
with the great Tree of Life, which fills with its dead and broken
branches the crust of the earth, and covers the surface with its
ever branching and beautiful ramifications.'[33]

Indeed, this graphic image might have made even the chronological movement of evolution seem familiar to those of Darwin's first readers familiar with the work of philologists (probably a significant percentage, since philology was an exciting new discipline). The tree was routinely used by historians of language not just to indicate relationships among languages but to illustrate a genealogical process almost exactly analogous to that postulated by Darwin's theory of descent with modification. At several points in the *Origin* Darwin explicitly invoked this similarity by way of explanation. Thus, specifically, 'a breed, like a dialect of a language, can hardly be said to have had a definite origin' and, more generally, 'it may be worth while to illustrate this view of classification by taking the case of languages'. Indeed in the case of humanity, analogy might be too weak a characterisation of the relationship between linguistic history and biological evolution: 'If we possessed a perfect pedigree of mankind, a genealogical arrangement of the races of man would afford the best classification of the various languages now spoken throughout the world.'[34]

And often Darwin's choice of language and metaphor in the *Origin* figuratively connected his argument not just with contemporary scientific discourse but with the outmoded but still familiar discourse of an earlier age, thus casting the net of association and recognition still wider. Thus he chose to express one of the most important components of his evolutionary theory, the genealogical connection between ancestral and descendant species, in the terminology of the Enlightenment. The imagery of linkage, recalling the ostensibly superseded chain of being, recurred again and again. He referred, for example, to 'the discovery of intermediate linking forms', to 'extreme groups ... connected together by a chain', and to the 'Ornithorhynchus [platypus] ... which ... connect[s] to a certain extent orders now widely separated in the natural scale'.[35] Indeed, Darwin's foregrounding of this trope also gave it renewed life outside the universe of scientific discourse. In the latter part of the nineteenth century the search for the 'missing link' between humans and non-human animals became (as it has remained) a compelling popular preoccupation.

If Darwin's evolutionary theory threatened no major revision in the practice of taxonomists, it did suggest a certain redirection of their attention. Previously, once a group of plants or animals had been identified as a variety (often referred to as a 'mere' variety) of another species, it lost much of its scientific interest. The nested hierarchy of taxa was often conceived to reflect intrinsic merit, and 'to attain the rank of species' was thus characterised as a kind of achievement on the part of the organisms in question.[36] So dead was this metaphor, indeed, that Darwin habitually used it himself, even though his redefinition of varieties as 'incipient species' suggested that their mutability, far from branding them as taxonomically negligible, gave them the greatest systematic importance.[37] (Another example of the old hierarchy of values persisting in Darwin's vocabulary, after he had discarded it from his theory, was his choice of the word 'hybrid' to denote the product of a cross between related species and of the less dignified 'mongrel' to denote the product of a cross between related varieties.)[38]

As with his revision of taxonomic theory, Darwin chose to cast this potential shift of perspective in terms that emphasised familiarity rather than novelty. It has often been remarked that Darwin began the *Origin* with a description of artificial selection as practised by farmers, stock breeders and pet fanciers, thus using a reassuringly homely example – one recognisable by the general public as well as by members of the scientific community – to introduce the most innovative component of his evolutionary theory.[39] The first chapter opened by identifying the author with the reader, and by referring to their mutual experience of garden-variety domesticates, rather than to the massive accumulation of technical data that he subsequently deployed to buttress his theory of natural selection: 'When we look to the individuals of the same variety or subvariety of our older cultivated plants and animals, one of the first points which strikes us, is, that they generally differ much more from each other, than do the individuals of any one species or variety in a state of nature.'[40]

Accessible and reassuring as it was, however, the analogy between natural and artificial selection was far from perfect. Most of the problems it presented were implicit in the nature of comparison. That is, if the things compared are not identical, they must differ from as well as resemble each other, and these differences can distract attention from, or even completely undermine, the focal similarity. The purpose of Darwin's analogy was to make the idea of natural selection seem plausible, and perhaps even to suggest that, like evolution itself, it was implicit in understandings already shared by his audience, by describing it as a grander version of a well-known process. Simultaneously, the analogy emphasised the efficiency and shaping power of natural selection. Thus Darwin noted that fancy pigeons bred by members of the London Pigeon Clubs were so divergent in size, plumage, beak shape, flying and vocalising technique, skeletal development and many other characteristics that 'at least a score ... might be chosen, which if shown to an ornithologist, and he were told that they were wild birds, would ... be ranked by him as well-defined species. Moreover, I do not believe that any ornithologist would place the English carrier, the short-faced tumbler, the runt, the barb, pouter, and fantail in the same genus.'[41] As he put it more generally, if the relatively feeble selective efforts of human breeders, whether applied 'methodically, or ... unconsciously', had produced 'the most distinct and useful domestic breeds ... There is no obvious reason why the principles which have acted so efficiently under domestication should not have acted under nature.'[42]

But as Darwin acknowledged, there were some fairly obvious reasons why the two processes might diverge. The more profound and concentrated power of natural selection – 'Man can act only on external and visible characters: nature ... can act on ... the whole machinery of life. Man selects only for his own good; Nature only for that of the being which she tends' – might constitute a difference of kind rather than degree, as might the much greater stretches of time available for natural selection.[43] And further, the results of the two processes tended to be different. Natural selection, as illustrated by the tree diagram, produced a constantly increasing and diversifying variety of forms. Anyone familiar with artificial selection would have realised that it could not be represented by the same spreading diagram. Even though, as Darwin pointed out, 'our oldest cultivated plants, such as wheat, often yield new varieties', and though there was no evidence that 'our domestic varieties manifested a strong tendency to reversion' to their wild forebears, the strains produced by human selection were neither as prolific nor as hardy as those produced by nature.[44] The animals and plants celebrated as the highest achievements of the breeder's art were especially liable to delicacy and infertility. Thus highly bred strains, long isolated from others of their species to preserve their genealogical purity, far from serving as a springboard for further variation, often had to be revivified by infusions of less rarefied blood.[45]

Despite these difficulties, Darwin not only sustained this analogy throughout the *Origin* as an illustration of natural selection, but he also extended it to specifically taxonomic issues. That is, he used it to explain and underline the enhanced significance of sub-specific categories in the light of his evolutionary theory. By studying varieties, scientists would 'gain a clear insight into the means of modification and coadaptation', the major unexplained component of Darwin's theory.[46] But, for many pragmatic reasons, not least the glacial slowness Darwin attributed to the working of natural selection, variation in nature was not easy to examine. If, however, the activities of the breeder shadowed those of nature, then the results of those activities should also be analogous. Since varieties were incipient species, the farmyard and the garden plot provided the closest available approximation of a laboratory of evolution. As Darwin stated, in explanation of the unusual amount of attention he had devoted to domesticated animals and plants in the *Origin*, 'in ... all ... perplexing cases I have invariably found that our knowledge, imperfect though it be, of variation under domestication, afforded the best and safest clue'.[47]

Darwin thus balanced the novel blurring of the line between the species and its sub-division with an implicit confirmation of an ingrained classificatory habit. The fact of domestication alone was traditionally considered sufficient to qualify a group of animals or plants for the rank of independent species, even if it could freely interbreed with its wild progenitor and differed little from it physically. Thus, for example, although the late-eighteenth-century naturalist Thomas Pennant acknowledged that the European wild cat was the 'stock and origin' of the domestic cat, one was *Felis sylvestris* and one was *Felis catus*. Sub-divisions of domestic 'species' were often treated with equal dignity. Thus many of Pennant's contemporaries (and successors) analogously included domestic dog breeds (as well as breeds of cattle, sheep and horses) in their catalogues of the natural world, often endowing them with latinate species labels such as *Canis sagax* (the hound) and *Canis pomeranus* (the pomeranian).[48]

This widespread taxonomic practice was at least inconsistent with the professedly objective principles of Enlightenment and post-Enlightenment systematics. Under close examination it could even appear somewhat subversive, since it suggested that earlier anthropocentric ways of viewing the natural world, allegedly discarded at the advent of the modern ideology of science, persisted within classificatory systems that claimed to be based entirely on the description and analysis of nature. But if natural selection and artificial selection were as similar as Darwin proposed, domestic animals were most appropriately considered as analogous to wild animals, not as categorically different from them. There was no scientific reason to relegate them to lesser taxonomic categories. By the same token, domestic breeds were analogous to wild varieties, and neither could be firmly differentiated from natural species. Thus it became possible for Darwin to use the English racehorse, which was distinct from other equine strains because simultaneous selection pressures had been exerted on all members of the breed, rather than because all racehorses shared descent from a single distinctive pair, as an argument for locating evolutionary change primarily within populations rather than individuals, without even acknowledging his slide from artificial to natural selection.[49] And thus his readers could understand the complex and potentially troublesome implications of his evolutionary theory as a whole within a context of familiar understandings and observations.

Darwin's sustained effort, embodied in his language, his analogies and his explicit reassurances, to integrate the argument of the *Origin* into the context of existing understanding can be understood partly in public relations terms. Of course, people are more likely to be receptive to a novel idea if they perceive it as an extension or revision of what they already know and believe than if they fear it will require them to jettison the intellectual or spiritual capital of a lifetime. But Darwin may also have recognised that revolutions in theory need not precipitate revolutions in practice – and that even incontestable revolutions have their conservative aspects. (It is these aspects that later chroniclers, with their understandable tendency to focus on innovation, may be inclined to overlook.) With regard to classification, what he offered could be seen as an explanation – even a justification – of traditional practices and understandings in what had become, by his period, one of the least forward-looking branches of natural history. And, although systematic theory duly absorbed his theoretical revisions, the practice of taxonomy did not in fact need to change much to accommodate them, as it has not, at bottom, needed to change much in response to the profound recent developments in genetic analysis. Thus, in response to the current biodiversity crisis, the distinguished biologist E. O. Wilson proposed 'the discovery and classification of all species', a formulation pragmatically untroubled either by Darwin's revision of the notion of species or by any subsequent complications of taxonomic theory.[50] And perhaps we can wonder, faced with this relatively tranquil surface overlaying stormy deeps, whether something similar might not be said about the impact of evolutionary theory as a whole, outside of rarefied intellectual or clerical circles. After all, even now, when it has long been a matter of scientific orthodoxy, relatively few people feel compelled to bother themselves about the theory of evolution by natural selection, and fewer still feel constrained to believe it.

Notes

1 Mark Ridley, *Evolution and Classification: The Reformation of Cladism* (London: Longman, 1986), p. 4. As Ridley points out, this generalisation applies only to cladists and evolutionary taxonomists, and not to the much smaller group of pheneticists, for whom 'classification aims to represent a hierarchy of similarity of form among living things' (p. 3).

2 Ernst Mayr, *The Growth of Biological Thought: Diversity, Evolution, and Inheritance* (Cambridge, MA: Harvard University Press, 1982), pp. 209, 501. Mayr's predecessors are profusely cited on pp. 880–1.

3 Darwin, *Origin*, p. 66

4 Darwin, *Origin*, p. 397.

5 Darwin, *Origin*, p. 399.

6 Darwin, *Origin*, p. 418–19.

7 For example, in titles of the form of Mary Frederick's *Religion and Evolution since 1859* (Chicago: Loyola University Press, 1934) or Stephen Jay Gould's *Ever Since Darwin* (New York: Norton, 1977).

8 Harriet Ritvo, 'The Power of the Word: Scientific Nomenclature and the Spread of Empire', *Victorian Newsletter* (spring 1990), p. 7.

9 Adrian Desmond and James Moore, *Darwin* (London: Michael Joseph, 1991), p. 485. Silvan S. Schweber surveys Darwin's more general intellectual affinities in 'The Wider British Context in Darwin's Theorizing', in David Kohn, ed., *The Darwinian Heritage* (Princeton: Princeton University Press, 1985), pp. 35–70.

10 See Adrian Desmond, *The Politics of Evolution: Morphology, Medicine and Reform in Radical London* (Chicago: University of Chicago Press, 1989), for a comprehensive account of these debates.

11 Darwin's respect for non-scientific sources of information was evident throughout his works; he was particularly interested in the experiences of farmers and fancy breeders of domesticated animals and plants. For an account of his connection with pigeon fanciers, which figured prominently in the discussion of artificial selection in the *Origin* (pp. 82–8), see James A. Secord, 'Nature's Fancy: Charles Darwin and the Breeding of Pigeons', *Isis* 72 (1985), pp. 163–86.

12 Desmond and Moore, *Darwin*, pp. 492–9.

13 Harriet Ritvo, *The Animal Estate: The English and Other Creatures in the Victorian Age* (Cambridge, MA: Harvard University Press, 1987), pp. 33–4.

14 Darwin, *Origin*, p. 404.

15 Darwin, *Origin*, p. 455.

16 Darwin, *Origin*, p. 114.

17 Darwin, *Origin*, p. 455.

18 Darwin, *Origin*, p. 210.

19 Darwin, *Origin*, p. 107.

20 Darwin, *Origin*, p. 456.

21 This debate is far from over, and it has generated an enormous amount of commentary. For recent historical accounts, see Peter F. Stevens, 'Species: Historical Perspectives' in *Keywords in Evolutionary Biology*, ed. Evelyn Fox Keller and Elisabeth A. Lloyd (Cambridge MA: Harvard University Press, 1992), pp. 302–11; Scott Atran, *Cognitive Foundations of Natural History: Towards an Anthropology of Science* (Cambridge: Cambridge University Press, 1990), chapter 6; and Mayr, *Growth of Biological Thought*, chapter 6.

22 Darwin, *Origin*, p. 206.

23 Darwin, *Origin*, pp. 270–1.

24 Darwin, *Origin*, p. 155.

25 Darwin, *Origin*, p. 106.

26 Darwin, *Origin*, p. 443.

27 The chain of being derived ultimately from the work of Aristotle (David

Hull, *Science as Process: An Evolutionary Account of the Social and Conceptual Development of Science* (Chicago: University of Chicago Press, 1988, p. 82). On the chain generally, see Arthur O. Lovejoy, *The Great Chain of Being: A Study of the History of an Idea* (Cambridge MA: Harvard University Press, 1936), esp. chapter 8.

28 Hull, *Science as Process*, p. 85; Oliver Goldsmith, *A History of the Earth and Animated Nature* (London: J. Nouse, 1774), vol. IV, p. 187; Harriet Ritvo, 'New Presbyter or Old Priest? Reconsidering Zoological Taxonomy in Britain, 1750–1840', *History of the Human Sciences* 1 (1990), pp. 259–76.

29 Recent discussions of the quinary system include David Knight, *Ordering the World: A History of Classifying Man* (London: Burnett Books, 1981), pp. 93–105; Mary P. Winsor, *Starfish, Jellyfish and the Order of Life: Issues in Nineteenth-Century Science* (New Haven: Yale University Press, 1976), pp. 82–7; and Alec L. Panchen, *Classification, Evolution, and the Nature of Biology* (Cambridge: Cambridge University Press, 1992), pp. 25–30.

30 Hugh Strickland, 'On the True Method of Discovering the Natural System in Zoology and Botany', *Annals and Magazine of Natural History* 6 (1841), p. 192.

31 For Darwin's interpretation of this diagram, see the *Origin*, pp. 159, 162–8, 404–6.

32 Darwin, *Origin*, p. 171.

33 Darwin, *Origin*, p. 172 .

34 Darwin, *Origin*, pp. 97, 406. The connection between philological (or historical linguistic) and evolutionary metaphors has been the subject of repeated commentary. See, for example, the essays collected in Henry M. Hoenigswald and Linda F. Wiener, eds, *Biological Metaphor and Cladistic Classification: An Interdisciplinary Perspective* (Philadelphia: University of Pennsylvania Press, 1987).

35 Darwin, *Origin*, pp. 112, 409, 151.

36 Darwin, *Origin*, p. 107.

37 Darwin, *Origin*, p. 107.

38 Darwin, *Origin*, p. 285.

39 Among these discussions are L. T. Evans, 'Darwin's Use of the Analogy between Artificial and Natural Selection', *Journal of the History of Biology* 17 (1984), pp. 113–40; John F. Cornell, 'Analogy and Technology in Darwin's Vision of Nature', *Journal of the History of Biology* 17 (1984), pp. 303–44; C. Kenneth Waters, 'Taking Analogical Inference Seriously: Darwin's Argument from Artificial Selection' *PSA 1986*, eds Arthur Fine and Peter Machamer, pp. 502–13; and Mary M. Bartley, 'Darwin and Domestication: Studies on Inheritance', *Journal of the History of Biology* 25 (1992), pp. 307–33.

40 Darwin, *Origin*, p. 71.

41 Darwin, *Origin*, p. 83.

42 Darwin, *Origin*, p. 441.

43 Darwin, *Origin*, p. 132.

44 Darwin, *Origin*, pp. 71, 77.

45 Such vitiation of purebred strains has occurred in the history of most domesticated animal species. For examples in several breeds of toy dogs,

see Judith Neville Lytton, *Toy Dogs and Their Ancestors, Including the History and Management of Toy Spaniels, Pekinese, Japanese and Pomeranians* (London: Duckworth, 1911).

46 Darwin, *Origin*, p. 67.

47 Darwin, *Origin*, p. 67.

48 Thomas Pennant, *History of Quadrupeds* (London: B. and J. White, 1793), vol. I, pp. 16–17; George Shaw, *General Zoology* (London: G. Kearsley, 1800), vol. I (2), pp. 277–80. For an extended discussion of this issue, see Ritvo, 'New Presbyter or Old Priest?', pp. 266–9. For a definitive recent discussion of this issue, see Juliet Clutton-Brock, 'The Definition of a Breed', in *Archeology* (Proceedings of the IIIrd International Archaeozoological Conference), ed. Marian Kubasiewicz (Szczecin, Poland: Agricultural Academy, 1979), pp. 35–44.

49 Darwin, *Origin*, p. 351–2.

50 Edward O. Wilson, *The Diversity of Life* (Cambridge,MA: Harvard University Press, 1992), p. 313.

3

Science, ideology and culture: Malthus and *The Origin of Species*

TED BENTON

Introduction: Methodological bearings

Any new biography must take account of the recent upheaval in the history of science, and its new emphasis on the cultural conditioning of knowledge. Gone is the day when Darwin could be depicted as a seer, a genius out of time. Ours is a defiantly social portrait. We make contact with the public events and institutions of Victorian England, with reform bills, poor law riots, learned societies, industrial innovation, radical medicine, Church debates, and, not least, with the new views of creation among reforming naturalists and the old practices of museum keepers. We see Darwin on the streets, sitting in with apes at the zoo, picking up pigeon lore in gin palaces, conniving with his heterodox dining circle, living a squire's life, investing in factories, worrying about religion and confronting death. Viewed in this light, his fears and foibles become intelligible and his evolutionary achievements make sense.[1]

This vivid and trenchant statement comes from a widely, and justly, acclaimed biography of Darwin. This chapter takes issue with the last quoted sentence only: and, even then, only with one of its two claims. Desmond and Moore are quite right to celebrate the new emphasis on the 'cultural conditioning' of knowledge. For writers in the English language, it was probably the work of Thomas Kuhn which did most to dismantle a prevailing orthodoxy about science. According to that orthodoxy, rigorous empirical testing of scientific theory and hypothesis, the close logical links between evidence and scientific claims, and the esoteric, technical character of scientific language all conspired to set it apart from other, more familiar, everyday social institutions and cultural practices – from moral and political controversy, and from artistic creation. History and sociology might tell us something about the formation of scientific institutions, the professionalisation of scientists, and the wider cultural conditions for, or obstacles to, the establishment of modern science. They could, however, tell us little or nothing about the *content* of scientific knowledge-claims.

By contrast, the post-Kuhnian consensus reminds us that 'there is more to seeing than meets the eyeball'[2] and that scientific theory is radically underdetermined by observational or experimental evidence. Not only are 'the facts' a discursive construct, but any single set of facts is in principle capable of assimilation by an indefinite variety of alternative theories. For Kuhn himself, whilst it might be difficult to display the *rationale* governing the revolutionary transition from one paradigm to another, the process was one whose *rationality* could be relied upon, as a choice made by 'the scientific community'. But once the Kuhnian cat was out of the bag there was no catching it. Feyerabend's self-avowed anarchism insisted that 'the scientific community' should have no more authority than the proponents of 'myth, religion, magic, witchcraft and ... all those ideas which rationalists would like to see forever removed from the surface of the earth ...'[3]

The contents of scientific belief-systems now move out of the dry specialist journals, into the open and up for critical scrutiny. For many scholars this has meant simultaneously *demoting* science from its authoritative role in policy formation, *debunking* its claim to special cognitive status, and *reintegrating* it with the wider structure of social and political interests. But for some, especially those working within one or another of the traditions of twentieth-century Marxism, this intellectual strategy seemed somewhat double-edged. Since scientific research is now closely linked to the state and big business, and since many on the Left have come to see science and technology as a central mechanism of social domination in modern capitalism, the implications for sociology and history of science seem clear:

science is to be understood as an aspect, or element, in the workings of the dominant ideology. But, if this is so, then what is now to be said about the status of the discourse within which this very claim is made?

Marxism itself claimed scientific status – and, indeed, in some of its versions, did play the role of a ruling ideology in the 'formerly existing' bureaucratic regimes of eastern Europe. For critical historians and sociologists of science there was a real dilemma: *either* reduce science to the play of social interests, and so abandon any special cognitive claims on the part of the critical study of science itself, *or* back-track on the 'strong programme' of social analysis, at least for some categories of knowledge-claims.

Subsequent developments have tended to ease this dilemma by a virtual obliteration of one of its terms. First, the authoritative status of the 'dominant ideology thesis' was challenged by feminists and others who objected to its focus on *class* as the central moment of social domination, and by cultural theorists who insisted that 'interests' could not be identified independently of their discursive (i.e. cultural, ideological) articulation. Second, a wave of post-structuralist rhetorics swept away the last bastions of the idea of objective knowledge, even as a regulative ideal. Linguistic meaning flows unconstrained from text to text, unanchorable in any extra-textual referent, while 'knowledge' becomes a discursive regime inseparable from sinister 'strategies of power'.

So, in 'Darwin studies', it is now possible to move, smoothly and without argument, from taking into account 'the cultural conditioning of knowledge' to an outright *assimilation* of 'knowledge' to 'culture':

> 'Social Darwinism' is often taken to be something extraneous, an ugly concretion added to the pure Darwinian corpus after the event, tarnishing Darwin's image. But his notebooks make plain that competition, free trade, imperialism, racial extermination, and sexual inequality were written into the equation from the start – 'Darwinism' was always intended to explain human society.[4]

But there is something paradoxical in this. As we saw, Desmond and Moore have two aims – one is to make Darwin's 'foibles and fears' intelligible, the other is to 'make sense' of his 'evolutionary achievements'. The former aim they achieve superlatively, but the latter they render problematic. If Darwinism was always 'intended to explain society' it seems that his 'evolutionary achievements' disappear from view. Indeed, the reduction of Darwin's explanatory achievements to expressions of the prevailing mid-Victorian culture even begins to corrode their account of his 'foibles and fears'. What, exactly, did he have to worry about? Presumably, solely that he arrived at his conclusions a couple of decades before they could become socially acceptable.

Literature, science and ideology

Comparable, though different, reductionist moves are made in Gillian Beer's literary approach to Darwin.[5] She is able to show how illuminating it can be to employ a literary critic's conceptual tools, and sensitivity to linguistic usage in reading a scientific text such as Darwin's *Origin*. She explores, persuasively, parallels and commonalities between Darwin's creative strategies and textual devices and those of nineteenth-century writers of fictional works. She also shows, I think quite convincingly, how uncontrolled 'surplus meaning' in some of Darwin's key metaphors provided points of anchorage for the myriad of diverse cultural, moral and political appropriations of Darwinism.

However, the theoretical moves by which she legitimates her analytical practice in relation to Darwin's text threaten to undermine some of her most important insights. Why, for example, was the authority bestowed by a textual anchorage in Darwin so keenly and pervasively sought? Why did people trouble to appropriate Darwin, instead of just getting on with what they wanted to do? And why, after all, were the implications of evolution by natural selection found so shocking and, as Beer suggests, controversial? This is particularly surprising if, as Beer suggests, Darwin's language allowed his readers so much licence to read the *Origin* according to their own protocols.

Like Desmond and Moore, Beer objects to the sequestration of science from its cultural context:

> Through the work of writers such as Bloor and Robert M. Young there has also been a movement away from the assumption that

science inhabits an absolute domain of its own, exempt from the ideological, and exempt also from the preoccupations of the society which the scientists inhabit.[6]

In Beer's case, the reintegration of the scientific text into its cultural surrounds is achieved, not by way of the concepts of 'ideology' or 'interests' but through a certain appreciation of language. First, she notes that 'In the mid-nineteenth century, scientists still shared a common language with other educated readers and writers of their time. There is nothing hermetic or exclusive in the writing of Lyell or Darwin.'[7] This meant that their works could be read 'very much as literary texts', and, also, that scientists could themselves draw upon literary, philosophical and historical sources. As they stand, those claims are unobjectionable. However, must we suppose that the reader of Lyell or Darwin and of Dickens or Eliot would have been impervious to genre, would have been insensitive to the difference between the communication of a scientific discovery and a work of fiction? And must we suppose that in *drawing* upon literary, philosophical and historical texts scientists did not do so for purposes and according to discursive constraints which derived from specific disciplinary requirements? Beer does not explicitly pose or answer these questions but the flow of her own text, rather like one of Lyell's geological forces, tends to efface their profile.

Beer goes on to make more specific and substantive claims for her literary approach to the text. The first seems to amount to a claim that the metaphorical excess and polysemy which made Darwin's text 'so incendiary'[8] was somehow inevitable. This is partly because analogy and metaphor are ineliminable features of scientific discourse. This is a widely shared view in post-Kuhnian approaches to scientific thinking, but it by no means implies that the roles of metaphor are the same in science and literature. Nor does it preclude the possibility that the elaboration of metaphor in science is subject to constraints of logical rigour, ontological plausibility and empirical testing which do not apply in the same way in non-scientific contexts of intellectual creation.

But Beer's claim also seems to be supported by the particular character of Darwin's object, 'life'. She acknowledges the attempt, in Darwin's circles, to eliminate metaphor, and to use a clear, direct form of scientific language, but quotes the authority of George Eliot to the effect that such a language 'will never express life'. As Beer concludes, 'the exuberantly metaphorical drive of the language of *The Origin* was proper to its topic'.[9] So why, one wonders, did Darwin take so many pains, in successive drafts of his earlier sketches, and then, in subsequent editions of the *Origin*, to rein in the excesses of his metaphorical language, to qualify and differentiate explicitly the 'large and metaphorical use' he makes of such a phrase as 'struggle for existence'? Why did Darwin's co-discoverer, Alfred Russel Wallace, express serious reservations about the metaphorical and teleological connotations of Darwin's term 'natural selection'? Beer is certainly aware of Darwin's struggle with his own language in this respect – she offers some very insightful analyses of it. So perhaps the heart of her claim about the unavoidability of metaphorical *excess* is not so much to do with the unavoidability of metaphor, or, indeed, the special features of 'life' as a topic of scientific investigation, but rather has to do with the nature of language itself.

Beer recognises that Darwin's theoretical intent is to resist anthropocentrism – to provide an account of organic change and the diversity of life which is independent of human purpose, and indifferent to human values. But his difficulty in his project derives, she claims, from the fact that language is by nature anthropocentric. It is difficult to know exactly what Beer means by this, or why she thinks it is true, but perhaps we can get some clues about this from her more specific instantiations of it. She says it is difficult to distinguish 'agency' from 'intention', and so Darwin often misleadingly uses 'Creationist' language. This is compounded by Darwin's own struggle against Natural Theology, which in fact biases him towards its teleological descriptions of living forms.[10] Finally, in writing for the general reader, Darwin uses metaphors whose meaning may 'overflow' to the point of reversing Darwin's actual argument.

In each case, it seems to me, Beer hits the mark. However, in doing so, she undermines the force of her own more general claim. She clearly understands that Darwin's intellectual project is anti-anthropocentric, that his theory does not attribute

Concrete

conscious intention to natural forces, and that he does not think that living organisms are designed by a creator. His more careful readers, and most certainly his scientific readers, understood all this perfectly well. There are two possibilities here. Either Darwin's theoretical achievements must be distinguished from their often misleading particular linguistic expositions, or somehow Darwin manages to press a recalcitrant 'anthropocentric' language into stating non-anthropocentric knowledge-claims. If the latter is the case, then Beer is just wrong about the unavoidability of Darwin's problems with language. If the former is the case, then what is exposed is a certain limitation in her literary approach: to analyse Darwin's *language* is not the same thing as to analyse his *theory*. Perhaps we might go further and say that a measure of the scale of Darwin's *theoretical* innovation is the difficulty he has in putting it into words: the gap between what Darwin *wants* to say and what the available language *enables* him to say. Darwin was engaged in two interconnected but still analytically distinguishable struggles – to understand the mechanism by which new species were formed, and to find a clear, rigorous and unambiguous way of stating what he had discovered.

Finally, Beer's most ambitious substantive claim is that Darwin's literary tastes were important in the formation of the concept of evolution by natural selection itself. This specific claim is made on behalf of Shakespeare's historical plays, and Milton's poetical writings. Shakespeare's plays, Beer argues, are important for their focus on inheritance, family fortunes and choice in breeding, and so as a source for Darwin's all-important contrast between artificial and natural selection. This rather speculative claim seems to me to be vulnerable on several grounds. First, the relevance to the question of the origin of species of variation under domestication was well established in natural history circles well before Darwin's first formation of the idea of natural selection. Darwin himself was at great pains to learn about selective breeding, the origins of domesticated breeds of plants and animals, and their relationships to wild stock. Darwin began his *Origin* with a chapter reviewing this evidence, and did likewise in his earlier sketches. After reviewing the evidence about variation in nature, and introducing the idea of a struggle for existence, Darwin proceeds (at the beginning of chapter IV of the *Origin*) to ask 'Can the principle of selection, which we have seen is so potent in the hands of man, apply in nature?'.[11] Since Darwin makes it so plain that the source of his analogy is with the breeding of domesticated strains of animals and plants, what grounds are there for supposing it might lie in the historical plays of Shakespeare? What is missing from the rather obvious and banal reading which the more exciting and esoteric one offers? It would be ungenerous to answer, 'an expanded role for literary analysis', but it is hard to see what other answer might be given.

Beer's claim on behalf of Milton's poetical works is that Darwin's reading of Malthus was decisively affected by what he took from Milton. There are, in fact, three claims here: first, that Darwin's 'crucial insight' was 'derived directly' from his reading of Malthus's *Essay*; second, that the *way* Darwin read Malthus was affected by his reading of Milton, and, third, that this different reading of Malthus was somehow crucial for the formation of the idea of natural selection. I find all of these claims very interesting and challenging. The first of them is, of course, widely shared, though still controversial. Most of the rest of this chapter will centre on its significance. The other two claims are, so far as I know, special to Beer: 'What has gone unremarked is that it [Darwin's crucial insight] derived also from the one book he never left behind during his expeditions from the *Beagle*: *The Poetical Works of John Milton*'.[12]

Beer notes that although his reading of Malthus 'precipitated' the idea of natural selection, Darwin, in the process, 'transformed the imaginative tone and emotional balance and hence the intellectual potentialities of Malthus's concept.'[13] Central to both Darwin's and Malthus's thinking was a recognition of nature's immense fecundity, but Malthus's response was part celebration, and part alarm. By contrast, to Darwin, 'fecundity was a liberating and creative principle, leading to increased variability, increased potential for change and development'.[14] This transformation of Malthus is understood by Beer as an imaginative residue of his reading of Milton, and his celebration of the diversity and profusion of nature. She also comments on Darwin's ecstatic descriptions of tropical nature in the *Journal of Researches*, as if in support of her claim.

However, Darwin's ecstasy at his first experience of tropical nature might equally be taken to be the *source* of both his affection for Milton *and* his affective transformation of Malthus. Even as a very old man, Alfred Russel Wallace, for example, could still recall his first encounter with the Amazonian forests with extraordinary vividness:

> Looking back over my four years' wanderings in the Amazonian valley, there seem to me to be three great features which especially impressed me, and which fully equalled or surpassed my expectations of them. The first was the virgin forest, everywhere grand, often beautiful and even sublime. Its wonderful variety with a more general uniformity never palled.[15]

So far as is known, Wallace's ecstasy was unmediated by Milton.

But none of this is quite to the point. Perhaps Beer is right and perhaps in Darwin's *particular* case Milton did make possible a distinctive transformative reading of Malthus. But if so, the question arises, why did Darwin take from Milton his celebration of diversity and profusion, and not something else? Beer emphasises that Milton's writing is riven with an anthropocentrism which Darwin rejoiced in overturning. Can Beer's approach offer any answer to the question why Darwin took one aspect of his reading of Milton into his reading of Malthus, but not the other? Perhaps it can, but in Beer's text the selection is made to appear quite arbitrary.

The suggestion I would like to make – and to explore in the rest of this chapter – is that Darwin *did* transform Malthus in the process of forming the idea of natural selection, but that in order to understand how and why, we need to appreciate the *specificity* of Darwin's explanatory purposes. Further, to recognise what *they* were requires us to situate Darwin's thought in the context of a distinctive discourse of natural history as it emerged and was sustained in the circle of naturalists and scientists to which Darwin belonged, through their letters and discussions, in the clubs and societies they formed, and in the periodicals they produced and read. Of course, it is true that there were no hermetic boundaries around this circle and its practices, and that its participants also discussed and were concerned with many issues other than natural history. These facts are important if we are to understand the *connections* between the concerns of natural history and those of the wider culture, but they should not lead us to forget the specificity of the discourse of natural history itself. Analytical procedures which seek to assimilate Darwin's *Origin* to the 'common culture' also tend, if they remain unqualified, to efface the significance of the profound conceptual innovation achieved in the former.

In this respect, Beer's work resembles that of Robert M. Young, despite other significant differences between them. Young's distinctive combination of political vision and rigorous scholarship is exemplary, but I think he, too, assimilates Darwin's *Origin* too readily to its cultural context:

> In a sense, I want to marry history of socioeconomic theory and history of biology or – to alter the metaphor – to show that Malthus, Paley, Chalmers, Darwin, Charles Lyell, Herbert Spencer, A. R. Wallace, and others were part of a single debate.[16]

Young acknowledges that 'The role of science as ideology is relatively over-emphasized' in his major essay on the nineteenth century debate on 'man's place in nature'. He says he does this 'to counterbalance the existing bias in the literature towards the internal history of ideas'.[17] Certainly, the case he builds against much traditional historiography, and also against some Marxist writers who stress the autonomy of science, is a powerful one. However, Young does not fully address some of the dilemmas and difficulties of his own position. As he points out, the Marxist tradition has tended to acknowledge Darwin's scientific achievements, but to follow Marx and Engels themselves in reviling Malthus as an ideologist of the ruling class. Young's account cements Darwin and Malthus together, as participants in a single debate, refusing to acknowledge in natural science a limit to the applicability of ideological analysis. Darwin and Malthus are, alike, participants in the imposition of a reifying ideology encouraging fatalistic acceptance of property and injustice as a law of nature, and so disabling liberatory opposition:

> Adam Smith, Paley, Malthus, Darwin, Chambers, Spencer, the

'Social Darwinists', and the emergence of functionalism, pragmatism, psychoanalysis and numerous other theorists and their schools can then be seen as part of a continuous development. That development was the substitution of one form of rationalization of the hierarchical relations among people for another – from the projection of natural theology to the reification of society through biologism.[18]

I shall stress the issue at stake here is not the historical and cultural role of biologism (with some reservations, I agree with Young about this) but whether it is right to see in Darwin's scientific achievement *nothing but* the dominant role it was made to play in the culture. As Young himself shows, there were *numerous* uses of Malthusian ideas. So, also, have there been many, often wildly contradictory, uses of Darwin's ideas. Perhaps some of these are more 'liberatory' than others? But, in any case, their very diversity shows that a distinction may be made between Darwin's thought and the various uses made of it. More seriously, it seems to me that Young, however he situates himself in relation to the Marxian tradition, shares some of its dilemmas.

In refusing to prise Malthus and Darwin apart, he is, presumably, committed to rejecting Marx and Engels's positive valuation of Darwin's scientific achievement. That Young does take this step is implicit in his 'constructionist' view of knowledge: 'Of course, external nature exists, but all attempts to know it – to qualify or quantify it in any way – are inescapably mediated through human consciousness and consciousness is a sociopolitical and ideological mediator.'[19] This statement strongly suggests a socio-political relativism about knowledge, a position to which Young is clearly tempted, but from which he eventually draws back: 'Relativism and contextualism are useful as first approximations, but they are ultimately useless to socialists unless they are subsumed under a strong ideological approach.'[20] Earlier in the essay, what this ideological approach should be is made clear:

> The politically partisan nature of these activities and their parent ideological positions must, however, be made explicit. We can then get on with determining whose view of science and its history is just and liberating rather than whose is 'rational'.[21]

The choice between approaches turns on which is just and liberating, rather than which is rational. But why should reason, justice and liberty come apart in this way? Why should we *need* to choose between them? And, if we *do* choose between them, what *grounds* do the struggles for justice and liberty stand upon? Are they an arbitrary taking of sides, or can they be reasoned and argued for? Even Malthus, though he was on the other side, saw the necessity to give reasons. Are we so impressed that we must fall back on an *unreasoned* appeal to our moral values? If not, then I suggest that Darwin's view of our place in nature has much to recommend it as a source for radical and liberatory visions. To show this will, however, require a more direct engagement, first with the *textual* discrepancies between Malthus and Darwin, and, second, with the course of Darwin's thought and the origin of the *Origin*.

Malthus and *The Origin*: divergences

In a much-quoted passage from his *Autobiography*, Darwin says this about his relation to Malthus:

> In October 1838, that is fifteen months after I had begun my systematic enquiry, I happened to read for amusement 'Malthus on Population', and being well prepared to appreciate the struggle for existence which everywhere goes on from long-continued observations of the habits of animals and plants, it at once struck one that under these circumstances favourable variations would tend to be preserved and unfavourable ones to be destroyed. The result of this would be the formation of new species.[22]

It is worth noting both that Darwin claims to have read Malthus 'for amusement' (not for insight into the species-problem!) and that he acknowledges his reading as a 'prepared' one. Beyond that, he tells us little about the *content* of his encounter with Malthus's ideas. Something of this we can reconstruct from letters and notebooks, and from successive sketches for his book on species, which eventuated in the *Origin*. However, before I go on to say something about that *process*, it will be instructive to consider its product: the use Darwin makes of Malthus in the *Origin* itself.

After assembling facts and generalisations about variation

under domestication and in nature, Darwin embarks on his chapter on the 'struggle for existence'. The emergence of new species, he tells his readers, follows inevitably from the struggle for life. De Candolle, Lyell and the horticulturalist W. Herbert have all shown how severe is the 'competition' to which all organic beings are exposed. Then follows the crucial passage[23] in which he exemplifies and qualifies the 'several senses, which pass into each other' of the term 'struggle for existence' as he will use it.

Since, for every species, more are produced than could possibly survive, there must 'in every case be a struggle for existence'. This struggle is carried on between the individuals of a species, between them and the individuals of other species, and 'with the physical conditions of life': 'It is the doctrine of Malthus applied with manifold force to the whole animal and vegetable kingdoms: for in this case there can be no artificial increase of food, and no prudential restraint from marriage.'[24]

Darwin read the 1826 edition of Malthus's *Essay* which Malthus himself considered to offer a certain 'softening' of the very harsh implications of his first (1798) *Essay*. This proclaimed softening consisted mainly in Malthus's distinguishing, and raising to prominence, 'moral restraint', alongside vice and misery, as the inevitable consequences of his law of population. Malthus himself begins in both versions of the *Essay* by presenting his principle as a natural law governing all animal and plant life. Nature's 'profuse and liberal hand' scatters the 'seeds of life' abroad, but is relatively sparing in the means available for their nourishment. The matter is simple with plants and 'irrational animals', which have an instinct to increase their number. Where possible, this instinct expresses itself, and increased numbers are then checked by 'want of room and nourishment'. Humankind 'cannot by any efforts of reason escape' this law, but its effects are more complicated in the human case. The instinct to procreate is no less, but human reason enables us to ask whether we may bring into the world beings for whom we have no means of support. This consideration may lead to avoidance or delay of marriage, but all too often this leads to vice. Alternatively, the instinct may be indulged, with the effects also found in the non-human world

– population rising beyond the means of subsistence, and consequent 'positive' checks to the population.[25]

In the later editions, much is made of voluntary restraint from marriage *not* followed by 'irregular gratifications'. This must, as a suppression of a natural instinct, cause some unhappiness, but it entails less suffering than the alternatives and so is a virtue Malthus implores us to practise. But as if recognising the insufficiency of mere injunction Malthus argues for social policies and institutional forms which will exert a constant pressure to family limitation. The English Poor Laws positively encourage the poorest in society to produce more children than they can provide for, and, by imposing a tax burden on others, threaten to drive more families into poverty than would otherwise be the case. Moreover they undermine the virtue of independence among those who receive relief. As for the utopian schemes of Wallace, Condorcet and Godwin, Malthus makes short work of their optimistic view that problems of absolute scarcity might arise only in the distant future. The immediate threat of poverty or of loss of social position is necessary both to encourage moral restraint and to stimulate industry, without which means of subsistence may not be increased at all.

The use Darwin makes of Malthus involves him in a reversal of the direction of Malthus's own argument. Darwin rightly takes Malthus's primary concern to be with the human case, whereas Darwin 'applies' Malthus back to the 'animal and vegetable kingdoms'. As a consequence, there are two orders of discrepancy between Darwin's and Malthus's concern with population: first, the direct consequences of the shift from the human case, and, second, transformations worked by Darwin in his conception of Malthus's principle in the course of this reverse shift. Two of the direct consequences of the shift in focus to non-human organisms are noted by Darwin himself: the absence of Malthus's third category of (preventive) check – prudential restraint – and of artificial increase in the food supply. This must mean, as Darwin points out, that the positive checks operate in non-human populations with a still greater intensity – as he says, 'with manifold force'. As we shall see, this is of considerable significance. The third direct consequence of Darwin's re-direction of Malthus's principle to non-human animals and plants is already implicit in the other two: it is the non-voluntary character of the 'struggle for life' in the natural world. As we have seen, Darwin lays great stress on this in his careful qualifications of his metaphorical use of the term 'struggle', and in his frequent use of plants as illustrations, where the absence of intentionality makes his meaning plain.

Now to the transformations worked by Darwin in his use of Malthus's principle. In reversing the direction of Malthus's argument, it is clear that Darwin does not, after all, arrive at Malthus's starting point.[26] He is much *closer*, admittedly, to the 'harsher' view of the principle which Malthus offered in his first *Essay*. He also *seems* to agree with Malthus when he says that 'The amount of food for each species of course gives the extreme limit to which each can increase'.[27] However, an 'extreme limit' is not the same thing as an 'ultimate cause'. The whole moral and political force of Malthus's argument depends on the differential rates of increase between population and food-supply. So, whilst Malthus has to recognise that starvation is not the *sole* cause of human mortality, he has a powerful ideological motive for treating shortage of food as a primary cause which operates *by way* of other, immediate causes of premature death. So, among the positive checks, many diseases, and customs which 'weaken and destroy the human frame', are attributed to shortage of means of subsistence, whilst 'moral restraint' and the other preventive checks are only effective when there is a tangible and perceived threat of poverty and loss of social position with reduced income.[28]

Even Malthus has to concede a category of 'immediate causes' independent of scarcity, but this sets up an unresolved tension in his argument: in what sense are these causes 'immediate', if, in their case, shortage of means of subsistence is not functioning as 'ultimate' cause? The most he could consistently claim, in the face of this category of causes of premature death, would be that, if they were not in operation, scarcity *would* take their place.

Darwin, by contrast, stresses our *ignorance* of the checks to population. We know that they must operate with great intensity, otherwise the world would be overrun with the progeny of a single pair of any species, but: 'We know not exactly what the checks are in even one single instance. Nor will this surprise any one who reflects how ignorant we are on this head, even in regard to mankind, so incomparably better known than any other animal.'[29] Darwin then embarks on an open-ended discussion of the 'web of complex relations' between climatic conditions, seasonal and geographical conditions, food supply, predation, parasitism, disease-epidemics and so on and the populations of particular species, concluding:

> In the case of every species, many different checks, acting at different periods of life, and during different seasons or years, probably come into play; some one check or some few being generally the most potent, but all concurring in determining the average number or even the existence of the species.[30]

Where Malthus speaks of a 'simple' relation of population to means of subsistence, Darwin insists upon an irreducible variety and complexity in the struggle for existence in nature. What the checks to population are will vary from species to species, and different checks will act with varying intensity in different places and times, and at different stages in the life-history of individuals. All of this requires empirical investigation in each particular case. More than this, variation in the action of these various checks through time implies a *changing* web of interdependencies, as 'spaces' open up in the economy of nature, and are filled by adjacent populations, so that: 'The face of Nature may be compared to a yielding surface, with ten thousand sharp wedges packed close together and driven inwards by incessant blows, sometimes one wedge being struck and then another with greater force'.[31] Gillian Beer may be right in suggesting that the uncontrollably intense and repellant anthropomorphism of this famous metaphor led to its being excised from later editions of the *Origin*.[32] However, its role in the *formation* of Darwin's thought is evident right from his 'transmutation' notebooks through to the *Origin*.

Finally, it may be necessary to mention the complete absence from Darwin's use of Malthus in the *Origin* of any concern with the moral and metaphysical implications of Malthus's principle. This is hardly surprising, since Malthus is centrally concerned with the human case only – with the causes which have 'impeded the progress of mankind towards happiness' — and with the prospects for their removal.[33] His arguments against Wallace, Condorcet, Godwin and the English Poor Laws all depend on the assumption of human capacities for moral or prudential regulation of activity in the light of fear, interest or reason. Given the non-voluntary character of the metaphorical 'struggle for existence' in the rest of nature, none of these implications has any purchase. Animals and plants struggling for existence either survive and reproduce or they do not. They are not pressured into late marriage or small families, or tempted to 'vicious practices to conceal the consequences of irregular connections', and nor are they stimulated to abandon idleness and dependency in favour of autonomous industriousness. Malthus and Darwin were *not* 'part of a single debate'.[34]

However, this is most certainly *not* to argue that what Darwin took from Malthus amounted to little or nothing, that Malthus was more-or-less irrelevant to Darwin's explanation of the origin of the species. Darwin's own recollections and the evidence of his notebooks and early sketches are relevant but not decisive here. Perhaps somewhat more telling is the fact that A. R. Wallace attributed his own independent invention of the idea to his recollection of Malthus.[35] A thorough comparative reconstruction of Wallace's and Darwin's routes to their independent discoveries would undoubtedly be very revealing, but all I have space for here is a preliminary sketch of that process in the case of Darwin.

The formation of the concept of natural selection

After his return from the *Beagle* voyage, Darwin became increasingly obsessed with the question of the transmutation of species, so much so that he began a series of notebooks devoted to the topic. The first of these was commenced in July 1837. This question could itself only have arisen for Darwin on the basis of a prior intellectual and practical labour of considerable scale and scope. He had read Lyell's *Principles of Geology* during the voyage and, simultaneously observing geological formations, fossil remains and the patterns of distribution and variation of living forms, he had become convinced by Lyell's uniformitarian approach. Throughout its long history, the earth's crust had undergone enormous transformations, but these were to be explained as the outcome of causes such as climatic conditions, volcanic action, earthquakes and so on which we find in operation today. Moreover, the earth's transformations were to be explained as to the outcome of long-run, continuous accumulations of small-scale changes, rather than extreme cataclysmic events.

Lyell noted the differences in the organic remains contained in successive strata, and the extent of their adaptations to their existing conditions of life. He supposed that, as such conditions changed, some species would have been no longer adapted, and would have become extinct. However, he remained entirely opposed to the suggestion that adaptation to new conditions of life might explain the emergence of *new* species. He, like Darwin's other geological mentor, Sedgwick, scornfully rejected the Lamarckian transformationist hypothesis (to which Darwin had himself been introduced by Robert Grant, during his student days at Edinburgh). Gruber,[36] along with many others, has pointed out the tension between the broad principles of Lyell's approach to geological questions – historical transformations as outcomes of continuously acting causes and accumulated small-scale change – and his commitment to Creationism and fixity of species in the case of living forms. It seems likely that Darwin's observations of small-scale variations among closely related species on adjacent islands, as well as his own work of geological and palaeontological exploration during the *Beagle* voyage, eventually convinced him of the necessity to extend Lyell's uniformitarian approach to include living forms: they, too, must somehow have undergone transmutation, along with their physical conditions of life, by some unknown cause or causes.

Darwin's simultaneous struggle towards a materialist view of mental operations,[37] together with his shock at first encounter with 'primitive' humanity in the shape of the beleaguered Fuegians, may have been important in removing one obstacle to accepting transmutation: belief in the special moral and intellectual status of the human species. The ultimate anathema to

Lyell was the consideration that humans might be descended from the apes. As Desmond and Moore point out: 'Even for Lyell the prospect was appalling, because he feared that an ape ancestry would brutalize mankind and destroy his "high estate."'[38] Darwin's first (March 1838) encounter with a great ape – the orang-utan 'Jenny' – at London Zoo also deeply impressed him: 'Let man visit Ourang-outang in domestication, hear expressive whine, see its intelligence when spoken; ... & then let him dare to boast of his proud preeminence.'[39]

But if Darwin's increasingly naturalistic approach to human nature was removing a major *obstacle* to his transformationist view of species, it did not help him with what was now his key problem: the *causes* of transmutation, and the formation of new species. Between their commencement in July 1837 and Darwin's reading of Malthus in late September 1838, his notebooks abound with rehearsed responses to expected objections to 'his theory', and with discussions of phenomena, such as 'useless structures', and the patterns of variation between island and continental forms, which were accountable on the Creationist doctrine only with extreme implausibility. But Darwin himself never doubts that new species are formed from varieties of pre-existing ones, and that the enormous variety of present and past living organisms has arisen in this way from some common ancestor or ancestors.

So, the topic of Darwin's enquiry in the transmutation notebooks is *how* new species arise. But his question was a more complex and demanding one than this formulation suggests. As Darwin recounts in his autobiography:

> But it was equally evident that neither the action of the surrounding conditions, nor the will of the organisms (especially in the case of plants), could account for the innumerable cases in which organisms of every kind are beautifully adapted to their habits of life ... I had always been much struck by such adaptations, and until these could be explained it seemed to me almost useless to endeavour to prove by indirect evidence that species have been modified.[40]

Speciation-as-adaptation to changing conditions of life was Darwin's problem (see note 35). Transmutation in plants, as well as other objections to Lamarck's teleology, set a further constraint on what was to count as an adequate solution: some causal mechanism must be found which did not attribute adaptation, as an outcome of modification, to the will, or purpose of the adapted organism. Lyell's uniformitarian geology also provided Darwin with epistemological and methodological guidelines – with a definite model of the *kind* of account which would be acceptable: infinitessimally small changes as a result of constantly acting causes, over enormous spans of time, cumulatively bringing about large-scale transformations. Finally, Darwin took it as a criterion of the success of a theory that it linked together a large range of facts under a common explanatory principle: 'In comparing my theory with any other. it should be observed not what comparative difficulties (as long as not overwhelming) What comparative solutions & linking of facts.'[41] This is why Darwin's notebooks range so apparently eclectically over questions of fossil remains, comparative anatomy, geographical distribution, inheritance and variation in domestic and wild species, metamorphosis and development, taxonomy and so on: Darwin was constantly alive to the pertinence of all these classes of facts to his central questions of organic change and adaptation.

On uniformitarian principles, Darwin was searching for some mechanism by which individual variations, some of which, at least, were inheritable, might be passed on and progressively augmented. This would lead to a growing differentiation from the original stock, until 'good' species were formed, and so on though to genera, families and the higher taxonomic levels of differentiation. Intermediate forms, or their relative absence, were problems – but Darwin emphasised the incompleteness of the fossil record, and also noted the absence of extant intermediate forms between different breeds of domesticated animals. No one doubted that intermediate forms *had* existed in these cases. Another problem, which Darwin returned to again and again, was that, according to the 'blending' view of inheritance which was then in favour, variations should be eliminated by cross-breeding. This was, indeed, thought to be necessary to explain the *stability* of species, despite considerable individual variation.

In tackling this problem Darwin was drawn more and more

into his study of domestic breeds – searching out the literature on pigeons, ducks and farm animals, as well as making intensive personal inquiries of William Yarrell, Mr Wynne (his father's gardener), William Darwin Fox, Sir J. Sebright, and others. He showed particular interest in hybrids, and the fertility or otherwise of varieties and closely related species. In this and other respects, Darwin used the 'rules of thumb' employed by breeders of domesticated species to shed light on variation and inheritance in the wild. In the notebooks, his attention fixes on cases of inter-breeding in which the offspring resemble one or other of the parents, or are heterogeneous, rather than following the expected pattern of blending. In the case of wild forms, geographical isolation, as in the Galapagos, might offset the stabilising consequences of 'blending', and allow new varieties to diverge. By his own account, Darwin did not resolve this problem to his own satisfaction until much later.[42]

But what Darwin's excursions into the world of pigeon fanciers and dog breeders *did* achieve was to suggest to him the possibility of some analogy between the domesticated varieties produced by selective breeding and the mechanism of organic modification in nature. At its first appearance, the analogy is abortive: 'The changes in species must be very slow, owing to physical change slow & offspring not picked. – as man do. when making varieties. -'[43] Unfortunately the notebooks do not give us more evidence about the formative role of this analogy in Darwin's thinking prior to his reading of Malthus. However, his very adoption of the metaphorical term 'natural selection' and the order of his exposition in the 1842 sketch (not to mention subsequent drafts[44]) strongly suggest that this analogy was Darwin's route through to the mechanism of organic change. The 1842 sketch begins by pointing out the extent of modification achieved by selective breeding in a relatively short time. Why would not new species be produced in nature over a much longer period? But is there a 'creative agency' in nature which could bring about these results?

In the sketch, Malthus is brought in at this point. However, to refer back to the notebooks, one further concept is required for Darwin's use of Malthus to do the explanatory work

demanded of it. Only some twenty pages prior to his breakthrough in the notebooks, Darwin includes the following:

> Owen says 'the necessity of combining observation of the living
> habits of animals, with anatomical & zoological research, in order
> to establish entirely their place in nature, as well as fully to
> understand their oeconomy, is now universally admitted'.[45]

With the qualification that this 'oeconomy' is in constant
process of change, this clearly conforms exactly to Darwin's
own practice, and is a restatement of the problem he has set
himself to solve: the 'adaptation' of organisms to their conditions of life as a complex web of interconnections between the
anatomy, physiology and behaviour of the members of different co-existing populations in relation to one another and to
their physical environments. This concept of a flexible economy
of nature was, as we shall see, quite decisive.

The first impact of Darwin's reading of Malthus comes in
his note of 28 September 1838: 'Even the energetic language of
Decandoelle does not convey the warring of the species as inference from Malthus.'[46] Immediately we get not Malthus's
Principle but the implications of the far greater intensity of its
action in nature: 'in Nature production does not increase, whilst
no checks prevail, but the positive check of famine & consequently death.' Then comes the astonishingly condensed theoretical breakthrough:

> [T]ake Europe on an average, every species must have same
> number killed, year with year, by hawks. by. cold & c. – even
> one species of hawk decreasing in number must effect instanta-
> neously all the rest.- One may say there is a force like a hundred
> thousand wedges trying force every kind of adapted structure
> into the gaps in the economy of Nature, or rather forming gaps
> by thrusting out weaker ones. The final cause of all this wedg-
> ings, must be to sort out proper structure & adapt it to change.
> – to do that for form, which Malthus shows, is the final effect,
> (by means however of volition) of this populousness, on the
> energy of Man.[47]

When Darwin read Malthus, he was 'prepared' by more than
his own observations of the struggle for existence in nature. He
was prepared by his central *question* – the source of adaptive
organic change - by his study of *inheritable variation* among

populations of animals and plants, by his concept of *a changing economy of nature* and by his uniformitarian methodological precepts. Because and *only* because he read Malthus through this dynamic conceptual grid was he able to see that a consequence of the *great intensity* of the struggle for existence in the non-human world is *qualitative* change in populations towards a multi-dimensional fit between organisms and their environments. Ever-changing organisms, increasingly adapted to their place in a dynamic economy of nature, will be the unwilled outcome.

Those writers, such as Gerratana,[48] who have argued that Malthus was unnecessary to Darwin − 'a mere literary reminiscence' − are mistaken. Malthus's geometrical ratio and its implications for *non*-human nature brought home to Darwin just *how* powerful a selective force was operating in nature. This was necessary for the colossal imaginative leap required to see what an immense, teeming diversity of organic life, including structures as complex and finely tuned to their functions as the eye or ear, could result from this force, given a long enough interval of time. Darwin's E notebook, commenced just after his reading of Malthus, explicitly acknowledges the difficulty of this imaginative leap: 'The difficulty of multiplying effects & to conceive the result with that clearness of conviction, absolutely necessary as the basal foundation stone of further inductive reasoning is immense.'[49]

Equally, his own comment notwithstanding, Darwin does *not* become a Malthusian. At no point does Malthus's principle of population enter into Darwin's thought. It serves, as Althusser[50] would have said, as a 'theoretical raw material', which is profoundly *transformed* as it is appropriated and set to work by the complex apparatus of Darwin's thinking about the species question. And Darwin's thinking itself, as we have seen, was formed, constrained and enabled by the wider discourse of early-nineteenth-century natural history. Gillian Beer is right to emphasise the *affective* dimension of Darwin's reading, and its transformative character. However, my analysis suggests that, rather than Milton affecting Darwin's reading of Malthus, it was Darwin's reading of Malthus which profoundly changed the affective tone of Darwin's own appreciation of nature: 'It is difficult to believe in the dreadful but quiet war of organic beings. going on the peaceful woods. & smiling fields.'[51] Far from finding satisfaction in this view of nature, his notebooks and the *Origin* itself are replete with expressions of dread and disquiet, combined with feeble utilitarian attempts at 'consolation'.[52] This is evidence of Darwin not as someone swimming with the tide of mid-century cultural change but as like Schoenberg, in a different context, a 'reluctant revolutionary', pushed by the rigour of his own struggle with an intellectual problem into a profoundly innovative scientific advance – an advance which he knew would shake the foundations of what had become a ruling ideology: 'Once grant that species one genus may pass into each other. – grant that one instinct to be acquired ... & whole fabric totters & falls'.[53]

But Darwin's achievement was not a ready-made buttress for any alternative 'cultural dominant'. As Desmond and Moore (with dubious consistency) point out, 'Darwin's non-human orientation was a total departure from radical wisdom, let alone religious convention'.[54] Darwin's breaching of the 'species barrier' opened up in a radically new way two fields of moral and metaphysical speculation. Human *kinship* with non-human animals affords new ways of thinking about human nature itself, and, conversely, about the moral status of non-human animals:

> Animals – whom we have made our slaves we do not like to consider our equals. – Do not slave-holders wish to make the black man other kind? ... the soul by consent of all is superadded, animals not got it, not look forward if we choose to let conjecture run wild then animals our fellow brethren in pain, disease, death, & suffering & famine; our slaves in the most laborious work, our companion in our amusements. they may partake, from our origin in one common ancestor we may be all netted together.[55]

And, as part of that complicated web of interdependencies which make up nature's 'economy', humans are ecologically, as well as by relations of descent, bound together with non-human species. Only in the last few decades of the twentieth century are the full consequences of Darwin's re-location of humanity *within* nature coming into their own.[56]

Notes

1 A. Desmond and J. Moore, *Darwin* (Harmondsworth: Penguin, 1992.
2 N. R. Hanson, *Patterns of Discovery* (Cambridge: Cambridge University Press, 1965) p. 7.
3 P. K. Feyerabend, *Against Method* (London: New Left Books, 1975) chapter 18.
4 A. Desmond and J. Moore, p. xix.
5 G. Beer, *Darwin's Plots: Evolutionary Narrative in Darwin, George Eliot and Nineteenth-Century Fiction* (London: Routledge & Kegan Paul, 1983).
6 Ibid ., p. 90.
7 Ibid., p. 6.
8 Ibid., p. 100.
9 Ibid., p. 38.
10 Ibid., p. 53.
11 Darwin, *Origin*, p. 130.
12 Beer, *Darwin's Plots*, p. 7 (my parenthesis).
13 Ibid., p. 33.
14 Ibid., p. 34.
15 A. R. Wallace, *My Life* (condensed edition) (London: Chapman and Hall, 1908), p. 149.
16 R. M. Young, *Darwin's Metaphor: Nature's Place in Victorian Culture* (Cambridge: Cambridge University Press, 1985), p. 24.
17 Ibid., p. 166.
18 Ibid., p. 240.
19 Ibid., p. 241.
20 Ibid., 246.
21 Ibid., p. 225.
22 C. Darwin and T. H. Huxley, *Autobiographies,* ed. and introduced by G. De Beer (Oxford and New York: Oxford University Press, 1986), p. 71.
23 Darwin, *Origin*, p. 116.
24 Ibid., p. 117.
25 T. R. Malthus, *An Essay on the Principle of Population,* ed P. James in 2 vols. (Cambridge: Cambridge University Press,1989), chapter 1.
26 Compare Robert Young's analysis: 'It appears, then, that it was the removal of Malthus's idea of "moral restraint" and an emphasis on the concept of "population pressure", which left a natural law about plants and animals, that characterised Darwin's interpretation. He was, in effect, reverting to the purity of the inescapable dilemma of Malthus's first edition' (Young, *Darwin's Metaphor*, p. 45).
27 Darwin, *Origin*, p. 120.
28 Malthus, *Essay*, pp. 16-7.
29 Darwin, *Origin*, p. 120.
30 Ibid., p. 125.
31 Ibid., p. 119.
32 Beer, *Darwin's Plots*, p. 72.
33 Malthus, *Essay*, p. 9.
34 Young, *Darwin's Metaphor*, p. 24.

35 The route to Wallace's concept was, however, significantly different.
    Wallace certainly considered the relevance of domestic breeding of
    animals and plants, but did not arrive at his view of the origin of species
    by way of the analogy between natural and 'artificial' selection. The facts
    of variation, affinity and geographical distribution were the focus of his
    concerns in the Malay Archipelago. Less influenced than Darwin by
    natural theological arguments about adaptation and design, Wallace was
    correspondingly more disposed to see 'progressive' organic change as an
    outcome of the struggle for existence. This probably represents a colour-
    ing of Wallace's view by his generally much more radical political views,
    but it was an obstacle to his arriving at the non-anthropocentric view of
    evolution which surfaces in Darwin (if only to disappear again when he
    directly confronts the question of human descent). See the analysis in H.
    L. McKinney, *Wallace and Natural Selection* (New Haven and London:
    Yale University Press, 1972) (esp. Appendix IV) and my own essay
    'Where to Draw the Line? A. R. Wallace in Borneo', in eds. F. Barker,
    P. Hulme and M. Iversen, *Writing Travels* (Manchester: Manchester
    University Press, forthcoming).
36 H. E. Gruber and Paul. H. Barrett, *Darwin on Man* (London: Wildwood
    House, 1974), p. 133.
37 C. Darwin, *Charles Darwin's Notebooks 1836–1846* ed. P. H. Barrett, P.
    J. Gautrey, S. Herbert, D. Kohn and S. Smith, British Museum (Natural
    History)/Cambridge: Cambridge University Press, 1987), pp. 517-60.–
    Notebook M.
38 Desmond and Moore, *Darwin*, p. 221.
39 Darwin, *Notebooks*, p. 264 – Notebook C 79.
40 Darwin and Huxley, *Autobigraphies*, p. 70.
41 Darwin, *Notebooks*, p. 356 – Notebook D 71.
42 Darwin & Huxley, *Autobigraphies*, pp. 71-2.
43 Darwin, *Notebooks*, p. 242 – Notebook C 17e.
44 See C, Darwin, *The Foundations of the Origin of Species*, ed. F. Darwin
    (Cambridge: Cambridge University Press, 1909); and C. Darwin, *Charles
    Darwin's Natural Selection: Being the Second Part of His Big Species Book
    Written from 1856 to 1858*, ed. R.C. Stamffer (Cambridge: Cambridge
    University Press, 1975).
45 Darwin, *Notebooks*, p. 369 – Notebook D 115.
46 Ibid., p. 375 – Notebook D 134.
47 Ibid., pp. 375-6 – Notebook D 135e.
48 V. Gerratana, 'Marx and Darwin', *New Left Review* 82 (Nov./Dec. 1973),
    p. 72. Lest this seems too dismissive of Gerratana's work, I should make
    it clear that in several important respects my approach here endorses
    Gerratana's analysis – especially his judgement that Malthus's theory
    remains 'essentially foreign' to Darwin's thought.
49 Darwin, *Notebooks*, p. 398 - Notebook E 5e.
50 L. Althusser, *For Marx* (London: New Left Books, 1969) especially in the
    essay 'On the Materialist Dialectic'. The analysis I offer here uses, in a
    fairly open-ended way, concepts derived from the French tradition of
    historical epistemology, associated with Bachelard and Canguilhem, from

Althusser's concept of knowledge as a form of (intellectual) production, and from Roy Bhaskar's approach to realist philosophy of science (see R. Bhaskar, *A Realist Theory of Science* (Brighton, Harvester, 1978) and *Realism and Human Emancipation* (London: Vergo,1986); T. Benton, *Philosophical Foundations of the Three Sociologies* (London: Routledge and Kegan Paul, 1977) and *The Rise and Fall of Structural Marxism* (Basingstoke: Macmillan 1984); and A. Collier, *Scientific Realism and Socialist Thought* (Hemel Hempstead: Harvester 1989), and *Critical Realism* (London: Verso 1994)).

51　Darwin, *Notebooks*, p. 429 – Notebook E, 114, 12 March 1839.

52　Compare with Desmond and Moore: 'At last he had a mechanism that was compatible with the competitive, tree-trading ideals of the ultra-Whigs. The transmutation at the base of his theory would still be loathed by many. But the Malthusian superstructure struck an emotionally satisfying chord; an open struggle with no hand-outs to the losers was the Whig way, and no poor-law commissioner could have bettered Darwin's view' (*Darwin*, p. 267).

53　Darwin, *Notebooks*, p. 263 – Notebook C 76.

54　Desmond and Moore, *Darwin*, p. 232.

55　Darwin, *Notebooks*, pp. 228-9 – Notebook B 231-2.

56　For a further development of this argument, see T. Benton, *Natural Relations: Ecology, Animal Rights and Social Justice* (London: Verso 1993).

4

The Origin of Species and the science of female inferiority

FIONA ERSKINE

> Sexual selection will give its aid to ordinary selection, by assuring to the most vigorous and best adapted *males* the greatest number of offspring.   *Origin of Species*

> If women comprehended all that is contained in the domestic sphere, they would ask no other.   Herbert Spencer[1]

During the second half of the nineteenth century, the 'woman question' increasingly dominated public discourse as reforms were demanded that threatened to transform the relations between the sexes. Married women's property legislation was passed, recognising a wife's independent existence; educational opportunities were expanded with the founding of Queen's College and Bedford College in 1848 and 1849 and with the subsequent opening of further schools and colleges for the daughters of the middle classes; new career opportunities were being seized. Women learned that they could organise around issues of gender: the campaign against the Contagious Diseases Acts, finally repealed in 1886, brought together women of all classes across the nation in protest against the sexual double standard. Political rights were demanded: Barbara Bodichon set up the Women's Suffrage Committee in 1866 and Parliament debated the issue for the first time the following year. And yet for all its apparent strength and vitality the women's movement all but disappeared with the First World War and re-emerged only half a century later.

The rise of feminism in the 1970s was accompanied by that

of sociobiology, which emphasised biological limits to women's aspirations. Viewing this as a deliberate attempt to subvert the women's movement, feminist historians of science were prompted to look for a causal link between the rise of gendered science and the demise of the first woman's movement. Their thesis was that, in response to women's achievements and their continuing demands, the anti-feminist opposition looked to science, and in particular to Darwinian evolution, for a most potent weapon: tracts, essays and lectures flowed abundantly from the 1860s on, demonstrating how natural and sexual selection had operated to produce the physical and mental inferiority that could be proved anatomically and demonstrated empirically. Already by the turn of the century feminism was defeated ideologically, although the campaign for the suffrage postponed its public disintegration. The success of the scientific attack on feminism was a consequence of the unassailable authority vested in evolutionary science in the late nineteenth century and of the unanimity of the evolutionists commitment to the subordination of women.[2]

Although polemically attractive, this interpretation raises difficulties. The paradox of Darwin's scientific radicalism and social liberalism on the one hand, and his conservative views on gender on the other, is not addressed. The success of gendered science is assumed rather than explained: the suggestion that this success can be attributed simply to the contemporary prestige of science underestimates the degree to which scientific ideas were subjected to critical scrutiny from within and without the scientific community. More importantly, it diverts attention from the fundamental contradiction in the women's movement, that of demanding expanded opportunities for women, whilst denying any need for a reappraisal of the male role or of the patriarchal foundations of contemporary society. This chapter will attempt to address some of these issues by looking first at Darwin's views on gender as elaborated in the *Origin* and in other private and public communications; second at the development of those ideas by Darwin's disciples and at the use made of them in the cause of anti-feminism and third at the response of some of the women involved in the 'woman question'.

Darwin on gender

The relevance of the *Origin* to the debate about gender derives initially from the fundamental role played by sexual reproduction as the mechanism through which variability becomes heritable. Without sexual reproduction, natural selection cannot operate. For this reason, Darwin argued, one of the earliest developments in evolution was the separation of the male and female reproductive role. Sexual divergence occurs in two ways: through natural selection and through sexual selection. Natural selection operates to increase sexual differentiation because such differentiation enhances functional adaptation, in accordance with the established principle of the physiological division of labour.[3] The basic principles of Darwinian theory therefore include gender specialisation.

Sexual selection, Darwin's secondary mechanism of sexual differentiation, depends on the struggle between males for possession of females, a struggle explained by the fact that success in leaving progeny is as important an element in the struggle for existence as the life of the individual. Sexual selection explains the development of courtship rituals as well as of peculiarly male characteristics in many species. Some such characteristics enhance the attractiveness of the male, whose success ultimately depends on female choice: the plumage of the peacock has evolved through sexual selection as a means of pleasing the peahen. Others enhance the ability to fight off rival males: the antlers of the deer are so explained. The effect in all cases is to encourage divergence between the males and females of a species.[4]

The central role of sexual selection in the evolution of man was further elaborated in the *Descent*. Darwin first reiterated the general principle: 'It is certain that amongst almost all animals there is a struggle between the males for the possession of the ... female. Hence the females have the opportunity of selecting one out of several males.' But in man, the power of selection has been transferred to the male: 'Man is more powerful in body and mind than woman, and in the savage state he keeps her in a far more abject state of bondage than does the male of any other animal; therefore it is not surprising that he should have gained the power of selection.' Given the determination

with which Darwin resisted human exceptionalism when
proposed by those, like Wallace and Lyell, who feared the mate-
rialistic implications of Darwinism, his ready accommodation of
the male power to select is remarkable. But Darwin disclaimed
any disjuncture between man and brute: he referred to a species
of monkey wherein male choice prevailed, as well as to prehistoric society, in which female choice was responsible for the
evolution, through sexual selection, of the beard. The transfer
to the male of the power to select was a symbol of evolutionary advance: 'for in utterly barbarous tribes the women have
more power in choosing, rejecting, and tempting their lovers,
or of afterwards changing their husbands, than might have
been expected.'[5]

Other explanations of change detailed in the *Origin*, not
explicitly concerned with sex differences, also had a bearing on
the relations between the sexes. In the section on the 'Laws of
Variation', Darwin advanced causes of change in organisms
additional to and complementary to natural selection. These
included the effect of external conditions, or the direct influence of the environment, and change through use and disuse.
Darwin claimed to be sceptical of any significant degree of
modification brought about by the effect of external conditions;
rather, he suggested that changes in the environment induce
variability, 'and natural selection will then accumulate all prof-
itable variations, however slight, until they become plainly
developed and appreciable by us'.[6] This passage, in raising the
controversial issue of the inheritance of acquired characters,
caused bitter debate among naturalists, but to reformers in
many fields, including that of women's rights, it appeared to
provide a pathway by which cultural change could adjust
human potential and human relationships.

This optimistic interpretation of the theory of evolution by
natural selection depended on a theory of heredity that allowed
environmentally induced change to be transmitted to the next
generation. Meanwhile, the existence of gender differences,
increasing under the impact either of sexual selection or of
natural selection, depended upon a theory of heredity which
allowed characteristics to pass to one sex only. Darwin made no
pretensions to a theory of heredity, claiming only that obser-

vation supported such assumptions. As Weisman's theory of the germ plasm and Mendelian genetics were synthesised to produce a new theory of heredity at the turn of the century, both were undermined. For the reformers, the loss of Darwin's supplementary agents of change proved a major blow. For the anti-feminists, the damage was more easily repaired: anthropologists relied instead on aboriginal rather than evolutionary sexual difference. They found sanction for this concept in the *Origin*, where Darwin wrote that the two sexes might be regarded in the light of two separate species.[7]

When Darwin came to address the issue of gender explicitly in the *Descent*, there had already been produced a substantial body of work by his friends and supporters arguing for biologically determined female inferiority. Darwin endorsed and reinforced this work, expressing his conviction not only of female inferiority but also of innate differences in the quality of female thought. He had long believed that women had a greater capacity for religious belief (or a greater credulity) than men. He now claimed that while women were tenderer and less selfish, they were also more emotional and less capable of reasoned thought.[8] (It was, Darwin argued, 'the tenderness of their hearts', coupled with 'their profound ignorance', that made women support Frances Power Cobbe's anti-vivisection agitation; an agitation which he vehemently opposed, in the interests of 'abstract truth'.)[9] Women remained for ever childlike, physiologically and mentally.

It has been argued that ideas contained in the *Descent of Man* can not be used to judge of Darwin's opinions when he wrote the *Origin*, and that the *Origin* is neutral on the question of sexual difference. The development of sexual selection to accommodate the male power to select is held to indicate that it was only in the 1860s, under the pressure of the debate about women then raging, that Darwin developed his views of biologically-determined female inferiority and grafted them on to his evolutionary theory.[10] In many areas, it is undoubtedly true that the *Descent* reflects major developments in Darwin's social thought during the 1860s. Undeniably, too, the *Descent* speaks on gender difference with a certainty and dogmatism quite absent from the *Origin*. But in the case of Darwin's attitude to women, the expression in the *Descent* represents a change in purpose rather than in attitude. Sexual selection is intrinsically anti-feminist: outlined in the *Origin* as the means by which males become stronger, fitter, more beautiful or more talented, it can only be a mechanism for the disproportionate development of male prowess.

The *Descent* gives voice to Darwin's deeply-rooted beliefs. If his *Origin* statements appear neutral, it is only because patriarchy and the subordination of women were for him unchallenged assumptions. As a young bachelor he had dreamed of 'nice little wives'; in notes on matrimony, he described a wife as 'object to be beloved and played with. – better than a dog anyhow'; in his transmutation notebooks he likened the female to the young of a species, the woman to the child; Emma Wedgwood, the well-educated, intelligent woman whom he married in January 1839, was valued for her abilities to nurse him and to bear and raise his children. Both intimidated by and scornful of intellectual women, he found his brother's friend Harriet Martineau overpowering and considered a visit from his blue-stocking niece, Julia Wedgwood, 'rather a bore'.[11] Darwin saw the role of women in orthodox terms. Women were born to suffer, to nurture and to redeem and were equipped for these tasks with fortitude, altruism and an elevated moral sense.

For Darwin patriarchy was entrenched, and there was close conformity between his findings on sex differences and those of conventional opinion. The sex stereotyping of the *Descent* is best understood in terms of an appreciation that evolutionary biology could be employed to counter the undue ambitions of women. Darwin's long-standing sympathy for women's education was now subordinated to the hard fact of female inferiority. In his early transmutation notebooks, true to the Wedgwood– Darwin tradition of support for advances in education, he had written 'improve the women. (double influence) and mankind must improve –' . But in the *Descent* he argued that there was little potential for the advancement of women's mental powers as there was no survival value in it. Indeed, it was fortunate that the laws of inheritance allowed a degree of transmission of 'male' characteristics to the 'female'. For otherwise the gulf between the mental powers of male and female would be even

greater: 'it is probable that men would have become as superior in mental endowment to women, as the peacock is in orna-
mental plumage to the peahen.' For the tendency was for sexual
differences to increase over time, owing to the greater pressure
under which males were placed by natural and sexual selection,
and the consequently greater variability of the male.[12]

The *Origin*, seen in the wider context of Darwin's views on
women, implies female subordination. The central focus on
sexual reproduction, and the female's role as a vessel for the
development of the next generation, meant that success in that
role took on primary importance. Sexual selection forced males
to become ever stronger and fitter, whilst making females
progressively more passive. The female was akin to the infan-
tile form, so different from the male as to be regarded in the
light of separate species.

Science and the subordination of women

Only Darwin's self-denying ordinance to avoid discussion of
man in the *Origin* allowed his views on gender to be obscured.
It remained initially for others to tease out the implications of
his theories for the 'woman question'. The legitimacy of trans-
lating his ideas to such a purpose was not in question: it had
always been his intention to supply universal laws to explain
human development.[13] In the *Origin* he claimed that 'Psychology
will be based on a new foundation, that of the necessary
acquirement of each mental power and capacity by gradation.
Light will be thrown on the origin of man and his history.' But
Darwin was hesitant about the potential for engineering change
by means of natural selection. His belief in relative adaptation
led him to reject perfectibilism while his commitment to grad-
ualism and uniformitarianism caused him repeatedly to emphasise the extremely slow pace of evolutionary change. Change
was intermittent rather than continuous, adaptive rather than
progressive. Whilst the struggle for existence was constant, the
status quo was the norm. 'Battle within battle must ever be
recurring with varying success; and yet in the long-run the
forces are so nicely balanced, that the face of nature remains
uniform for long periods of time ...'.[14]

The central ambiguity of Darwin's attitude to change and persistence allowed a wide variety of interpretations of the import of his theories for the debate about gender, but they resulted in comparable rejections of female aspiration. Herbert Spencer argued that the process of evolution could be accelerated through submission to its laws; since sexual divergence was one such law, the women's movement was necessarily an obstacle to evolution. George Romanes on the other hand could argue that even if conditions were right for female advance, the pace of change through natural selection was so slow that no amount of female education could ever bridge the intellectual gap that had opened up over the centuries.[15] Underlying these, and divers other interpretations, lay a common agreement on fundamental and unremitting differences in the temperament and abilities of males and females. This agreement depended not on scientific research but on the separate sphere ideology that now found legitimation in science. The idea of innocent, intuitive woman, presiding over, yet contained and protected by, the home, was a commonplace of Victorian writing. Tennyson described the ideal in *The Princess*, in 1847:

> Not learned, save in gracious household ways,
> Not perfect, nay, but full of tender wants,
> No angel, but a dearer being, all dipt
> In angel instincts, breathing Paradise,
> Interpreter between the Gods and men

Ruskin described woman as the helpmate of man and summarised the ideal type of both sexes:

> His intellect is for speculation and invention; his energy for adventure, for war, and for conquest, wherever war is just, wherever conquest necessary. But the woman's power is for rule, not for battle, – and her intellect is not for invention or creation, but for sweet ordering, arrangement and decision.[16]

In the 1850s anthropologists began to argue a scientific basis for separate sphere ideology and to make explicit its implication of sexual hierarchy. Although the manner of expression varied according to whether the authors wished to confront or conciliate, their findings as to gender differences were remarkably similar to those of the men of letters, for all that they were couched in the language of science. But until anthropology tied itself to evolutionary theory there was no mechanism to explain how and why gender differences should exist.[17] Nor was there any defence against John Stuart Mill's charge that they were merely a cultural artefact: 'I have before repudiated the notion', Mill wrote in *The Subjection of Women*, 'of its being yet certainly known that there is any natural difference at all in the average strength or direction of the mental capacities of the two sexes, much less what that difference is'.[18] He argued that the only way of ascertaining the truth of gender difference was to subject both sexes to the same conditions over a long period of time. Without such empirical evidence he denied that any definitive statement could be made.

As the prestige of evolutionary theory grew, social anthropologists looked for an alliance that would invest their findings with greater authority. A succession of studies appeared in the 1860s, demonstrating that the subordination of women to men was a hallmark of civilisation: whilst primitive societies enjoyed near equality between the sexes, evolutionarily advanced societies experienced increasing sexual divergence. Building on the recently established antiquity of man, Darwinian explanations were grafted on to a scale of civilisation that showed the ascent of man from universal primitive savagery, unspecialised and communal, to the highly differentiated patriarchal culture that obtained in Victorian England.[19]

Herbert Spencer played an important role in developing the link between this new social anthropology and Darwinian evolution. He declared the universality of evolutionary law, in *First Principles* in 1862, and allied to it progressivism; evolution thence became a mechanism for perfectibility. Its defining characteristics, such as sexual divergence, became prescriptions for evolutionary success: the degree of difference between the sexes indicated the degree to which the species or the race had evolved. Evolution could be hindered (for example by misguided feminists), but not denied, for Spencer stressed its necessitarian character: the necessity of specialisation of function, the necessity of suffering, the necessity, by implication, of the subordination of the will of the individual to the demands of the species.[20]

Spencer discussed the relationship between the sexes in *Principles of Biology* (1864–7). He argued that any enlargement of the role of women could occur only within strict limits. Women's physical inferiority was increasing as higher stages of evolution progressively freed them from physical labour; meanwhile the law of conservation of energy dictated that any energy consumed in intellectual activity was energy diverted from woman's primary, reproductive role. Here too, Spencer could find authority in Darwin s theories. Crediting Geoffroy and Goethe, Darwin wrote in the *Origin*: 'if nourishment flows to one part or organ in excess, it rarely flows, at least in excess, to another part; thus it is difficult to get a cow to give much milk and to fatten readily.'[21] For Darwin there was no real need to appeal to a special law of conservation, since the same phenomena were explicable by natural selection: 'natural selection is continually trying to economise in every part of the organisation.'

Prominent Darwinists in the 1860s presented their evidence of female inferiority. In 1864, Carl Vogt's *Lectures on Man* were published in English, confirming the suggestion made in Darwin's transmutation notebook that the brain of the woman was child-like, and arguing that the difference between her brain and that of the male became greater as the racial hierarchy was ascended. 'It is a remarkable circumstance', Vogt wrote, in a passage subsequently quoted by Darwin in the *Descent*, 'that the difference between the sexes, as regards the cranial cavity, increases with the development of the race, so that the male European excels much more the female, than the negro the negress.'[22] The female, like the savage, exhibited arrested development, and in developmental terms was, as Darwin had maintained since the 1830s, on a par with a child.

T. H. Huxley, instrumental in bringing anthropology within the evolutionary paradigm, presented similar anatomical evidence in the Hunterian lectures in 1864. Nature had condemned women to subject status, but Huxley was conciliatory. 'The duty of man is to see that not a grain is piled upon that load beyond what Nature imposes; that injustice is not added to inequality.' Educating women would not alter their status: 'The most Darwinian of theorists will not venture to propound the doctrine, that the physical disabilities under which women have hitherto laboured in the struggle for existence with men are likely to be removed by even the most skillfully conducted process of educational selection.' Huxley put his finding to practical use by engineering the expulsion of women from the Ethnological Society and preventing their admission to the Geological Society.[23]

Having established gender difference on a scientific basis, the men of science worked to reconcile women to their evolutionary lot. In a major article in *The Nineteenth Century* in 1887, George J. Romanes rehearsed the arguments for female inferiority: the greater brain size of the male (a specious argument which should not have survived J. S. Mill's retort in 1869 that brain size had necessarily to be proportional to overall body size), women's lack of originality and judgement, weaker willpower and poor concentration. These sex differences had their origin in the Darwinian principles of natural and sexual selection. They had been exaggerated by the poor quality of women's education, but education could never compensate for natural inferiority: had there existed a female potential for genius, claimed Romanes, echoing Galton, it would have shown itself. 'The strong passion of genius is not to be restrained by any such minor accidents of environment. Women by tens of thousands have enjoyed better educational as well as better social advantages than a Burns, a Keats, or a Faraday; and yet we have neither heard their voices nor seen their work.'[24]

The popular press played its part in alerting readers to the findings of the men of science. The 'new woman', product of a generation of middle-class girls' education, first made her appearance in the 1870s and was a journalistic commonplace by the 1880s.[25] Characterised as mannish and criticised for emasculating British manhood, she was attacked for being selfish, putting her own individual desires before the interests of society. Her perverted demand for independence was responsible for the decline in the middle-class birth rate, noted by the turn of the century, and for the increase in the number of 'surplus', that is unmarried, women. The failure to marry and reproduce was compounded by the failure properly to perform that other task for which nature had fitted women, that of child rearing.

This failure, particularly evident in the case of working mothers, accounted for the general debility of the population. The strength and vigour of the race was being undermined as a consequence of the women's movement.

The publications in 1889 of *The Evolution of Sex* by Patrick Geddes and J. Arthur Thomson and in 1894 of *Man and Woman* by Havelock Ellis, marked attempts to provide women with a substitute for equality. *The Evolution of Sex* rejected both the proponents of equal rights and the anti-feminists. The two sexes were 'complementary and mutually dependent', but inevitably and essentially different.[26] In *Man and Woman*, Ellis maintained that the role of women both in rearing children and in supporting male endeavour was critical: 'In women men find beings who have not wandered so far as they have from the typical life of earth's creatures; women are for men the human embodiments of the restful responsiveness of Nature.'[27] Thirty-five years of scientific investigation had produced the conclusion that woman was functionally adapted to be the companion of man, the servant of his needs and the mother of his children.

The case against male domination

The *Origin of Species* had not been expected to feature as defender of the status quo. Its publication was greeted with acclaim by many intellectual radicals, including prominent supporters of women's rights. Individual struggle as the engine of change implied the rejection of artificially contrived barriers to competition; environmental adaptation suggested that sexual convergence could result from social pressures for greater equality. Mental exertion could reverse the atrophy of women's intellectual faculties attributable to disuse. The *Origin* provided a theory of the universe that rejected the appeal of tradition and that was based on reason and understanding. In the context of an increasing faith in progress, Darwin's theories of evolution could be regarded optimistically.

Advanced thinkers applauded Darwin's enterprise, but there was initially scant recognition of any specific application to the 'woman question' of the theories contained in the *Origin*. Writing to Charles's brother Erasmus, feminist freethinker

Harriet Martineau had praise only for the scientific spirit that confronted traditional authority with reason and knowledge:

> I am not pretending to speak about the science; though I fancy I follow his argument as a learner. If we could follow no further, the unconscious disclosure of the spirit and habit of the true scientific mind would be a most profitable and charming lesson to us. I believed and have often described, the quality and conduct of your brother's mind, but it is an unspeakable satisfaction to see here the full manifestation of its earnestness and simplicity, its sagacity, its industry, and the patient power by which it has collected such a mass of facts, to transmute them by such sagacious treatment into such portentous knowledge.[28]

John Stuart Mill, writing to his friend Alexander Bain in April 1860, was interested only in the validity of Darwin's argument, while others, like George Henry Lewes and George Eliot, already familiar with and sympathetic to doctrines of progressive development, became firm proponents of Darwinism.[29]

With the linking of Darwinist evolution to anthropological findings of female inferiority and with the decline of meliorist interpretations in favour of an emphasis on the limitations on change, women were forced to consider the implications of Darwinism for the role of women in society. Many subscribed to and were constrained by a belief in innate sexual difference. Many were, like Harriet Martineau, profound admirers of a science they saw as objective and free from the prejudices of traditional authority. For such as these it was difficult to view scientific discovery as an instrument of oppression. Only a few voices were raised in defiance and in warning of the dangers of accommodation with gendered science.

Frances Power Cobbe found the strength to resist the new orthodoxy in a deep religious faith, to which all man-made artefacts, including science, were subordinated. An acclaimed and prolific writer on ethics and on the role of women in society, she was a friend of many of the eminent men of science, until divided from them by her campaign against vivisection in the 1870s. She had admired the *Origin*, and had discussed its implications for human society with Darwin on more than one occasion. But increasingly she viewed science as hostile to the spiritual well-being of humanity, especially in the way that, in

their 'priest-like arrogance', men of science arrogated to themselves the right to judge of human behaviour. She portrayed the
materialism of science as undermining aspirations to a higher
morality, and she depicted the men of science as jealously
guarding their male preserve from invasion by well-qualified
and competent women. Particularly interested in the problem
of domestic violence, she drew a parallel between the abuse of
women in the home and the activities of the vivisectors, in that
both resulted from the corrupting influence of absolute,
unchecked male power.[30]

Even before the *Descent of Man* had given Darwin's imprint
to the alliance of evolution with gendered anthropology, Frances
Power Cobbe was arguing that the new science could not be
used to deny the demands of women. Even if women were
proved to be inferior, this would not justify the refusal to grant
them civil rights. For such rights were owed to all those held
to possess moral responsibility for their actions. In any event,
if there were inferiority in some respects, it was balanced by
superiority n others. In *Fraser's Magazine* in 1868, she wrote:

> If men choose to say that women are their inferiors in everything,
> they are free and welcome then to say so. Women may think that
> they are the equivalents of, not the equals of men; that beauty is
> as great a physical advantage as the strength which man shares
> with the ox; that nimble wits and quick intuitions are on the
> whole as brilliant, though not as solid intellectual endowments as
> the strong understanding and creative imagination of men; and
> finally, that for morality, that old man is happy whose conscience
> as he leaves the world is as void of grave offence as that of the
> majority of old women.[31]

Cobbe accepted that women were essentially nurturant, com-
passionate and dutiful; it was these very qualities that made it
necessary for women to be fully emancipated and take their due
role in shaping society into a more spiritually acceptable mould.
She maintained that the domestic confinement of women was
responsible for their enfeeblement (like most other commentators on both sides of the argument, Cobbe used the leisured,
middle-class woman as the archetype of her sex). She cited
Darwin as her authority for the effect of disuse on brain size,
whilst admitting that the author of the *Origin* might not approve

of her appropriation of his words. Society's false ideals of womanhood were responsible for any mental inferiority as well as for much of the physical weakness of women. Indoctrinated in these ideals by parents and teachers, and regulated by doctors, women were forced to submit to a socially constructed semi-invalidism.[32]

In writings and lectures, Cobbe called upon women to work for their own advancement, and sought to instil a feminist consciousness: 'Ours is the old, old story of every uprising race or class or order. The work of elevation must be wrought by ourselves or not at all.' Women must fight for their rights, on the basis of equivalence rather than equality. Intellectual or physical inferiority was irrelevant, for the goal of life was moral self-improvement, in preparation for the life hereafter.[33]

Cobbe condemned the depressing effects of evolutionary theory on spiritual ambition and she ridiculed Darwin's explanation of the evolution of the moral sense: 'Love thy Neighbour' was a spiritual, not an evolutionary canon. The idea of common descent should have called forth sympathy towards all races of man and towards the lower animals, instead, 'Science has taught her devotees to regard the world as a scene of universal struggle'. Cobbe's strong religious sense gave her the licence to judge a scientific theory and find it wanting. In her review of the *Descent of Man*, she warned her readers against too readily accepting extrapolations from the theory of evolution by natural selection:

> When a great natural philosopher weaves mental phenomena into his general theory of physical development, it is to be feared that many a student will hastily accept a doctrine which seems to fit neatly enough into a system he adopts as a whole; even though it could find on its own merits no admission into a scheme of psychology.[34]

It might have been expected that there would have been a natural affinity between socialism and opposition to the subordination of women. Certainly socialism provided a theoretical basis for a critique of contemporary science. Engels rejected the claims to 'truth' of a culturally determined science, and elaborated a powerful critique of patriarchy, in *The Origin of the Family, Private Property and the State*, published in 1884. He

condemned marriage, in all its sexual hypocrisy, as merely an
institution for the protection of property rights.

> In fact, for men group marriage actually still exists even to this
> day. What for the women is a crime entailing grave legal and
> social consequences is considered honourable in a man, or, at the
> worse, a slight moral blemish which he cheerfully bears ...
> Monogamy arose from the concentration of considerable wealth
> in the hands of a single individual – a man – and from the need
> to bequeath this wealth to the children of that man and of no
> other. For this purpose, the monogamy of the woman did not in
> any way interfere with open or concealed polygamy on the part
> of the man.[35]

Engels's critique did not, however, provide the starting point
for a socialist attack on gendered science. Engels and his followers saw feminism as a bourgeois movement irrelevant in the
context of the fight against capitalism. Eleanor Marx recognised
women's genuine grievances, but distanced herself even from
the fight for the suffrage, which she saw as a distraction from
the main task of bringing about a fundamental restructuring of
society: 'Women are the creatures of an organised tyranny of
men, as the workers are the creatures of an organised tyranny
of idlers ... no solution of the difficulties and problems that
present themselves is really possible in the present condition of
society'.[36]

   If the followers of Marx saw feminism as an irrelevance,
other socialists resisted it on tactical grounds, considering that
an attack on male supremacy would alienate potential support.
Others simply considered it wrong: Robert Blatchford, for
example, subscribed fully to the concept of woman as angel of
the home, removed from the corrupting taint of public life.[37]
But while there was no necessary link between socialism and
feminism, individual socialist intellectuals did promote an alternative interpretation of the relations between the sexes. Olive
Schreiner, a South African living in London between 1881 and
1889, was one of a group of freethinking intellectuals which
included Eleanor Marx, psychologist Havelock Ellis and committed male supremacist, mathematician Karl Pearson. She was
a fervent admirer of Darwin and fully committed to evolution,
but was undeterred either by the growing attacks on environ-

mental agents of change or by the new emphasis on stasis. Schreiner believed Darwin's message for women was an optimistic one, and she began to write a 'sex paper' that was 'purely scientific in principle' as 'an attempt to apply the theory of evolution to elucidate sex problems'.[38]

Accepting that sexual divergence had occurred, according to the principle of the division of labour, she argued in *Woman and Labour* that the current restlessness of women was evidence that sex roles had become maladaptive in evolutionary terms. Deprived by industrialisation and modern civilisation of traditionally female forms of labour, the rebellion of women reflected a recognition of the threat to the future of humanity that must result, if one sex became increasingly parasitic and wanting in vigour and vitality: 'The two sexes are not distinct species but the two halves of one whole, always acting and interacting on each other through inheritance, and reproducing and blending with each other in each generation.' They resemble 'two oxen tethered to one yoke: for a moment one may move slightly forward and the other remain stationary; but they can never move farther from each other than the length of the yoke that binds them; and they must ultimately remain stationary or move forward together'. Access to the new areas of activity demanded by women would produce change in the relations between the sexes and a convergence of sexual characters. Schreiner argued that this result must advantage men as much as women. Nor need men fear women's penetration of fields for which they were unsuited: following John Stuart Mill, she argued that free and open competition was the best way to discover capacities and limitations. She denied that the demands of women were hostile to men:

> We have called the Woman's Movement of our age an endeavour on the part of women among civilised races to find new fields of labour as the old slip from them, as an attempt to escape from parasitism and an inactive dependence upon sex function alone; but, viewed from another side, the Woman's Movement might not less justly be called a part of a great movement of the sexes towards each other, a movement towards common occupations, common interests, common ideals, and towards an emotional sympathy between the sexes more deeply founded and more indestructible than any the world has yet seen.[39]

American feminist and socialist Charlotte Perkins Gilman, like Schreiner, accepted the fundamentals of Darwinian evolution, and she subscribed to the conventional depiction of the nurturant female and the aggressive combatant male. But she, too, rejected orthodox interpretations of the import of Darwinism for the position of women in society. In *Women and Economics*, 1898, she described anti-feminism as evolutionarily retrograde, and attributed to the economic dependence of women on men the widespread evidence of female discontent and female ill-health. Herself a victim of the expert medical opinion that prescribed total rest and proscribed intellectual activity in the treatment of female ailments, she bitterly denounced the effects of extreme sexual divergence. The present subordination of women actually distorted the operation of natural selection. In all other mammals, the participation of females in the struggle for survival ensured that the pressure of natural selection placed a brake on the degree of sexual divergence occasioned by sexual selection. This brake was absent in man, with deleterious consequences. Like Schreiner, Gilman insisted that men were just as much the losers as women in the current structure of society, but added that human progress was the greatest loser of all.[40]

A small number of radical feminists on both sides of the Atlantic were prepared to confront more aggressively the gendered science of Darwin and his disciples. Both Eliza Burt Gamble, in *The Evolution of Woman*, 1894, and Mona Caird, in *The Morality of Marriage*, 1897, rejected the orthodoxy of progress and the necessitarian character of evolution, by eulogising that ancient, female-dominated society described by anthropologists. Gamble argued that the subordination of women was the product not of evolution but of barbarism. The concept of female inferiority could not be logically deduced from the *Descent of Man* but was a consequence of the strength of the idea of male supremacy, so deeply rooted that neither Darwin nor other biologists working in the area were capable of challenging it. It was patriarchy that held women's intellectual development in check; patriarchy that was the enemy of progress, interfering with the free operation of natural selection; patriarchy which, by holding women back, retarded the advance of the species. The overruling of female choice through the economic dominance of the male, meant that the unfit male was no longer eliminated by sexual selection and the course of evolution was perverted.[41]

In similar terms Mona Caird claimed that anthropology provided evidence of a culturally, rather than biologically, determined female subservience, a subservience that was evolutionarily destructive. Far from sexual differentiation being a mark of a higher stage of evolution, it presented an obstacle to progress by keeping women in an artificially backward stage. In a series of articles published in the *Westminster Review* between 1888 and 1894, she developed her arguments against the contemporary relations between the sexes, and the institution of coercive marriage, which made the relationship of wife to husband little different from that of slave to master.[42]

Caird maintained that separate sphere ideology had brought ill-health and disease to women; over the long generations of male dominance this had become constitutional. And all that the men of science could suggest to tackle this constitutional debility was an even more obsessive concern with the reproductive role. Hopes of the improvement of the race through education and science were forlorn so long as one half of the race was kept in ignorance, for through heredity the feebleness of the women was passed on to the next generation. Caird challenged women to rebel against the tyranny of scientific findings. People must believe in their ability to control their destiny. 'Evolution! the word awes us. We are like children frightened at our own shadows.' Women were kept subservient with phrases like, 'Nature intends' or 'Nature desires'. 'She intends and desires nothing – she is an abject slave. *Man* intends, *man* desires, and "Nature", in the course of centuries, learns to obey. This worship of "Nature" is a strange survival in a scientific age of the old image-worship of our ancestors.'[43]

Patriarchy and the decline of the women's movement

Despite such examples of women who found in religion or in freethought, or in an unusually heightened feminist consciousness, the means to resist the social prescriptions of the evolutionists, for most this was not possible. The difficulty was that few subscribed to philosophical egalitarianism and many had based their demands for greater opportunities on the benefits to be gained by society through making use of the unique qualities of womanhood. Harriet Martineau, a lifelong campaigner for greater participation in society by women, insisted on woman's predilection for a life devoted to the welfare of others and on her predisposition to housewifery, needlework and other such womanly attributes. Martineau's purpose in raising women's aspirations was that they should employ their moral superiority to elevate the moral nature of men. Florence Nightingale, who campaigned so vigorously for opportunities for women to use their talents and energies, rejected any idea of competing with men in what she recognised to be men's sphere of action. Behind much of the thinking of the movement for women's education lay the belief that women were by nature suited to vocational work, involving service to others. George Eliot was ambivalent about any generalised rights for women: she favoured women's suffrage and gave limited support to women's education, but took no active role in the promotion of such causes and was compliant with the patriarchal culture in which she had found fame.[44]

Those involved in the women's movement in the nineteenth century subscribed to a consensus around the need for women's different, but complementary, qualities to be respected, and given equal value in society. It was this consensus that dictated the unity of Martineau and Nightingale in support of Josephine Butler's opposition to the Contagious Diseases Acts, 'hygienic' measures largely supported by the scientific community and promoted by physicians, which enshrined the sexual double standard, stripping women alike of human rights and female dignity.[45] The consensus did not address the questions of whether difference implied hierarchy, and in what realms if at all women must accept subordination to men. Such ideological questions now began to obtrude, and not simply because of scientific developments. The very success of women's campaigns in the realms of education and careers meant that the limit was approaching beyond which the advance of women could no longer be contained within the framework of separate sphere ideology but was bound to encroach on the traditional sphere of men.

Separate sphere ideology could not be relinquished lightly: it gave women a defined role as protectors and guarantors of Victorian civilisation and distanced that civilisation both from the lower classes and the lower races, amongst whom the sexuality of the women as much as the brutality of the men was a distinguishing mark of inferiority. If the social and racial hierarchies upon which their civilisation depended entailed an acceptance of sexual hierarchy, and if such a sexual hierarchy were threatened by the demands of women, many were prepared to relinquish their demands and accept that hierarchy. For the liberal bourgeois social order, from whose ranks were drawn the reformers, separate sphere ideology provided the necessary complement to the competitive ideology of the marketplace. The public world promoted economic prosperity, the private guaranteed domestic and social harmony. The public world provided work for the middle-class man, suited to business; the private for the middle-class woman, fitted for the transmission of the values of bourgeois society to her own household and to the wider community. There was scant support for any philosophically articulated feminism: women's rights campaigners argued for greater access to social influence within the broadly consensual social framework of patriarchy. It was this endorsement of sexual difference, this complicity in the social construct of Victorian patriarchy that rendered the Victorian women's movement so vulnerable to the attack of scientific anti-feminism.[46]

Charles Darwin's niece, Julia Wedgwood, was one of those who told her readers that the existence of innate sex differences was no longer open to question. John Stuart Mill, in *The Subjection of Women*, in 1869, may have been uninfluenced by the doctrines of the *Origin of Species*, but 'since that time there is no department of thought which they have not influenced'. And whilst cultural pressure in the modern age 'tends towards obliteration of the dividing line of male and female, a much older and wider set of influences are at work, tending to make every generation of women in some sense more feminine, every generation of men in some sense more masculine'. The only option was to promote the value of generally accepted female characteristics. Women enjoyed moral superiority, being innately predisposed to a sense of justice and of humanity, senses which could only be culturally acquired by men.[47]

Many contemporaries followed Wedgwood's argument. Popular journalist Eliza Lynn Linton accepted the absolute limits prescribed for the woman's sphere. She approved the acquisition of property rights, rights of divorce and limited rights to education, but beyond this she denounced the demands of the 'wild women' who tried to defy biological determinism, and, in the process, devalued woman's true nature. Widely attacked by feminists, Lynn Linton's views mirrored those of many women who sought an increased role in society only within the parameters of the biologically determined women's sphere: suitable occupations included teaching, medicine and social work.[48]

By the turn of the century, the growing emphasis on the role of the mother as the guardian of civilisation provided one means of enhancing the status of women without unduly encroaching on male preserves. It was compatible with the emerging notion of aboriginal sexual difference and could allow a reconciliation with the men of science, based on the essential role of motherhood. It appeared, too, to address the needs of a society beset by fears of a falling birth rate and racial degeneracy, as well as to speak to the concerns of ordinary working-class mothers, whose appalling living conditions had been exposed in the poverty surveys of the 1890s, and in the publications of movements such as the Women's Cooperative Guild. 'Old' feminists could be regarded as selfishly pursuing the interests of the prosperous few at the expense of women as a whole, whilst 'new' feminists promoted instead a higher status for all women as nurturers of the next generation. Maternity services would be provided, resulting in significant improvements in the health of mothers and babies. Women's education would be defended not on the grounds of abstract rights but by reference to the need to equip women for their vital role in raising children. Traditional policies such as the right to the vote, justifiable on the 'separate but equal' test, remained common to 'old' and 'new' feminism.

'New' feminism achieved some important advances in field of women's welfare, but in the process it yielded t. concept of natural rights and equal opportunities. In accepting that women's needs, capacities and interests were fundamentally different from those of men, it no longer challenged the implied assumption of sexual inferiority. The price was to entrench women of all classes ever more firmly in the domestic sphere. Furthermore, the very elevation of the maternal role now rendered it too important to be entrusted to the women themselves. Society must ensure their competence for the task. Increasingly women were subjected to control by a range of experts, predominantly male, in the fields of medicine, child development, nutrition and education.[49] Women were not supreme, even within the confines of the home; here too they must surrender to supervision.

By the time that the Representation of the People Act conferred limited franchise on women in 1918, the women's movement had effectively disintegrated. Some women continued to campaign for the vote on equal terms with men, others for the endowment of motherhood through the introduction of family allowances, still others for a variety of causes from divorce reform to widow's pensions. A few, like Winifred Holtby, resisted the 'powerful movement to reclothe the female form in swathing trails and frills and flounces to emphasise the difference between men and women'.[50] For the majority of women, the inter-war period was characterised by a passive acceptance of the establishment-promoted ethics of femininity and domesticity.

Undeniably, and quite deliberately, the men of science played their part in the dissolution of the women's movement, by conferring the imprint of evolutionary science on traditional concepts of female difference and female subordination. Darwin's personal contribution to the debate on gender was modest and cautious by comparison with those of his disciples and followers, but his doctrines provided the basis for the science of female inferiority. Subordination to male dominion was a pervasive assumption of the *Origin of Species*, and those who used it as a basis for gendered anthropology were applauded by Darwin in the *Descent*. The employment of

Darwinism in the cause of anti-feminism ensured that the issue of women's rights was no longer subsumed in the wider agenda of individual liberty, but was discussed rather in terms of biological fitness. Innate gender difference became an accepted canon, disputed only by a few isolated researchers whose arguments made little impression.[51]

Darwin's theories were conditioned by the patriarchal culture in which they were elaborated: he did not invent the concept of sexual difference. The late-nineteenth-century elaboration of that concept took place in the context of the growing demands of women. Its success owed much to women's own ambivalence about their role in society and the nature of womanhood. The defeat of the movement did not depend on the intervention of the men of science. But the support offered by a science that was for the most part accepted in its day as objective and value-free immeasurably strengthened patriarchy for decades to come. The *Origin* provided a mechanism for converting culturally entrenched ideas of female inferiority into permanent, biologically determined, sexual hierarchy. Its legacy resides in the depth of the split that opened up between old and new feminism, in the complex divisions that beset the women's movement in the decades that followed, and in the length of time that was to elapse before a new women's movement should once again challenge patriarchy.

Notes

1 *Origin*, p. 170 (my italics); Spencer, 'Biology and Women's Rights', 1878–9, quoted in Cynthia Eagle Russett, *Sexual Science: The Victorian Construction of Womanhood* (Cambridge, MA: Harvard University Press, 1989).
2 Anne Fausto-Sterling, *Myths of Gender: Biological Theories about Women and Men* (New York: Basic Books, 1985). Ruth Hubbard, 'Have Only Men Evolved?', in Sandra Harding and Merrill B. Hintikka, eds, *Discovering Reality* (Dordrecht: Reidel, 1983) p. 61.
3 *Origin*, p. 141.
4 *Origin*, p. 116, pp. 136–8, p. 227.
5 *Descent*, pp. 326, 911–12, and see Evelleen Richards, 'Darwin and the Descent of Woman', in D. Oldroyd and I. Langham, eds, *The Wider Domain of Evolutionary Thought*, (Dordrecht: Reidel, 1983), p. 78.
6 *Origin*, p. 131, pp. 173–5.
7 *Origin*, p. 76, p. 194. Patrick Geddes and J. Arthur Thomson, *The Evolution of Sex* (London, 1889).

8 *Descent*, pp. 857–61.
9 Frederick Burckhardt and Sydney Smith, eds, *Calendar of the Correspondence of Charles Darwin, 1812–1882* (London: Garland, 1985), 10546, Adrian Desmond and James Moore, *Darwin* (London: Michael Joseph, 1991), p. 615. On Darwin, Cobbe and anti-vivisection, see *Life of Frances Power Cobbe as told by Herself*, (Sonnenschein, 1904), vol. II, p. 128.
10 Elizabeth Fee, 'Women's Nature and Scientific Objectivity', in Marion Lowe and Ruth Hubbard, eds *Woman's Nature: Rationalisations of Inequality* (Oxford: Pergamon, 1983), p. 13; compare Phillip Barrish, 'Accumulating Variation: Darwin's On *The Origin of Species* and Contemporary Literary and Cultural Theory', *Victorian Studies* 34: 4 (1991), pp. 431–53, which suggests that the feminisation of Nature in the *Origin* and the endowment of Nature with the nurturing and selfless qualities of Victorian femininity, reveals the 'latently misogynist gender alignment in his theory'.
11 *Correspondence*, vol. 1, p. 286; vol. 2, p. 444; *D* 76; vol. 1, p. 518–19, 2, pp. 80, 86; CD to William Darwin, 17 February 1857, vol. 6.
12 Examples of Darwin's conventional opinions on gender may be found in two letters to Emma, 25 April 1858 and 28 April 1858, *Correspondence*, 7; *C* 220; *Descent*, p. 860.
13 Paul H. Barrett, P. J. Gantrey, S. Herbert, D. Kohn and S. Smith, eds, *Charles Darwin's Notebooks 1836–1844* (Cambridge: Cambridge University Press, 1987), see, e.g., *N* 5.
14 *Origin*, pp. 458–9, cf. pp. 153, 162, 167, 229, 232, 348: p. 124.
15 George J. Romanes, 'Mental Differences between Men and Women', *The Nineteenth Century* 21 (1887), pp. 654–72. For a discussion of the near unanimity of scientists' views on female inferiority, see Eagle Russett, *Sexual Science*, pp. 189–206.
16 Ruskin, *Sesame and Lilies*, 1865, quoted by Deirdre David, *Intellectual Women and Victorian Patriarchy: Harriet Martineau, Elizabeth Barrett Browning, George Eliot*, (London: Macmillan, 1987), p. 15.
17 Elizabeth Fee, 'The Sexual Politics of Victorian Social Anthropology', in Mary S. Hartman and Lois Banner, eds, *Clio's Consciousness Raised: New Perspectives in the History of Women* (New York: Harper & Row, 1974); J. McGrigor Allan, 'On the Real Differences in the minds of Men and Women', *Journal of the Anthropological Society* (1869), pp. clxxxix–cxcv.
18 John Stuart Mill, *The Subjection of Women*, 1869 (London: Everyman, 1965), p. 282.
19 D. R. Oldroyd, *Darwinian Impacts* (Milton Keynes: Open University Press, 1980), pp. 298–308.
20 J. D. Y. Peel, *Herbert Spencer: The Evolution of a Sociologist* (London: Heinemann, 1971).
21 *Origin*, pp. 185–6.
22 *Descent*, p. 861.
23 Evelleen Richards, 'Huxley and Woman's Place in Science: The Woman Question and the Control of Victorian Anthropology', in James R. Moore, ed., *History, Humanity and Evolution: Essays for John C. Green*, (New York: Cambridge University Press, 1989), p. 260, passim.

24 Mill, *Subjection*, p. 280; Romanes, 'Mental Differences', p. 665; for a rebuttal of arguments of female inferiority, see David G. Ritchie, *Darwinism and Politics*, 1890, quoted in Susan Sleeth Mosedale, 'Science Corrupted: Victorian Biologists Consider "the Woman Question"', *Journal of the History of Biology* 11 (1978), pp. 1–55.

25 Patricia Marks, *Bicycles, Bangs and Bloomers: the New Woman and the Popular Press* (Lexington, Ky: University Press of Kentucky, 1990).

26 Geddes and Thomson, *The Evolution of Sex*, 1889, quoted by Flavia Alaya, 'Victorian Science and the Genius of Woman', *Journal of the History of Ideas* (1977), pp. 261–80.

27 Ellis, *Man and Woman*, 1894, cited by Eagle Russett, *Sexual Science*, p. 96.

28 Harriet Martineau to Erasmus Darwin, 2 February 1860, W/M 32974–57, reproduced by courtesy of the Trustees of the Wedgwood Museum, Barlaston, Stoke-on-Trent, Staffordshire.

29 J. S. Mill to Alexander Bain, 11 April 1860, *Letters of John Stuart Mill* (London: Longmans, Green & Co., 1910), p. 236. Lewes was one of the first to draw attention to the patriarchal assumptions in Darwin's reasoning: Gillian Beer, *Darwin's Plots* (London: Routledge & Kegan Paul, 1983), p. 223.

30 *Life of Frances Power Cobbe as told by herself*, II, pp. 89, 128.

31 Frances Power Cobbe, 'Criminals, Idiots, Women and Minors', *Fraser's Magazine* 78 (1868), pp. 777–94, 793.

32 'The Subjection of Women', *Theological Review* 6 (1869), pp. 355–75, 362; 'The Little Health of Ladies', *Contemporary Review* 14 (1877–8), pp. 276–96.

33 Francis Power Cobbe, *Duties of Women: A Course of Lectures*, 1881 (London: Swan Sonnenschein & Co., 1905), pp. 8, 46.

34 Cobbe, *Duties*, p. 90; 'The Scientific Spirit of the Age', *Contemporary Review* 54 (1888), pp. 126–39, 136; 'Darwinism in Morals', *Theological Review* (1871), pp. 167–92, 186.

35 Engels cited in Hubbard, 'Have Only Men Evolved?', p. 56.

36 Shiela Rowbotham, *Hidden From History* (London: Pluto Press, 1973), p. 70.

37 Rowbotham, p. 73.

38 Schreiner to Havelock Ellis, 1887, quoted in Rosaleen Love, 'Darwinism and Feminism: The "Woman Question" in the Life and Work of Olive Schreiner and Charlotte Perkins Gilman', in Oldroyd and Langham, eds. *The Wider Domain of Evolutionary Thought*.

39 Olive Schreiner, *Woman and Labour*, 1911 (reprinted London: Virago 1978), pp. 79, 250–1, 258–9.

40 Love, 'Darwin and Feminism'; Eagle Russett, *Sexual Science*, p. 86.

41 Eliza Burt Gamble, *The Evolution of Woman* (reprinted as *The Sexes in Science and History: An Inquiry into the Dogma of Woman's Inferiority to Man*, New York, 1916), Preface, p. 376 and passim.

42 Mona Caird, *The Morality of Marriage and Other Essays on the Status and Destiny of Women* (London: George Redway, 1897).

43 Caird, *Morality*, pp. 115, 173.

44 On the quality of her feminism see *Harriet Martineau's Autobiography* (London: Smith, Elder & Co., 1877), vol. 1, pp. 400–2. and *Society in*

America (1837). On George Eliot, see David, *Intellectual Women*. On Florence Nightingale see Forster, *Significant Sisters* (London: Secker & Warburg, 1984), p. 94.

45 J. R. Walkowitz, *Prostitution and Victorian Society* (Cambridge: Cambridge University Press, 1980).

46 Anita Levy, *Other Women: The Writing of Class, Race and Gender, 1832–98* (Princeton: Princeton University Press 1991); Barbara Caine, *Victorian Feminists* (Oxford: Oxford University Press, 1992), chapter 2. Rosalind Rosenberg, 'In Search of Women's Nature, 1850–1920', *Feminist Studies* 3 (1975), pp. 141–54.

47 Julia Wedgwood, 'The Boundaries of Science', *Macmillans Magazine* 2 (1860), pp. 134–8, 136; and 'Male and Female Created He Them', *Contemporary Review* 56 (1889), pp. 120–33, 122–3.

48 Richards 'Huxley', p. 279; for a zfeminist response to Lynne Linton, see Caird, *Morality*, pp. 159–91.

49 Barbara Ehrenreich and Deirdre English, *For Her Own Good: 150 Years of the Experts' Advice to Women* (London: Pluto Press, 1979).

50 Quoted in Rowbotham, *Hidden from History*, p. 126.

51 See e.g. Rosenberg, 'In Search', pp. 147–52.

5

Proliferation and its discontents: Max Müller, Leslie Stephen, George Eliot and *The Origin of Species* as representation

DAVID AMIGONI

Theorising proliferation was a major challenge for Charles Darwin in the *Origin of Species by Means of Natural Selection:* imagining the systems of dispersal through which organisms were distributed to geographically divergent regions, and then reproduced with variations, would help to invalidate the myth of separate, individual acts of creation.[1] Darwin scholars have persistently enquired into ways in which the language of the *Origin* proliferated throughout nineteenth-century intellectual culture.[2] This chapter traces an emergent perception amongst some nineteenth-century intellectuals that Darwin's *Origin* comprised not simply a methodology but a language which proliferated widely beyond the book cover which contrived to contain it, varying as it moved. It will examine the political anxieties provoked by the perception of proliferation, and look at the ideological strategies devised for limiting proliferation, which involved making the figure of Darwin into an individual intellectual creator who named and had authority over his creations. I shall focus on these strategies as they emerged in and were exchanged between the theoretical and critical writings of two intellectuals working in different fields: Friedrich Max Müller in the field of comparative philology (the historical study of the origin and development of languages); and

Leslie Stephen, working in the fields of philosophy and literary criticism. It will be clear from the range of positions woven together in the essay that, for me, cultural analysis of the *Origin* must recognise that the text provoked cross-fertilisation between endeavours of intellectual labour. At the same time, contemporary resistance to particular aspects of this cross-fertilisation needs to be acknowledged, and it is in this sense that I will analyse Leslie Stephen's ideological resistance to a woman writer's use of 'Darwinian' language – that writer being George Eliot. I will begin by seeking to place the *Origin* in cultural history by drawing on and entering into debates with the work of Michel Foucault, Gillian Beer and V. N. Volosinov. I will go on to examine the relationship between the *Origin* and the discipline of philology, showing how Max Müller took the relationship in new directions. Finally I shall explore how this had an impact on Leslie Stephen's literary-critical evaluation of George Eliot.

The Origin of Species in cultural history

It is not always easy to plot a new sense of the subtle ideological connections that linked dispersed cultural discourses in the nineteenth century on the basis of existing cultural-historical maps. For instance, while the relationship between the sciences of life and the science of language in the nineteenth century have been, as we shall see, convincingly plotted, literary-critical discourse is not on this map.

First the map with well-marked routes. It is now well established that a relationship between the *Origin* and philology existed.[3] Darwin's biological thesis was grounded in geology and palaeontology. There were links between the possibilities of reading rock formations and fossils and the etymological dissection of words in ancient texts, which Darwin's *Origin* itself alluded to in searching for the secrets of the earth's composition, natural life, and humankind.[4] Following the work of the French philosopher and radical intellectual historian Michel Foucault, it is possible to see that the affinities between the *Origin* and philology were not incidental. According to Foucault in *The Order of Things: An Archaeology of the Human Sciences*, biology and philology were disciplines which emerged in the late eighteenth and early nineteenth centuries as new and parallel ways of ordering knowledge about organic life and language. The basis of their enquiry into these new objects of knowledge was a search for origins, or a search which placed the emergence and development of both organic life and language in the great depths of history. For Foucault, this new orthodoxy expelled an earlier way of thinking, and during the nineteenth century knowledge could no longer come about by 'relating one form of language to another' or by means of finding resemblances and differences between dense and interrelated *representations*.[5]

But while philology was linked to life sciences, and so the *Origin*, it did not appear to have impinged on literary criticism, a practice concerned with the judgement and interpretation of representations. In much of the work that has been undertaken exploring the emergence of the modern academic practice of literary criticism, a point that is stressed is the distance that was observed between subjective literary criticism and philology and its monumental search for national and cultural origins.[6] Even so, late nineteenth-century practitioners of literary criticism like Leslie Stephen invoked Darwin when formulating judgements which were subjective, philosophical and literary:

> I happened last night to be reading Montaigne's essay upon preparing one for death, and, though he has nothing new to say, I thought that he was giving my own sentiments. He takes his consolations out of Lucretius, as I have taken mine from Darwin; and they do as well as anything else.[7]

In 1901 when the aged and melancholic Stephen was preoccupied with thoughts of death (he was to die in 1904), reading Montaigne through a matrix of Darwinian ideas was a new way of reconciling the self to the inevitability of extinction. In this sense, Stephen was claiming Darwin as a guide to action, or rather resignation, in the present, and situating him authoritatively in a tradition of rational thought about death.

In the same letter Stephen wrote about his other preoccupation of the moment; George Eliot (Mary Anne Evans), the nineteenth-century English novelist about whom he was writing a critical biography for the English Men of Letters series of primers. Stephen's appreciation of the Eliot canon was qualified: 'I admire the English country novels as much as I could wish; but the later performances are not to my taste ... the 'poetry' – does not appear to me to be poetry.'[8] Although Stephen does not draw a connection here between Darwin's ideas and George Eliot, one was to emerge in the biography that he eventually wrote. Indeed, this essay will argue that Stephen's reading of Darwin and his negative literary critical evaluation of George Eliot's poetry were linked through an ideological strategy of resistance to the proliferaton of language from the *Origin*. Tracing this link will take us into some of the fields which appropriated the language of the *Origin* after its publication, these being Müller's philology and Leslie Stephen's work on ethics. First though we should turn to the *Origin* or at least to Gillian Beer's reading of this text for Beer's reading of the *Origin* urges a reformulation of the Foucauldian map of nineteenth-century cultural knowledge which I have sketched previously.

In *Darwin's Plots* (1983), Beer establishes an important relationship between the writings of Darwin and the writings of George Eliot which needs to be seen in the overall context of her argument. Beer's study examines Darwin's narrative, metaphoric and mythic imagination as manifested in the *Origin*, and the way in which this rich discourse proliferated throughout Victorian intellectual and literary culture after 1859, undergoing variations as it entered fields adjacent to and distant from biology. The discourse of the *Origin* found a particularly powerful interpreter in George Eliot (the novelist named in Beer's subtitle), who both embraced and resisted Darwin's theoretical discourse by weaving versions of it into her own imaginative writings.[9] The important point to stress in Beer's account is the emphasis that she places on the narrative and rhetorical properties of the *Origin* that is to say its status as a derivative amalgam of representations and a generator of further representations.

To give an example from the *Origin*, let us return to one of those allusions to reading for origins which I cited in support of Foucault's notion of the common, historicising tendencies shared between geology, palaeontology, philology and biology. It is difficult to read this without becoming aware of its density as representation:

> I look at the natural geological record, as a history of the world
> imperfectly kept, and written in a changing dialect; of this
> history we possess the last volume alone, relating only to two or
> three countries. Of this volume, only here and there a short chap-
> ter has been preserved; and of each page, only here and there a
> few lines. Each word of the slowly changing language, in which
> the history is supposed to be written, being more or less differ-
> ent in the interrupted succession of chapters, may represent the
> apparently abruptly changed forms of life, entombed in our
> consecutive, but widely separated formations.[10]

In reading the geological record, the speaker looks for what it
will convey about the depths of History, but philological practice is invoked not as an adjacent branch of positive research,
but rather as a simile of reading which is constructed by
metonymically breaking down the objects of philological
research into smaller and more isolated fragments: the changing dialect, the last volume of a series of chronicle texts, the
chapter, the page, a few lines. All of this is done to register the
problem of reading signs of the past rather than confirming the
accessibility of origins. We could say, following Foucault's view
of the epistemology of representation, that Darwin here
produces knowledge not by an empirical method which is guaranteed by the privileged gaze of the observer but by relating
one language in terms of another, especially when we note that
Darwin begins by informing the reader how he is 'following
out [Sir Charles] Lyell's metaphor' in constructing his own variation on a representation. Beer's reading of the *Origin* encourages us to see this text as a contribution to the epistemology of
representation, and this has consequences for the way in which
we conceive the singular yet abundant nature of this text in
nineteenth-century intellectual culture.

Darwin scholars have had problems in reconciling their
desire to assert Darwin's authority in a particular field with the
daunting, yet often enigmatic, reputation that the *Origin* has
acquired. Robert Keefe's essay 'Literati, Language, and Darwinism' is a case in point. Keefe's essay is concerned with the
impact that Darwin's ideas had upon nineteenth-century intellectuals and their thinking about the human subject's relationship to language – questions that will be major concerns of this
chapter in its dealings with Max Müller and Leslie Stephen.

Keefe argues that the most momentous cultural earthquake caused by Darwin occurred in the field of language theory, where Darwin's developmental materialism set in place a conventionalist view of language (we are born into language and its conventions and have no real control over it: language speaks us). For Keefe, Darwin emerges as a proto-post-structuralist ushering in the age of Saussure, Lacan, Barthes and Derrida: 'This most fluent of scientists has no great ontological respect for the Logos.'[11] In asserting Darwin's capacity to cause an earthquake, Keefe is obliged to pay homage to the power of the *Origin*: 'the publication of that book in 1859 shook the ground under the feet of European intellectuals.'[12] The problem with a cultural earthquake, however, is that it is often difficult to locate its epicentre. Keefe presents us with the image of the European intelligentsia reeling under the shockwaves caused by the *Origin*, but in making his crucial point he writes 'listen to Darwin. Not the Darwin of *Origin of Species* ... [b]ut the *Descent of Man*.'[13] Keefe encounters a familiar problem: that at the level of direct statement, whether about anthropology, sexual selection, or, in our case, language, the *Origin*, though suggestive, is never quite the intellectual dynamite that speculations about 'the Darwinian Revolution' have led us to expect. As an alternative Beer's argument encourages us to see the representational power of language itself as a powerful engine of suggestiveness in cultural history.

Beer's reading of the *Origin* as a contribution to the epistemology of representation will help me to negotiate this problem in two senses. First, I shall argue that even when the *Origin* speculated on, for instance, problems relating to the evolution of domestic breeds, its tendency to use metaphor and analogy raised questions about the evolution of language – its relationship to human subjects, and its powers of proliferation – which were suggestive to intellectuals in other fields, such as Max Müller and Leslie Stephen. Second, both Müller and Stephen responded astutely to the *Origin* as a contribution to the epistemology of representation: both these intellectuals responded to the *Origin* as a manifestation of symbolic language which had the power to generate material effects in the present and the future.

In arguing the second point, it will be necessary to situate this reaction to the *Origin* as language in relation to overlapping responses. Philologists like Müller and philosophers and literary critics like Stephen first grasped the *Origin* as a methodological tool which would enable them to pursue the origins of language and ethics according to Foucault's sense of nineteenth-century intellectual priorities. However, in appropriating such concepts as natural selection and the struggle for existence, and introducing them into the fields of philology, ethics and literary criticism, Müller and Stephen saw that it had implications for their own conditions of existence as intellectuals involved in struggles waged over ideas and language – they argued and disagreed over the relationship between man, animals and language. That Müller and Stephen recognised the existence of intellectual struggle brings them close, in many ways, to the theorist who informs the methodology that governs my chapter: the Russian Marxist theorist of discourse, V. N. Volosinov. Volosinov argued that the word, or, as he conceptualised it, the sign, is the principal site of ideological contestation in communities divided by class, race and gender.[14] In his book *The Science of Ethics*, Stephen accorded the sign great importance, arguing that 'we may be said to feel through signs as well as to reason by signs'.[15] As I shall argue, Stephen came to see intellectual activity as an ideological struggle with the inherited values conveyed by the signs of language.

It is Stephen's patriarchal position in this ideological struggle that I wish to foreground and contest. In order to explain this, I will begin by questioning a formulation in Gillian Beer's *Darwin's Plots* which, for me, fails to grasp fully the cultural politics which framed the reception and further use of those ideas that we have come to call 'Darwinian'. To conceptualise the particular exchanges that passed between the *Origin* and its interpreters, Beer establishes this caveat: 'An ecological rather than a patriarchal model is most appropriate ... in studying [Darwin's] work.'[16] While Beer's ecological analysis of the proliferation of the discourse of the *Origin* undoubtedly captures a vital aspect of the text's cultural significance, it underestimates the extent to which patriarchal resistance became embodied in ideological discourses which attempted to set limits on the proliferation of Darwinian language, and Stephen's literary-critical biography of George Eliot was, as I shall argue, one such patriarchal discourse which held that for femininity to extend and develop 'Darwin's' language had degenerate implications. But before elaborating this argument, it will be helpful to advance towards it by looking more closely at the various questions which the *Origin* posed about researches into language development.

The Origin of Species and philology: methodological and metaphorical readings

Darwin's reference to the science of comparative philology in the *Origin* was one of the few explicit anthropological insights offered in a text which carefully evaded direct speculation on the natural history of humankind.[17] In asserting the primacy of genealogy as the natural basis for the classification of living and extinct species, Darwin sought methodological support from the natural history of languages:

> It may be worth while to illustrate this view of classification by taking the case of languages. If we possessed a perfect pedigree of mankind, a genealogical arrangement of the races of man would afford the best classification of the various languages spread throughout the world; and if all extinct languages, and all intermediate and slowly changing dialects had to be included, such an arrangement would, I think, be the only one ... this would be strictly natural, as it would connect together all languages, extinct and modern, by the closest affinities, and would give the filiation and origin of each new tongue.[18]

A telling indication of the hierarchical relationship of influence and dependence that was deemed to exist between Darwin's theory of species transmutation and comparative philology can be gleaned from the title of a short pamphlet written in 1863 and translated from the German original into English in 1869: *Darwinism Tested by the Science of Language*. For the author, August Schleicher, philology, or the science of language, was the senior discipline with the authority to 'test' the claims of the *Origin*. As the translator Alex Bikkers put it: 'the science of language, although still in its infancy, is the highest and at the same time the easiest test of Mr Darwin's theory'.[19]

Schleicher read Darwin's text as a methodological compatriot to philology in the great nineteenth-century quest for origins. The *Origin* presented a transmutational view of the emergence of individual species, as comparative philology viewed individual languages as transmutations of earlier languages. In the same way that comparative philology traced the great variety of languages that existed in the present and the past back to a primitive language, the *Origin* argued that the living organisms comprising genera, species and varieties present and past had descended from a common stock. To confirm this aspect of the convergence Schleicher's pamphlet was furnished with an illustration of a tree representing the evolution of language families based on Darwin's famous graphic representing the transmutation of species and variations from genera.[20] The key concept in the *Origin*, natural selection brought about by the struggle for existence, which explained success and succession, failure and extinction, was, Schleicher claimed, simultaneously grasped by comparative philology: 'I pronounced an opinion coinciding in a remarkable degree with Darwin's views on "the struggle for existence", on the extinction of ancient forms, on the widely spread varieties of individual species in the field of speech, as far back as the year 1860'.[21]

Schleicher's text is an example of a disciplinary perspective which framed the *Origin* as a scientific methodology which rendered visible origins and lines of succession. However, Schleicher's reading overlooks the extent to which the *Origin* was tentative and speculative in the presentation of its case, and the way in which its case was cast in prose organised by analogies and narrative strategies which posed questions and additional possiblities through connotation and implication. Thus, when the *Origin* discussed the problem of the origin of domestic breeds, a scepticism concerning the precise location of origins was posited in terms that bear close analysis when considering the relationship between biology and philology:

> A breed, like a dialect of a language, can hardly be said to have had a definite origin. A man preserves and breeds from an individual with some slight deviation of structure, or takes more care

than usual in matching his best animals and thus improves them, and the improved individuals slowly spread in the immediate neighbourhood. But as yet they will hardly have a distinct name, and from being only slightly valued their history will be disregarded. When further improved by the same slow and gradual process, they will spread more widely, and will get recognised as something distinct and valuable, and will then probably receive a provincial name. In semi-civilised countries, with little free communication, the spreading and knowledge of any new sub-breed will be a slow process. As soon as the points of value of the sub-breed are once fully acknowledged, the principle, as I have called it, of unconscious selection will always tend,– perhaps more at one period than at another, as the breed rises or falls in fashion, perhaps more at one period than at another, according to the state of civilisation of the inhabitants – slowly to add to the characteristic feature of the breed, whatever they may be.[22]

In speculating about slow processes of change pertaining to breeds under domestication Darwin seeks to represent the origin of varieties, their propensity to vary and the subsequent means by which they diffuse and proliferate. Darwin conceives of this process by using language development as an analogy, but this only complicates the picture, for the origins of a dialect, and by extension the origins of language, are admitted to be shrouded in obscurity. To compensate, Darwin becomes a narrator, and has to speculate and construct a story about the processes he is urging the reader to try to imagine. This narrative represents processes of selection and proliferation through two suggestive kinds of language. First, the process of domestic selection, one branch of which is described as 'unconscious selection'. 'Unconscous selection' differs from the conscious selection and breeding from individuals with slight deviations in that the breeder has no desire to change the breed, even though, inevitably, unsought variations will occur.[23] This is suggestively described through the language of human mind and the presence/absence of rational calculation, or the 'conscious'/'unconscious' opposition. Second, Darwin tries to describe the grounds on which breeders make choices and influence the choices of other breeders, and thus cause certain forms to proliferate. Here he uses a language of evaluation; breeders

select, even unconsciously, from the 'best', most 'valuable' of
their animals.

We should recall that we are plunged into this speculative
narrative through an analogy with the emergence of a dialect.
As Gillian Beer has remarked of metaphors and analogies in the
Origin, their peripheries remain undescribed; we can see how
they begin but we remain unsure about when, and whether, to
set them aside.[24] The analogy developed between domestic
breeds and the development and proliferation of linguistic
dialects is a case in point: it invites an opening-up of the relationship between biological and philological speculation into
the field of philosophy and questions of value posed therein.
For if 'unconscious selection' is taken to mean the habitual
preservation of linguistic forms based on custom and convention, then on what basis has evaluation been undertaken, and
what makes the form the 'best', or 'valuable'? The *Origin*,
through an anthropomorphic language of subjectivity, opens
up issues of the human subject's relation to language, and begs
questions about language as a system in which values are
inscribed, inherited and changed over time. As we shall see,
Friedrich Max Müller's contribution to philological theory
attempted to wrestle with these questions, as well as two other
issues: the variation of linguistic forms in the present; and the
extent to which the *Origin* as itself language was implicated in
this process. As we shall see, these matters were in turn taken
up by Leslie Stephen's theory of ethics and his literary-critical
practice.

Max Müller's *Science of Language*:
the *Origin* as language

The ex-patriate German Friedrich Max Müller was a Sanskrit
scholar and comparative philologist who came to public prominence in England in the early 1860s with the publication of his
Lectures on the Science of Language, delivered at the Royal
Institution in two series (1861 and 1863), and subsequently
published (1862-4). The early 1860s saw writers extending the
arguments of the *Origin* into the field of anthropology with the
publication of key texts such as T. H. Huxley's *Man's Place in*

Nature (1862), and Müller's *Lectures* were an intervention in anthropology, or 'the crown of all the natural sciences'.[25] However, for Müller, the science of language was the central philosophical defence of humankind in a field increasingly penetrated by biology, precisely because language seemed to ensure a unique position for humans in nature's economy. Müller's philosophical science of language asserted that 'language is our Rubicon, and no brute will dare to cross it'.[26] In being a philosophical contribution to anthropology, Müller's account wrestled with concepts of mind and value, and so entered into the kind of speculative opening generated by the representational powers of the *Origin*. Müller's actual response to the *Origin* was complex. Müller appropriated a key concept of the *Origin* – natural selection, which was assimilated into philology as an explanatory tool. In addition, Müller came to see such a concept as itself having a dense, representational identity, and so being immersed in the process of linguistic development and proliferation that his theory was seeking to explain. It is to Müller's theory that we should now turn.

The notion of the root was central to this theory. Roots, in Müller's definition, were 'the constituent elements in different families of language'. Müller asserted that roots 'are not interjections, nor are they imitations. They are phonetic types produced by a power inherent in human nature'.[27] This definition embraces two opposing theories of, first, the origin of language, and, second, the human subject's relationship to language as an evolving phenomenon in history.

In saying that roots are neither interjections nor imitations, Müller was opposing a materialist and conventionalist theory of the origins of language, characteristic of Enlightenment thought.[28] According to this theory, language originated when prehistoric humans produced noises which were either interjections – cries signifying the sensory experience of pleasure or pain – or imitations of noises made by natural phenomena – for instance animal noises, or water rushing. These sounds, prompted by stimuli or phenomena but only arbitrarily related to them, became signs for these stimuli or phenomena by means of convention; conventions which either became extinct, or were preserved and further developed by subsequent generations in a particular locale. If we think back to the passage in the *Origin* in which the text narrates the origins of domestic breeds and compares the process to the emergence of a dialect, we will recall that it is underwritten by a similar rhetoric of speculation.

We also need to recall that the *Origin* introduced concepts of mind and value into this speculation, and, when translated into the domain of language theory itself, it was precisely these human concerns which, according to Müller, could not be satisfactorily explained by means of the materialist/conventionalist theory of language. Embedded in the theory of the root was an alternative explanation of human mind and value. To go back to Müller's definition of the root, the root is a sound (a 'phonetic type') which responds to external stimuli, but which is primarily shaped by a 'power inherent in human nature'. There were, philologists believed, between four and five hundred phonetic types or roots underlying the numerous different families of language which had developed throughout human history. From a developmental point of view roots were building blocks, the means by which languages went through their agglutinative phases – or the process whereby the complex lexical and grammatical formations characteristic of a particular language were formed by the inflection of much simpler, common forms. But according to Müller's philosophical position, roots were the expression of human nature itself, or put another way, the product of a faculty capable of rational self-reflection and conscious evaluation.

Müller's analysis of the Sanskrit root MAR, meaning 'grinding down' is a good illustration of his philosophical presumption in practice. Because MAR is a phonetic type, it is manifest in Sanskrit compounds where written inscriptions appear different but sound similar. Thus phonetically it is present in the Sanskrit word *mritá*, meaning 'dead'; and is very clearly at the centre of the Sanskrit word *márta*, which Müller argues was 'one of the earliest names for man ... [meaning] the dying, the frail creature'. Müller traces this root to later languages in the historical sequence, as in the Latin *mortus* ('dead').[29] There are two points which can be made from this which make explicit the premises of Müller's theory. First it is assumed that language formation is based on the principle of discovering similarity in difference: that is to say it is metaphorical – there is an equivalence between the act of grinding down, mortality and the concept of man which necessitates dependence on the phonetic type MAR. This brings us to the second point. For Müller, there had to be some reasoning faculty which would generate the root and put it to work in different but suggestively similar ways. According to Müller this reasoning faculty was characterised by self-reflection – it could perceive a connection between processes of grinding down and processes of illness and ageing which culminate in the death of the human subject. Paradoxically, the ability to reflect on human death was the key to understanding the specificity and value of the human self, which is named accordingly as a reasoning being, distinct from animals.[30]

Value, which as we have seen tends to be deployed as a relative, conventional term in the *Origin*, emerges as an absolute in Müller's theory: it is inherent in linguistic roots which have been generated by human reason. Even so, this did not prevent Müller from actually turning to the *Origin* and appropriating the concept which made value into a wholly relative concept – natural selection, which argued that 'valuable' success-producing characteristics were never willed but randomly selected. Müller tried to turn natural selection against itself, so to speak. If the theory of natural selection stressed an operation which was non-telological, arbitrary, and outside the remit of will, for Müller, natural selection in the evolution of language was 'invairably rational selection'.[31] While attempting to use natural selection to stress a transcendent principle of rationality in the development of languages, Müller had to concede something to the forces of arbitrariness and randomness – this was manifested in similes depicting unconscious animal activity, and human consciousness and mind:

> We want an idea that is to exclude caprice as well as necessity – that is to include individual exertion as well as general co-operation – an idea applicable neither to the unconscious building of bees nor to the conscious architecture of human beings, yet combining within itself both these operations, and raising them to a new and higher conception. You will guess both the idea and

the word, if I add that it is likewise to explain the extinction of
fossil kingdoms and the origin of new species – it is the idea of
Natural Selection.[32]

In arguing this, as Gillian Beer has astutely pointed out in
Darwin's Plots, Müller comes to see the methodological framework of the *Origin* as language. As such, it was the object of
the very processes that his theory was seeking to grasp, evolving in the heart of the present: here Müller was following transmutational theorists such as Robert Chambers who saw in
language the best opportunity for observing actual processes of
variation, accelerated by the social and cultural contexts of
modernity.[33] If the *Origin* openly declared the metaphorical
basis of its theoretrical insights, then, as Beer has argued,
Müller took these declarations seriously, assimilating their
consequences into his own theory of language development.[34]
As we have seen, Müller's theory of language development
accorded metaphor a powerful role, but, as Beer points out, it
also played a degenerative role – Müller described it as a
'disease of language', whereby 'concrete' terms lost their original clarity and precision as they were passed unconsciously
from generation to generation, accumulating variations in
meaning and developing into systems of myth and religion.[35]
Beer observes Müller finding the concept of natural selection in
its first pristine state of meaning. However, while Beer sees that,
according to Müller's theory, the metaphor of natural selection
would degenerate as it proliferated and varied, she does not go
on to explore the extent to which its movement towards a
degenerative state challenged the theory of mind which was so
central to Müller's research. The concept of natural selection
might seek to transcend and describe natural processes which
lie in the undecidable territory between unconscious and
conscious operations; but what was implied about the limited
powers of human rationality as the concept itself proliferated
and became caught up in this territory, to be selected and then
unconsciously passed on with variations in meaning? It is in
this context that Müller's assertion of Darwin's rightful owner-
ship of the concept needs to be seen as an ideological strategy
of resistance to the degenerative effects of proliferation:
'[Darwin's] name will remain afixed to a new idea, a new genus

of thought'.[36] Müller invokes the name of Darwin as a kind of permanent reminder of the rational power of human reflection which fathered the concept of natural selection. The idea of fathering is introduced here quite deliberately, and can be connected to a gendered understanding of the evolutionary relationship between language and mind which Müller set forth in an arresting metaphor: 'Language has been a very good housewife to her husband, the Human Mind; she has made very little go a long way'.[37] If the patriarchal mind had supported rational lines of wifely expansion, it had also, presumably, sent some wanton spendthrifts, who had misused the meagre housekeeping represented by the root, to the wall. This metaphor represents a gendered ideology which, as we shall see, was elaborated further by Leslie Stephen in his attempt to limit the proliferation of the language of the *Origin*. I shall argue that this patriarchal construction of reason reappears in Stephen's critical account of George Eliot's language. The important point here is that it is the language of the *Origin* itself – its transmission and variation – that had become the concern.

Leslie Stephen and literary criticism: the development of symbolic language, George Eliot and gender

Stephen's route to this concern was complex, through an argument he entered into against Müller. It was in the early 1870s, a decade after the delivery of his Lectures on the Science of Language, that Müller lectured on 'Mr Darwin's Philosophy of Language', a response to Darwin's contribution to the anthropological debate, *The Descent of Man*, just then published. The *Descent* itemised the grounds on which the relationship between philology and biology had been built, and entered explicitly into a discussion of the origins of human language which relied heavily on conventionalism.[38] In response, Müller articulated the philosophy underwriting his account of the innate presence of reason in human language. Müller grounded his argument in Immanuel Kant's theory of the *a priori* categories of understanding comprising the human mind; these were the categories, Müller argued, which generated the roots of language and which separated humans from animals.[39] Müller argued that the theory of language displayed in the *Descent*, and his own oppositional position, was to be located as a part of an ongoing struggle between two philosophical traditions: the idealism of Kant and the deterministic materialism of David Hume.[40] It was this assertion that brought Leslie Stephen into the arena of argument with his essay 'Darwinism and Divinity' published in 1873. Using arguments claiming that dogs understand the words that are spoken to them and thereby display elementary reasoning powers, Stephen's essay argued that language did not separate man from beast. In arguing this, Stephen was also attempting to place limits on philosophical readings of the *Origin*, seeking to prevent it from being appropriated by a metaphysical arena where 'Kant and Hume must fight out their quarrel'.[41]

Stephen's response initially overlooked a wider range of implications. For Müller, philosophy had an improving ideological mission: 'the intellectual vigour and moral health of a nation depend no more on the established religion than on the dominant philosophy of the realm'. Moreover, ideas and their linguistic embodiment – Müller consistently argued that thought and language were inseparable – were subject to proliferation and appropriation: 'what is thought out and written down in the study, is soon ... discussed at the corner of the street'.[42]

By 1876 Stephen's position on language had changed subtly. Not with regard to first principles; Stephen was philosophically a descendant of the Hume school, an agnostic materialist, and aggressive towards any position (such as Müller's) which smacked of intuitionism and Creationism.   Rather, Stephen's position had changed in the way he conceptualised language as an object of enquiry; he framed it as a phenomenon which not only had developed but which was susceptible to proliferation and appropriation by ideologically 'regressive' positions. This was manifest in his essay 'Thoughts of an Outsider: The Ethics of Vivisection' which appeared in the *Cornhill Magazine* of April 1876, during the anti-vivisection campaign in which Darwin and the institution of scientific research were challenged. Stephen began his essay by bemoaning the level of debate conducted between the journalistic parties contesting the campaign. In doing this, he cited Müller, using philological paradigms as an authority for comparing the writing of the contestants to the vivisection question to the emotional interjections thought to underlie the origins of human language.[43] According to Stephen, this language, for all its apparent sophistication, had not evolved beyond a primal state so far as its reasoning powers were concerned. Three points are important here. First there is Stephen's concern with the transcendence of reason. Second, Stephen's object of enquiry has become the language deployed in the debate – from whence it had evolved, its rhetorical and representational powers and, in common with Müller, though Stephen articulates the concern more pessimistically, its capacity to proliferate 'rapidly amongst people of low sensibility'.[44] Finally, we should note his decision as to who, given the appropriate language of argumentation, had reason on their side in this contest: Stephen adjudicates that it is the pro-vivisectors, Darwin and the scientists.[45] It is significant that of those who were deemed not to have reason on their side, the anti-vivisectors, many were women, the campaign being led by Frances Power Cobbe.[46] Stephen's concerns with linguistic development, proliferation and appropriation as an object of enquiry in its own right and its relations to reason and gender shaped his literary criticism, particularly his biographical-critical study of George Eliot.

Stephen's literary histories used the methodological framework of the *Origin* much in the way that August Schleicher had used it in the field of philology. This is clear from his Ford Lectures on the relationship between literature and society in eighteenth-century England:

> In every form of artistic production ... schools arise; each of which seems to embody some kind of principle, and develops and afterwards decays, according to some mysterious law. It may resemble the animal species which is, somehow or other, stamped out in the struggle for existence by a form more appropriate to the new order ... the succession of literary species implies that some are always passing into the stage of 'survivals'.[47]

Here a literary or cultural history is assumed to be in place: the point is to find some mechanism (natural selection is implied) which can explain patterns of origin, development, extinction and succession. This would seem to confirm the view that nine-teenth-century men of letters were broad-brush-stroke histori-cists, and not very interested in the representational capacties of language in its own right.

Stephen's critical biography of George Eliot also situated its subject in a literary-historical frame cast in biological language.[48] However, it is striking to note that Stephen's localised judgements of George Eliot's language were under-pinned by a transmutational paradigm:

> Perhaps it was that George Eliot had not one essential gift – the exquisite sense for the value of words which may transmute even common thought into poetry. Even her prose, indeed, though often admirable, sometimes becomes heavy, and gives the impres-sion that instead of finding the right word she is accumulating more or less complicated approximations.[49]

In Stephen's view, Eliot was not conscious of the transmuta-tional power of language, which could be artfully exploited to produce a valuable form of expression, poetry. By contrast, Eliot's 'poetry' tended to irrupt in inappropriate forms, like prose, when she seemed to have lost control of language. The effect, for Stephen, was that Eliot's writings accumulated complex variations of meaning in themselves. Stephen's judge-ment needs to be seen in relation to Müller's theory of metaphor. For Müller, metaphor was less an effect than a prin-ciple of degeneracy inherent in the evolution of language. However, the proliferation of this development was something which could be checked by the rationality of the human mind, a rationality which Müller inscribed with a masculine gender. These connections can help us to grasp the politics behind Stephen's claim that Eliot lacked a fully developed conscious-ness and a sense of the value of language, politics which become still clearer when we look at his adjacent work on language and reason in *The Science of Ethics* (1882), bearing in mind that, for Stephen, the language and literature of a given society was a reflection of its ethical framework.[50]

In the Preface to *The Science of Ethics* Stephen styled himself as a 'disciple' to Darwin's *Origin*.[51] Stephen extended the faith by refuting intuitionist accounts of morality with a materialist history of ethics; the latter moving beyond the individualistic ethical theory of utilitarianism.[52] Stephen effected this move by theorising the place of ethics in an organic sociological model, conceptualised by Stephen as 'the social organism'. Conceptualising the clearly metaphorical 'social organism' in discourse was itself fraught with potential dangers given the transmutational powers of language, and Stephen significantly ponders 'what language will be best adapted to express the relations involved'.[53] Language was accorded a tremendous density and power in Stephen's theory of ethics, resembling the power of the 'symbolic order' of Lacanian psychoanalytic theory.[54] In being taught to speak, human subjects enter 'a mass of knowledge already elaborately organised'. Thus, acquiring 'language implies the unconscious absorption of a philosophy'.[55] This is indicative of Stephen's position in the intense debate about heredity – another structuring absence in Darwin's original theory as set out in the first edition of the *Origin* – which was going on in the 1880s and 1890s.[56] Stephen argued that in the 'social organism' it was language itself which was inherited by human subjects as they became socialised; the knowledges embedded in language were disseminated and passed on to future generations; it was primarily through this agency – rather than acquired advantageous physical characteristics – that social progress would be ensured.[57]

It is worth focusing on Stephen's formulation for a moment, because it harks back to the suggestive passage from the *Origin* which was examined in some detail earlier. For Stephen, acquiring language implies the 'unconscious absorption of a philosophy'; that is to say, the subject is at the mercy of pre-existing systems of thought, and there is little scope for transcending and evaluating the conventions which the subject has been born into. To counter this problem, Stephen championed the corrective powers of reason, for in addition to unconsciously imbibed philosophies acquired through the subject's absorption in language, there was the practice of philosophic reasoning: 'philosophy is in great measure a series of attempts to escape from the erroneous conceptions … [which language] introduced in the very earliest forms of speech'.[58] Müller's philological theory of the degenerative powers latent in metaphors, formed in early languages and then passed on to future language families

and the bodies of knowledge they organised, is clearly important in Stephen's account of the major impediment to the
successful transmission of reason throughout the sucession of
historically evolving 'social organisms'.

Philosophy was united with reason in *The Science of Ethics*
through a representational paradigm. Stephen still insisted that
reason was common to man and beast, arguing that instincts are
simple processes of reasoning while reasons are sophisticated
instincts – the development from lower into higher organisms
being the key to the difference.[59] Philosophy was then merely
an enormously sophisticated instinct which could take place
only through symbols (words), and that, while the values
attached to these symbols were inherited, they were amenable
to manipulation and variation to produce new concepts which
might overthrow erroneous old values and their symbolic
embodiments.[60] The means for judging whether or not they
were erroneous was vested in a trans-historical notion of reason
which Stephen defined as 'the faculty which enables us to act
with a view to the distant and the future'.[61] For late-nineteenth-
century intellectuals like Stephen, this implied two things: first
an appreciation of the laws which had determined things
distant (history), and second an understanding of the likely
consequences that these laws would have for developments in
the future – these would govern how the subject might act in
the present. Given Stephen's avowed discipleship to Darwin in
The Science of Ethics, the implication is fairly clear: Darwin's
Origin of Species was a manipulation of old erroneous symbol-
ism, like Natural Theology and its Creationist philosophy,
which invigorated the individual's powers of reasoning about
the past, the future and how to act in the present. This is where
we return to Stephen's critical evaluation of George Eliot's writings; for in Stephen's view their proliferation threatened to
vary Darwin's state-of-the-art line in reason beyond 'reasonable' limits.

Stephen's critical biography of Eliot argued for a division
between the early and late periods of her writings. The early
writings of the 1850s comprise a series of 'country' novels –
Scenes of Clerical Life, *Adam Bede*, and *The Mill on the Floss* –
of which Stephen by and large approved. The later writings of

the 1860s and 1870s– *Romola, Felix Holt the Radical, The Spanish Gypsy, Middlemarch* and *Daniel Deronda* – appeared flawed to Stephen because of their speculative and 'theoretical' tendencies.[62] The point here is not to analyse in detail the way in which Eliot wove Darwinian discourse into her writings – here I refer the reader to the rich researches of Gillian Beer – the point is rather to explore the grounds for Stephen's ideological resistance to the consequences. Even so, it will be necessary to sketch in two major topical concerns dramatised and linked in both *The Spanish Gypsy* and *Daniel Deronda*, concerns which Stephen's critical practice resisted.

The first was nationalism. Both *The Spanish Gypsy*, a long poem set in late medieval Spain, and *Daniel Deronda*, Eliot's last novel, set in mid nineteenth-century England, were concerned with the establishment of a nation belonging to a marginalised social and ethnic group – gypsies in *The Spanish Gypsy*, Jews in *Daniel Deronda*. Stephen was alert to this shared thematic concern, and the way in which it aped nationalistic sentiments echoing concerns with which his readers would have been familiar.[63] We should bear in mind that in the late nineteenth century English imperialism had made English nationalism a very powerful ideology, while resurgent forms of nationalistic resistance in lands ruled by England challenged the imperial system which dominated them. This was the case in Ireland, where, in the late nineteenth century, the argument over Home Rule constituted the major political and ideological problem facing English politicians of all parties, and intellectuals, or experts in ideological legitimation, like Stephen.

The second was heredity. In *Daniel Deronda* the instinctive, mystical sympathy that Deronda feels for Jewish sister and brother Mirah and Mordecai is explained through the revelation of his own Jewish descent, which is unknown to him at the beginning of the narrative. Stephen objected to the theme of descent in *Daniel Deronda*, arguing that it made heredity into a religion.[64] In *The Spanish Gypsy*, the heroine Fedalma, apparently a Catholic Spaniard, bride-to-be of the Spanish nobleman Don Silva, is confronted by the leader of a band of gypsies, Zarca. Zarca reveals to the unsuspecting Fedalma that he is her father; instinctively, she abandons her attachment to Don Silva and follows her father in his enterprise to establish a gypsy nation in Africa:

> Father, my soul is not too base to ring
> At touch of your great thoughts; nay in my blood
> There streams the sense unspeakable of kind
> As leopard feels at ease with leopard.[65]

Heredity is here *represented* metaphorically as an instinctual drive which overwhelms the individual's capacity to reason and evaluate. But it was the consequences of an alliance between such a language of heredity and nationalism that prompted Stephen's resistance: 'the discovery that my father was a Saxon or a Celt might be allowed to affect my sympathies, but surely should not change my views of home rule'.[66] Stephen's critical practice here is not solely that it rejects a theory of the overwhelming effects of heredity and its power to overturn reason by unconscious drives. Rather it is resistant to the unconscious absorption of a particular mystical *language* of heredity which had transmuted and varied beyond the limits established by reason. The proliferation of such a species of representation might result in an abundance of irrational acts.

One such irrational act in Stephen's view was the martyr's death pursued for nationalistic ends, which is threatened in *The Spanish Gypsy*. Fedalma, having submitted herself to Zarca's bloody goal on the grounds of descent from him, looks forward to 'marriage' to a violent death, through which Zarca's cause might spread further: 'That death shall be my bridegroom'.[67] It is in Stephen's reaction to this speech that one dimension of the specifically patriarchal nature of his criticism is registered: 'of course, the young lady is excited. She is in the state of mind in which irrationality is a recommendation'.[68] Light irony, directed at both representations of femininity and, in Stephen's view, failed representations of masculinity, is a recurring strategy in the biography. But this is part and parcel of a broader patriarchal contention which, Stephen claims, disqualifies George Eliot from speculative activity for 'she had not the experience which enabled her to describe contemporary life, with its social and political ambitions and the rough struggle for existence in which practical lawyers and men of business are mainly occupied'.[69] If, for Stephen, the *Origin* had reformulated the language of speculative thought with a view to eliminating erroneous speculations and advancing reason, then the conceptual language that he put in place – for example, the struggle for existence – could be extended and elaborated only by professional men who, given their privileged position within the 'social organism' as Stephen's symbolic language phrased it (or the 'separate-spheres' ideology as a progressive symbolic language of today would phrase it) had an experiential and concrete relationship to the 'necessity' which the concept grasped and the future which it promised. Professional men, and literary intellectuals such as Stephen, were to be the legitimate custodians of Darwin's language; women writers such as George Eliot were not to be entrusted with its resources.

This returns us to one of our starting points; it helps to explain the complex patriarchal ideological strategies connecting Stephen's reading of Darwin as a descendant of Montaigne – styling them both as philosophers of mortality – and his dismissive judgement of George Eliot's poetry. We have already seen how Müller recognised the representational density of the language of the *Origin*, and that Müller reacted by insisting on the presence of Darwin's name, which would remain authoritatively fixed to the metaphors of the *Origin*. Devising a parallel strategy, we need to recall that in the Preface to *The Science of Ethics* Stephen fashioned himself as a disciple to Darwin, a relationship based on reverence and recognition of supreme authority. Stephen fashioned Darwin as an authoritative father whose language was to be read in the context of a tradition of a reasoned, masculine approach to being – and death. As we have seen earlier, Müller's theory of language development argued that Man reasoned his way into existence and selfhood by means of perceiving and speaking of his own mortality; for Stephen, philosophical activity was a constant fight against the degenerative tendencies of metaphor that set in thereafter, developing erroneous systems of myth and religion (which the language representing heredity as power over reason in *Daniel Deronda* and *The Spanish Gypsy* threatened to fuel). For Stephen, Darwin's manipulation of an inherited symbolic language enabled the reader to come to imaginary terms with a death in which power relations and inequalities would be stoicly accepted to

promote the greater good of the 'social organism', taking as its
text the ministration on death in the *Origin*: 'when we reflect
on this struggle, we may console ourselves with the full belief
that the war of nature is not incessant, that no fear is felt, that
death is generally prompt'.[70] Stephen was clearly antipathetic
to representations of death which were noisy, rhetorical and
oppositional as with Fedalma's imagined martyrdom in George
Eliot's *The Spanish Gypsy*.

This antipathy was linked to a fear of the proliferation and
inheritance of a Darwinian language that had varied in accordance with 'feminine' tendencies – not only because it had been
appropriated by a woman writer like George Eliot but also
because of the ideological perception of the cultural soil in
which such a language might flourish and allow its kind to
propagate. We have seen how Stephen's reactions to George
Eliot's appropriation of the languages of nationalism and heredity were linked to his political anxieties about Ireland, and if
Stephen did not explicitly construct Ireland as a degenerate
'feminine' culture, there were in existence ideological construc-
tions of Ireland which did precisely this. Matthew Arnold's *On
the Study of Celtic Literature* (1867) was another instance of literary criticism which drew upon philology. In this text, Arnold
constructed the Celtic tradition as being based on 'sentiment'
which was 'always ready to react against the despotism of fact',
leading the Celt to unthinkingly give himself 'body and soul to
some leader'. This was, Arnold claimed, illustrative of a 'feminine' culture.[71]

Conclusion

My guiding interest in perceptions of the proliferation of the
language of the *Origin* has brought me to the ideological strategies of Leslie Stephen's literary criticism by way of his evolutionary social and ethical theory, and its relations in turn to the
philological researches of Max Müller. Both Müller and Stephen
wrote in response to the *Origin*, but whereas they began by
using that text as a point of departure for arguing against each
other about the relationship between man, animals and
language, they both simultaneously responded to the *Origin* as

a form of dense, linguistic representation. I have argued, building on Gillian Beer's lead, that the *Origin* should be seen as a sign of the insistence of an epistemology of representation during the nineteenth century. This should encourage us to rethink Foucault's arguments about the emergence of nineteenth-century sciences of man eliminating an epistemology of representation while organising knowledge around a search for origins, and to see instead ovelap between these two epistemologies. The dense, connotative power of the representational language of Darwinian speculations on the origin of species prompted intellectuals such as Müller and Stephen to reflect on Darwin's contribution to the historical process of elaborating and varying the symbolic language of philosophy. The need to reflect on such a process was heightened by the proliferation of the language of the *Origin* into a multiplicity of intellectual domains and written forms, such as the philological and philosophical researches of high culture, but also the domain of popular writing. If we take the practice of representation – an ideological struggle over the sign – to be common but contested cultural ground between a novelist and poet like George Eliot and a critic like Leslie Stephen, then this enables us to become more aware of the fact that ideological conflicts were being waged over the right to appropriate and further disseminate the representational power of discourse. It is in this sense that cultural historians need to grasp critically Stephen's desire to fashion himself as a disciple to Darwin, and to fix limits around Darwin as an authoritative arbiter of meaning. It is important then to grant significance to strategies of patriarchal resistance which made the *Origin* into an authoritative act of individual creation, pitched against an eco-system of print in which practices of representation dispersed their seeds far and wide.

Notes

My thanks to Karen Ellis and Jeff Wallace who read and made astute, very helpful comments on earlier drafts of this essay which I have gratefully acted upon.

1 Charles Darwin, *Origin of Species by Means of Natural Selection*, 1859, XI and XII.
2 See for instance Peter Morton, *The Vital Science: Biology and the Literary Imagination, 1860–1900* (London: George Allen and Unwin, 1984), and

The Darwinian Heritage (Princeton: Princeton University Press, 1985); for
a review of recent scholarship investigating this proliferation see David
N. Livingstone, 'The Darwinian Diffusion: Darwin and Darwinism,
Divinity and Design', *Christian Scholar's Review* 19:2 (1989), pp 186–99.

3 See Gillian Beer's essay 'Darwin and the Growth of Language Theory',
in *Nature transfigured: Science and literature 1700–1900* (Manchester:
Manchester University Press, 1989), pp. 152–170.

4 See Darwin, *Origin* ,p. 316, and p. 406.

5 Michel Foucault, *The Order of Things: An Archaeology of the Human
Sciences*, translated from the French by Alan Sheridan (London:
Routledge, 1989), p. 40.

6 Gerald Graff, *Professing Literature: An Institutional History* (Chicago and
London: University of Chicago Press, 1987), pp. 71–2.

7 Leslie Stephen to Norton, 20 June 1901; in F. W. Maitland, *Life and
Letters of Leslie Stephen* (London: Duckworth, 1906), p. 463; although it
is not made clear, Stephen must be referring to Montaigne's essay 'That
to philosophise is to learne how to die', *Essayes of Michael Lord of
Montaigne*, translated from the French by John Florio (1603), 3 volumes
(London: Henry Frowde, 1904), vol. I, pp. 73–94.

8 Ibid.

9 Gillian Beer, *Darwin's Plots: Evolutionary Narrative in Darwin, George
Eliot and Nineteenth-Century Fiction*, 1983 (London: Ark, 1985), chapters
5 and 6.

10 Darwin, *Origin*, p. 316.

11 Robert Keefe, 'Literati, Language, and Darwinism', *Language and Style*
19:2 (spring 1986), pp. 123–137; p. 133.

12 Keefe, 'Literati, Language and Darwinism', p. 131.

13 Ibid.

14 V. N. Volosinov, *Marxism and the Philosophy of Language*, translated from
the Russian by Ladislav Matejka and I. R. Titunik (New York and
London: Seminar Press, 1973), p. 9 and p. 23.

15 Leslie Stephen, *The Science of Ethics* (London: Smith, Elder and Co.,
1882), p. 63.

16 Beer, *Darwin's Plots*, p. 10.

17 For an illuminating discussion of the anthropological assumptions embedded in the early philological researches of Bopp see Foucault, *The Order
of Things*, pp. 287–294. For a general discussion of the place of philology
in nineteenth-century English intellectual culture, including accounts of
its major exponents (Sir William Jones, Baron Bunsen, Max Müller) see
J. W. Burrow, 'The Uses of Philology in Victorian England', in *Ideas and
Institutions of the Victorians: Essays in Honour of George Kitson Clark*,
edited by R. Robson (London: G. Bell, 1967), pp. 180–204; p. 185. The
best general discussion of the *Origin* – and other writings by Darwin –
in relation to nineteenth-century philology and language theory is Beer's
'Darwin and the Growth of Language Theory'.

18 Darwin, *Origin*, p. 406.

19 August Schleicher, *Darwinism Tested by the Science of Language*, translated from the German by A. V. W. Bikkers (London: John Camden

Hotten, 1869), translator's Preface, p. 9.

20 Darwin, *Origin*, pp. 160–61; Schleicher, *Darwinism*, Appendix.

21 Schleicher, *Darwinism*, p. 15; the *Origin* was not translated into German until 1860; the translation that Schleicher read would have been taken from the second edition.

22 Darwin, *Origin*, pp. 97–8.

23 For the concept of 'unconscious selection', see also Darwin, *Origin*, p. 138 and 148.

24 Beer, *Darwin's Plots*, p. 100.

25 Friedrich Max Müller, *Lectures on the Science of Language: Second Series* (London: Longman Green, 1864), p. 7.

26 Müller, *Lectures on the Science of Language: First Series*, second edition (London: Longman Green, 1862), p. 356.

27 Müller, *Lectures: First Series*, p. 387.

28 See for instance Müller's commentary on the project of Bishop Wilkins, *Towards a Real Character and a Philosophical Language* (1668) in the lecture 'Language and Reason', *Lectures: Second series*, pp. 47–62. This is a summary of what has come to be known as Enlightenment (or 'classical' in Foucault's terminology) thought on language, which Müller critiques. In the emphasis it places on arbitrariness and convention it is close to what we now know as Saussurean linguistics; see Ferdinand de Saussure, *Course in General Linguistics* (1916).

29 Müller, *Lectures: Second Series*, pp. 315–19.

30 Müller, *Lectures: First Series*, pp. 384–5.

31 See for instance Darwin *Origin*, p. 348; Müller, *Lectures: Second Series*, p. 306.

32 Müller, *Lectures: Second Series*, pp. 309–10.

33 'I have been told ... that the children of Manchester factory workers left for a great deal of the day, in large assemblage, under the care of perhaps a single elderly person, and spending the time in amusements, are found to make a great deal of new language. I have seen children in other circumstances amuse themselves by concocting and throwing into the family circulation entirely new words; and I believe I am running little risk of contradiction when I say that there is scarcely a family, even amongst the middle classes of this country, who have not some peculiarites of pronunciation and syntax, which have originated amongst themselves, it is hardly possible to say how'. Robert Chambers, *Vestiges of the Natural History of Creation*, 1844, (London: George Routledge & Sons, 1887), p. 234–5.

34 'I should premise that I use the term Struggle for Existence in a large and metaphorical sense'; Darwin, *Origin*, p. 116. Beer, *Darwin's Plots*, p. 122.

35 Müller, *Lectures: First Series,* p. 347.

36 Müller, *Lectures; First Series*, p. 310.

37 Müller, *Lectures: First Series*, p. 353.

38 Charles Darwin, *The Descent of Man and Selection in Relation to Sex*, 1871, second edition (London: John Murray, 1913), pp. 129–42; for itemised relationship between philological research into language development

and biological research into species development, see p. 138.

39 Friedrich Max Müller, 'Mr Darwin's Philosophy of Language I', *Fraser's Magazine* (new series) 7:41 (May 1873), pp. 525–541, p. 534.

40 Müller, 'Mr Darwin's Philosophy of Language II', *Fraser's Magazine* (new series) 7:42 (June 1873), pp. 659–678, p. 659.

41 Leslie Stephen, *Essays in Freethinking and Plainspeaking*, (London: Longman Green, 1873), p. 81.

42 Max Müller, 'Mr Darwin's Philosophy of Language I', p. 525, and *Lectures: Second Series*, p. 386.

43 Leslie Stephen, 'The Ethics of Vivisection', *Cornhill Magazine*, 33 (April 1876), pp. 468–478, p. 468. Müller did not totally reject the idea of interjections; rather he differed from Enlightenment theorists of interjections in his interpretation of what happened to them subsequent to their formation. Müller was concerned to eliminate arbitrariness and convention from the theory, insisting that the root that was selected proved the innate human power of reason to extract something of permanent value from the cry. See *Lectures: First Series*, p. 306.

44 Stephen, 'Vivisection', p. 475.

45 Stephen, 'Vivisection', p. 477–8.

46 See Fiona Erskine's chapter in this volume. See Adrian Desond and James Moore, *Darwin* (Harmondsworth: Penguin, 1992), pp. 615–16.

47 Leslie Stephen, *English Literature and Society in the Eighteenth Century* (London: Duckworth, 1904), pp. 20–2.

48 Leslie Stephen, *George Eliot*, English Men of Letters (London: Macmillan, 1902), pp. 66–7.

49 Stephen, *George Eliot*, p. 168.

50 Stephen, *George Eliot*, pp. 66–7.

51 Stephen, *Science*, p. v.

52 For an account of Stephen's role in the rejuvination of liberal ideology and its utilitarian philosophy by biological theory see Greta Jones, *Social Darwinism and English Thought* (Brighton: Harvester Press, 1980), pp. 47–53.

53 Stephen, *Science*, p. 93.

54 'We are metaphysicians in the cradle, and distinguish object and subject by methods instilled in us by our nurses'. Stephen, *Science*, p. 106. For an account of the 'symbolic order' see Rosalind Coward and John Ellis, *Language and Materialism: Developments in Semiology and the Theory of the Subject* (London: Routledge and Kegan Paul, 1977), pp. 114–21.

55 Stephen, *Science*, p. 106.

56 For an account of the various positions in this debate, see Jones, *Social Darwinism*, chapters 5 and 6.

57 See Stephen's essay 'Heredity' in *Social Rights and Duties: Addresses to Ethical Societies*, 2 vols (London: Swan Sonnenschein & Co., 1896), II, p. 46.

58 Stephen, *Science*, p. 106.

59 Stephen, *Science*, p. 63.

60 Stephen, *Science*, p. 63, p. 106.

61 Stephen, *Science*, p. 60.

62 Stephen, *George Eliot*, p. 112–3.
63 Stephen, *George Eliot*, p. 188–9.
64 Stephen, *George Eliot*, p. 190.
65 George Eliot, *The Spanish Gypsy*, Book I, in *Works: Warwick Edition*, 20 vols (Edinburgh and London: Blackwoods, 1906), vol. XI, p. 153.
66 Stephen, *George Eliot*, p. 166.
67 Eliot, *The Spanish Gypsy*, Book I, p. 163.
68 Stephen, *George Eliot*, pp. 165–66.
69 Stephen, *George Eliot*, p. 202.
70 Darwin, *Origin*, p. 129.
71 Matthew Arnold, *On the Study of Celtic Literature and Other Essays* (London: Dent, no date), p. 82, pp. 85–6. This view of Ireland as a degenerate culture links the work of Arnold and Stephen to a Europe-wide context of cultural anxieties about degeneration which has been brilliantly traced by Daniel Pick in *Faces of Degeneration: A European Disorder, c. 1848– c.1918* (Cambridge: Cambridge University Pres, 1989), p. 177. As Pick shows, degeneration was discursively linked to the problem of proliferation: 'Though originating in the viscious course of individuals, [degenerations] are not confined in their consequences to the guilty sufferers, but are passed on to the offspring, and then become year by year more generally diffused among the great mass of the people'. 'Race Degeneration', *The Lancet*, 1, (June 1866), p. 691, quoted by Pick, p. 191.

6

Origins, species and
Great Expectations

KATE FLINT

Great Expectations is a text obsessed with the idea of origins: the origin of wealth, the identification of parenthood. The theme of the disclosure of origins is responsible for the way in which the plot unfolds, and for the way in which the reader becomes actively enmeshed in the interpretive process, as Dickens leads his audience, at times, to be deceived or distracted by the same clues as those which mislead Pip. The formal organisation of the text ensures that the reader's attention becomes focused on several crucial issues: first, to what extent does the uncovering of origins, and the knowledge gained thereby, prove a useful exercise (or a timewasting and distressing one) when it comes to developing one's social and moral identity, and shaping the course of one future; and second, what part is played by culture and upbringing in deflecting, even radically altering, the determining factors of such origins? More pertinent still to its time was the implicit questioning of whether or not the human species obeyed the same laws of development as the rest of the organic world, and, if so, whether one could, indeed, find any signs of a 'progress towards perfection' – to use Darwin's words – in the social world as depicted in the novel.

Dickens's novel began publication in his magazine, *All the Year Round*, on 1 December 1860, just over a year after the appearance of Charles Darwin's controversial, widely discussed *The Origin of Species*. We cannot prove, even if we were to wish to do so, that Dickens is engaging directly with Darwin. There are no explicit references to the scientist's work in the pages of *Great Expectations*, no mentions of his name in the published *Letters* or in Forster's *Life*, although the catalogue of Dickens's library at Gad's Hill shows that a copy of the first edition of the *Origin* was in his possession at the time of his death. It would seem likely, though, that the two men had at least encountered each other (they were elected members of the Athenaeum Club on the same day, 21 June 1838, for example), and Dickens's editorial supervision of the pages of *All the Year Round* almost certainly ensured that he was familiar with the tenets of the *Origin*.[1] In any case, I am not concerned with determining *direct* influence; with searching, as it were, with a patriarchal anxiety for the *novel*'s origins, attempting to confirm its legitimate descent. In broad terms, I wish to show that Dickens shared a common set of concerns, and to some extent a common language — both descriptive and metaphorical — in which to discuss them, with those working in what were ostensibly different disciplines. As Peter Ackroyd has put it: 'Dickens's own understanding of the symbolic forces of the world is charged with the same group of perceptions defined by contemporary scientists and geologists.'[2] At the same time, I want to consider how *All the Year Round* functioned as a site on which various forms of response to questions of natural selection were displayed. This means looking not only at Dickens's own fiction, but at the two relatively lengthy articles (appearing on 2 June and 7 July 1860) in which the content and implications of Darwin's work were discussed, and at a number of less conspicuous references to the question of whether or not the same generalisations applied to human as to animal life. One should also note the immensely popular novel serialized immediately after *Great Expectations*, from August 1861-March 1862, Edward Bulwer-Lytton's *A Strange Story*, which, in a thoroughly fantastic plot, introduces a manuscript which allegedly reveals all the inner secrets of nature, and has the central characters engaged in an abortive attempt to brew the elixir of life. The question of whether or not human life and development could invariably be subject to rational explanations was thus kept continually before Dickens's public for over two years. And, as

Gillian Beer has written in relation to Darwin and *Daniel Deronda*, 'the process of interchange of metaphors and concepts between fields is at its most active "in areas of unresolved conflict or problem"'.[3]

In their magnificent biography of Darwin, Adrian Desmond and James Moore show how the *Origin* was not sprung on an unprepared public: rather, Darwin held back from publishing his deliberations and theories until he could be seen to be making a contribution to an established debate, rather than a sensational and wildly speculative intervention. Among non-specialist contributors to this debate, it was no novelty for Dickens to engage with issues of evolution and survival, along-side other scientific matters. Most notably, he introduces London at the opening of *Bleak House* – a novel which George Levine describes as working 'through many of the crises that Darwin's thought made explicit'[4] – as having:

> As much mud in the streets, as if the waters had but newly retired from the face of the earth, and it would not be wonderful to meet a Megalosaurus, forty feet long or so, waddling like an elephan-tine lizard up Holborn Hill. Smoke lowering down from chimney pots, making a soft black drizzle with flakes of soot in it as big as full-grown snowflakes – gone into mourning, one might imag-ine, for the death of the sun. Dogs, undistinguishable in mire. Horses, scarcely better; splashed to their very blinkers. Foot passengers, jostling one another's umbrellas, in a general infec-tion of ill temper, and losing their foot-hold at street-corners, where tens of thousands of other foot passengers have been slip-ping and sliding since the day broke (if this day ever broke), adding new deposits to the crust upon crust of mud, sticking at those points tenaciously to the pavement, and accumulating at compound interest.[5]

This paragraph links the murky condition of contemporary London with current apprehension concerning entropy – the slow exhaustion of the earth's stocks of energy – and the future cooling of the sun which would render earth uninhabitable.[6] Such apprehension is superficially at odds with the evolution-ary references which it also contains: references which suggest a parallel between the progression of organic life, and financial growth. The terms 'deposits' and 'accumulating at compound interest' invite one to consider whether economic laws, and what might be termed the survival of the fittest in the commercial world, may bear an intimate connection with natural growth. For by turning London into a muddy swamp – the environment from which life came; the slime into which it may sink again – Dickens demands that we should consider urban life in terms of very basic conditions of survival. Elemental environment is similarly highlighted in *Great Expectations* in the language which describes the marshes where the novel opens, a countryside of mud, water and mist. Most ominously, in this evolutionary parade which opens *Bleak House* – megalosaurus, dog, horse, man – the explicit threat of extinction is present. As the first of these species perished, so might the rest.

Dickens very probably drew this image of the megalosaurus (as William Buckland called the Great Lizard in 1824) from an article which Henry Morley had written for *Household Words*, published on 16 August 1851, shortly before he began writing the novel.[7] In this article, 'Our Phantom Ship on an Antediluvian Cruise', we meet, as in *Jurassic Park*, 'a land reptile, before which we take the liberty of running. His teeth look too decidedly carnivorous. A sort of crocodile, thirty feet long, with a big body, mounted on high thick legs, is not likely to be friendly with our legs and bodies. Megalosaurus is his name, and, doubtless, greedy is his nature.'[8] I will be returning to the subject of greed and carnivorousness in relation to *Great Expectations*: here, though, the article is to be noted as one among a number which Dickens included in *Household Words* and *All the Year Round* on this area of popular science. It followed a piece in December 1850 on the Hunterian Museum, where 'we come into absolute contact with some things that moved upon the earth before the Flood',[9] and preceded later post-*Origin* articles on similar subjects: one on the natural history collections in the British Museum in 1862, for example, and one on 'Mary Anning, the Fossil Finder' (she discovered the fossilised skeleton of the first dinosaur known to science) in 1865.[10] As Susan Shatto has argued, Dickens appears to add weight, by printing these, to Darwin's argument, in chapter XI of the *Origin*, that people have demonstrated egocentric unwillingness in their reluctance to believe in the annihilation of physically strong species: such annihilation undoubtedly took place.[11]

These articles dealt with topical issues. So did the 1860 pieces, 'Species' and 'Natural Selection.' Most unusually for *All the Year Round*, however, these took the form of a summary and assessment of a recent publication: the periodical contained very few articles which were explicitly based on current works, and the appearance of two pieces directly engaging with one text (followed by a third, 'Transmutation of Species', on 9 March 1861, which deals in part with the *Origin*) was exceptional. Moreover, as Alvar Ellegård has demonstrated in his study of the reception of Darwin's theories on evolution in over a hundred mid-Victorian periodicals, *All the Year Round* was atypical, among mass-circulation magazines (as opposed to the weeklies, monthlies and quarterlies more specifically targeted at certain literary, political and religious allegiances) in placing a good deal of weight on the *Origin*. The only other similar magazine to pay it as much attention was *Chambers's Journal*, and this was hardly surprising, since Robert Chambers, author of the *Vestiges of the Natural History of Creation* (1844), was one of its editors.[12]

'Species' and 'Natural Selection' isolated, for Dickens's readership, what their writer saw as Darwin's crucial premise: his belief in the fallacy of the idea that each species has been independently created. Rather, those belonging to what are termed the same genera are lineal descendants of some other, generally extinct species. Animals have descended from at most four or five progenitors, plants from an equal or lesser number. By analogy – although, of course, he cannot prove it – Darwin hypothesises that every living thing is derived from some single, primitive, rudimentary cell. As the *All the Year Round* articles were at some pains to point out, such a theory is, up to this point, not necessarily incompatible with Christian beliefs: even *one* original cell must have been 'created' somehow: moreover, the complexity of living organisms which now exist is such that it can 'only be sustained by an All-wise, Almighty Divinity.'[13] Sustained, perhaps – the writer builds on the conciliatory hints offered by Darwin in such phrases as 'laws impressed on matter by the Creator' – but not, Darwin would argue, developed, and here, for the *All the Year Round* commentator as for so many others, lay the controversial crux of the book, in Darwin's maintaining that all species have evolved according to a process of natural selection, a better organised, stronger, fitter creature with the characteristics best suited to its environment having a much better chance of survival than its fellows. This, the second of the articles made clear, was a belief directly opposed to those who maintained that:

> various species of plants and animals ... have been purposely fitted and adapted to the place in creation which they were intended to occupy by an Overruling Intelligence; for it is maintained that the more complex organs and instincts have been perfected, not at once in the first-created individual, by the Hand of the Maker, but by the accumulation of innumerable slight variations, each good for the individual possessor for the time being, during an exceedingly long succession of individuals from generation to generation. (NS, 296)

The consequence of this, explains the article in Darwin's words, is that 'We are no longer to look at an organic being as a savage looks at a ship – as at something totally beyond his comprehension; we are to regard every production of nature as one which has had a history' (NS, 299). Moreover, its history is not individualistic, discrete, but is intimately connected with that of all other living beings: to quote Darwin, in his Summary to chapter IV, there is an 'infinite complexity of the relations of all organic beings to each other and to their conditions of existence, causing an infinite diversity in structure, constitution, and habits' (169).

In *Great Expectations*, Dickens takes up the idea of unbreakable patterns of cause and effect working to determine present existence. 'Pause you who read this,' asks Pip – and/or Dickens commenting through Pip – 'and think for a moment of the long chain of iron or gold, of thorns or flowers, that would never have bound you, but for the formation of the first link on one memorable day.'[14] The clink of prisoners' fetters that can be heard through this metaphor recalls the meeting with Magwitch in the churchyard which so significantly shapes Pip's life: the churchyard being also the location of his own origins, since it is the resting place of his actual progenitors. Pip's own name suggests a seed, an origin. The significance of this is implicitly exploited at the opening of chapter 8, which functions as a linguistic confirmation of the link between Magwitch, and the way in which he flourishes, in economic terms, in Australia, and the boy. When Pip visits Mr Pumblechook's premises, he notices the many little drawers in his shop: .'..and I wondered when I peeped into one or two on the lower tiers, and saw the tied-up brown paper packets inside, whether the flower-seeds and bulbs ever wanted of a fine day to break out of those jails, and bloom' (83). The twin metaphors, of pip/seed and prisons, and the reminder that both may hold the potential to contain significant life, are both silently joined to the idea of primal matter by the organic resonances of the word 'cell.'

The *All the Year Round* article on 'Species', in emphasising that 'creatures so remote in the scale of being as plants and animals are still bound together by a web of complex relations' (S,177) carries with it the implication that different forms of *animal* life must be bound together by closer ties yet. This is, of course, exemplified through its plot, and it is worth recalling at this point Gillian Beer's reminder that the traffic between the *Origin* and other forms of Victorian culture was not one-way. The organisation of Darwin's book, she remarks, 'seems to owe a good deal to the example of one of Darwin's most frequently read authors, Charles Dickens, with its apparent unruly superfluity of material gradually and retrospectively revealing itself as order, its superfecundity of instance serving an argument which can reveal itself only *through* instance and revelations.'[15] Initially, however, I am here concerned not so much with the revelations which help to structure *Great Expectations* as with the closer texture of metaphorical language.

Dickens's novel is hardly a vegetarian tract. It emphasises an uncomfortably close dependency of one form of animal life upon another. Daily survival is made suspiciously similar to an act of cannibalism. Magwitch first works his threats, necessary to ensure that *he* obtains food, through licking his lips, commenting on the fatness of Pip's cheeks, speaking hungrily of the boy's heart and liver. These particular organs point not just to cannibalism but to the boy as human sacrifice. The way in which he eats the food Pip provides, gobbling mincemeat, meatbone, bread, cheese and pork pie all at once, with short sudden snapping bites, instantly recalls to Pip the way a large dog eats its meals (and thus links with the way in which Pip is fed by Estella). Such references to the ingestion of animal flesh are not limited to the melodramatic context of graveyard and convict, where they have a role in underscoring the fear Pip experiences, but occur in conjunction with the domestic ritual of the Christmas dinner. Mr Wopsle draws on the gluttony of swine as presenting an example to the young:

> 'What is detestable in a pig, is more detestable in a boy...
>
> 'Besides,' said Mr Pumblechook, turning sharp on me, 'think what you've got to be grateful for. If you'd been born a Squeaker _'
>
> 'He was, if ever a child was,' said my sister, most emphatically. Joe gave me some more gravy.

– hardly a consolatory gesture, in the circumstances.

> 'Well, but I mean a four-footed Squeaker,' said Mr Pumblechook.
>
> 'If you had been born such, would you have been here now? Not you -'
>
> 'Unless in that form,' said Mr Wopsle, nodding towards the dish.(58)

This idea seems to stick in Pumblechook's mind: later, he apostrophises the fowl he is feeding to Pip: '"You little thought ... when you was a young fledgling, what was in store for you"' (180). Similarly, Wemmick's pig meets a useful, but uncomfortably anthropomorphised, fate. When Pip hides out for a day in Wemmick's suburban residence, he is invited to have:

> '... a little bit of – you remember the pig?'
>
> 'Of course,' said I.
>
> 'Well; and a little bit of him. That sausage you toasted was his, and he was in all respects a first-rater. Do try him, if it is only for old acquaintance sake'.(386)

Even at the end of the novel, Pumblechook looks back to the young Pip, on the eve of his departure for London, as having been 'as plump as a peach' (483): eminently ripe for consumption.

This preoccupation with human edibility is found in *All the Year Round* articles contemporaneous with the novel's serialisation. A few months prior to its appearance, one of Dickens's own 'Uncommercial Traveller' pieces dwells with unpleasant relish on Captain Murderer, whose 'mission was matrimony, and the gratification of a cannibal appetite with tender brides.' He made tasty pies of successive wives, each culinary enterprise culminating with the refrain 'and he chopped her into pieces, and peppered her, and salted her, and put her in the pie, and sent it to the baker's, and ate it all, and picked the bones.'[16] James Marlow has drawn attention to Dickens' interest in cannibalism, particularly after the failure of Franklin's expedition and the information which emerged that Franklin had been driven to eat human flesh during his fatal search for the North-west Passage. But the 'real issue', claims Marlow, 'was neither the behavior of men who were never civilized nor even the behavior of civilized men like Franklin in a savage world; rather, the issue was the savage behavior of men in what purported to be the civilized world.'[17] Yet in *All the Year Round* in the early 1860s, these issues are shown to be completely interrelated, since all have a bearing on what it may mean to be human. In 'Life in Africa', the profusion of animal and vegetable life in central Africa, alongside the laziness of the inhabitants when it comes to tilling the land and rearing animals, is noted:

> They eat what comes to hand – elephant, hippopotamus, rat, mouse, dog, frog, slug – and when food runs short they fall back upon man. Some eat man cooked, others prefer him raw; some eat him young, some old; some eat enemies killed in battle, others have no objection to a friend, and kill him when he is ill and dying, or barter for his body after he is dead. They bring the traveller a plump slave as we should offer a fowl.[18]

Further articles claim that 'In the absence of all domestic animals, man would convert his fellow-men into beasts of burden, and even into butcher's meat',[19] and record Ethiopian practices ('when a lady presented her lord with twins, they used to get up a little family party, cook the twins, and eat them').[20] In 1861, du Chaillu's account of his travels on the swampy shores and hinterland of Africa south of the Guinea coast, which included detailed descriptions of gorillas, prompted a good deal of debate in the popular press about whether the gorilla provided the missing link between humans and apes (despite du Chaillu's disclaimers to the contrary). It would seem, though, that *All the Year Round* took the opportunity to press home the point that 'the most degraded' of all human tribes reach depths of behaviour to which advanced apes would not sink. Gorillas are vegetarian: the author, however:

> who describes to us the gorilla as the most hellish and fearful-looking monster that could be conceived, states that in the native African village he entered after bagging his first specimen of man-ape, he met a woman who 'bore with her a piece of the thigh of a human body, just as we should go to the market and carry thence a steak.'[21]

The tenuous nature of the division between animal and human – even vegetable – life in *Great Expectations* is notable on a broader scale than the half-comic, half-queasy gastronomic one we have just examined. The link between meat and institutionalised murder is made on the occasion of Pip's first walk through London. Waiting for Mr Jaggers, he takes a stroll which effortlessly stimulates his latent sense of guilt, first passing the meat market and slaughteryards of Smithfield – 'the shameful place, being all asmear with filth and fat and blood and foam, seemed to stick to me' (189) – and then turning into the street where Newgate prison was situated, and learning of the criminals who would be hanged the next morning. These same prisoners are termed 'plants' in a 'greenhouse', tended by Wemmick the 'gardener': vegetables waiting to play their part in the food chain. The animal/human connection is made at the simple level of sobriquet and simile. Pip is a 'young monkey' (something which, in this context, takes one back to earlier scientific speculation, via the reference in the first, genealogical chapter of *Martin Chuzzlewit* to 'the Monboddo doctrine touching the probability of the human race having once been monkeys');[22] the convicts going down on the coach to the hulks are described as having 'coarse mangy ungainly outer surface[s], as if they were lower animals' (249);[23] Orlick, in his slovenly confined porter's room at Miss Havisham's, 'looked like the human dormouse for whom it was fitted up' (255) – a misleadingly soporific image, in this particular case. For violent, predatory natures are what bring animals and humans close together time and time again. Mrs Joe is incapable of washing the young Pip without pouncing on him 'like an eagle.'

Jaggers's name for Bentley Drummle, 'the Spider', proves convenient for Pip to use too: 'So, the Spider, doggedly watching Estella, outwatched many brighter insects, and would often uncoil himself and drop at the right nick of time' (328). The most telling reference of all is that which Wemmick makes concerning Jaggers's housekeeper. He advises Pip to look out for her:

> 'Shall I see something very uncommon?'
> 'Well,' said Wemmick, 'you'll see a wild beast tamed. Not so very uncommon, you'll tell me. I reply, that depends on the original wildness of the beast, and the amount of taming'.(224)

Wemmick's choice of language shows that he has no worries about speaking of a human being as though she is an animal to whom motiveless violence comes naturally. But in fact, the text of *Great Expectations* queries this easy assumption, suggesting, when it comes to serious acts of aggression, that there is, after all, a distinction between animal and human: that the same laws cannot be seen to apply to both. This joins with a wider questioning concurrently found at the time in *All the Year Round* as to whether or not humans and animals can be generalised about together. Although the issue is barely raised explicitly in Darwin's work until *The Descent of Man* (1871), it was not just the tantalising remark towards the end of the *Origin* that 'In the distant future I see open fields for far more important researches ... Light will be thrown on the origin of man and his history' (458), but the whole tenor of the work that meant that a large number of commentators on the volume raised the issue themselves.

In *All the Year Round*, it would seem the linking of humans and beasts is acceptable when dealing with physiological factors such as gourmandism and digestion: 'Throughout the whole of the great class of animals headed by man, from the elephant down to the shrew mouse, there is one sort of tooth – the sweet tooth -common to all.'[24] Similarly, we learn that though

> Races and nations differ in the substances they feed on, and in the way they feed on them, but all these differences disappear in the final result; the blood of one race and one nation is the same as the blood of all races. So also the cow eats grass and turnip, converting them into blood; the lion declines those succulent

vegetables, but feasts upon the cow, and yet converts this food
into nothing better than blood.[25]

But when the 'higher affections' are in question, dividing lines
appear. Man, we are told, 'is the only animal that knows
how to kiss.' Cats may lick their kittens, donkeys rub noses,
pigeons and stock-doves bill and coo on branches, 'but none of
these creatures kiss. Even low-class savages do not kiss like
civilised men; so that we may take this habit and function to
be actual evidence of intellect and civilisation; which is a pleasant idea at any rate.'[26] Even more specifically, animals – even
those who physically appear the closest to humans – do not
possess the faculty of reason. Even the 'stupid weak savage will
still make a prey of the yet more stupid but enormously powerful gorilla, for the one uses reason, and the other has only his
instincts.'[27]

Aggression, in Dickens's novel, is an indeterminate quality.
It certainly links humans – at a relatively early, instinctual stage
of their personal development – to animals. When Pip fights
Herbert, the 'pale young gentleman', there is no apparent
pretext on either side. Scrapping seems to be a form of activity
natural to boys – 'Indeed', commented Pip, 'I go so far as to
hope that I regarded myself while dressing, as a species of
savage young wolf, or other wild beast' (120-1) – but is something to be abandoned in favour of more rational, verbal
discourse when adulthood is reached. For elsewhere in the
novel, violent actions are shown to have reasons behind them,
even if these actions are not, in themselves, necessarily morally
justifiable. Jealousy, as Darwin points out in *The Expression of
the Emotions in Man and Animals* (1872) may indeed be an
animal as well as a human sentiment, but it becomes a powerful factor in the plotting of the novel when accompanied by
logically planned and executed strategies. Thus Estella's mother
murders (presuming she does murder) out of jealousy: Magwitch
had cast her off in favour of another woman. Magwitch's anger
against Compeyson is a rational assault, not just against an individual, but against the power which external signs of social
status wield within society. When the two are tried together,
Compeyson's smart clothing, his schooling, clubs and societies,
ensured that he was given a sentence only half the length of

Magwitch's. Understandably, Magwitch waited until he could take direct revenge for this institutionalised unfairness. The most conspicuously violent figure in the novel is Orlick, but even his sadistic attack on Mrs Joe with a sawn-off leg fetter is, ultimately, shown as having motivation. In the scene which takes place in the old sluice house on the marshes, Orlick is repeatedly referred to in predatory animal terms – 'with his mouth snarling like a tiger's' (436); 'the tiger crouching to spring'(438). This bestial impression is reinforced by the way in which Orlick tries to bring Pip down to his own level by calling him 'wolf'; by tying him up and announcing that he is going to kill him 'like any other beast' – as, indeed, he claims he felled Mrs Gargery: 'like a bullock' (439). None the less, this language is once again fuelled by jealousy: it is premeditated and, in its way, logically justifiable. Orlick even shifts the blame for Pip's sister's murder back on to Pip himself: '… it warn't Old Orlick as did it; it was you. You was favoured, and he was bullied and beat … Now you pays for it' (437).

Rationality distinguishes man from beast in Dickens's novel, providing a 'line of demarcation … between species' (443) (something which Darwin denied existed). Such a challenge to Darwin's doctrines was found in contemporary sceptical receptions to the *Origin*, although rationality was not so frequently foregrounded as a differentiating characteristic as was the idea of the soul: something which, like rationality, allows a commentator to accept that Darwin's theories may be applied to the physical development of humans, but not to all aspects of their being. To acknowledge that humans have souls is to recognise that they may still act as a vehicle for the divine. For the general public, indeed, Darwinism was presented as much as a religious as a scientific question. Dickens adopts no overtly Christian premise: however, Pip's *bildungsroman* is a chronicle of the maturation of his conscience, altruism and self-knowledge – again, these are significantly non-animalistic characteristics.

There are further ways in which the novel signals its distance from some of Darwin's methods and implicit conclusions. The very question of whether or not it is worthwhile to spend time on the contemplation of what development from

one's origins may imply is called into question. As so often in
Dickens's fiction, this happens at a satiric as well as at an
entirely serious level: Mrs Pocket's family tumbles around her
chaotically, at some risk to its own imminent survival, whilst
she is immersed in reading about titles and family genealogies,
trying to find out when her grandfather should have come into
his baronetcy. More centrally, it is obvious how the revelations,
to Pip, of the source of his financial prosperity (or potential for
prosperity) and of Estella's parentage shock him deeply,
although ultimately they lead to a breaking down of his snob-
bish assumptions. His desire to establish more of a distance than
in fact exists is voiced through a verbal separation of his kind
from that of the creature before him: 'The abhorrence in which
I held the man, the dread I had of him, the repugnance with
which I shrank from him, could not have been exceeded if he
had been some terrible beast' (337). This repugnance is inten-
sified when Magwitch announces '''I'm your second father.
You're my son -more to me nor any son''' (337). So violently,
in fact, does Pip repudiate any such suggestion that he invokes
the most unnatural, shocking, and non-evolutionary of all
recent creation myths, that of Frankenstein and his monster:
'The imaginary student pursued by this mis-shapen creature he
had impiously made, was not more wretched than I, pursued
by the creature who had made me, and recoiling from him with
a stronger repulsion, the more he admired me and the fonder
he was of me' (354). The very perversion of this myth is itself
interesting, suggesting Pip's hazy acknowledgement that the
operation of chains of causation meant that, however involun-
tarily, he was a formative factor on Magwitch, as the convict
had been on him.[28] Simultaneously, the reference back to an
earlier nineteenth-century novel (like the Miltonic echoes
which this novel, like *Frankenstein*, contains), suggests that
authorship is in part an activity which involves the adaptation
of previous texts: that it partakes (here, at an artificial or
conscious level, but elsewhere at a natural, unconscious one as
well) of a selective, evolutionary process.

     In this novel, interest in family origins is related to class
prejudice, and hence to some of Pip's more unpalatable errors.
It is precisely in relation to snobbism that, when it comes to

individual histories, Dickens shows up the irrelevance of placing too much weight on origins. In this, he in fact shows himself
to have more in common with Darwin than the title of the scientist's work might suggest. The marriage of Herbert Pocket is
one of the two obviously happy marriages in the book (three,
if one counts the future partnership of Wemmick and Miss
Skiffins) and, as Herbert reminds Pip, 'The blessed darling
comes of no family ... and hasn't a notion about her grand-
papa. What a fortune for the son of my mother!' (460). In the
other successful pair, Joe's father's alcoholism does not recur in
his son; his habit of hammering away at Joe's mother is only
re-enacted upon a proper recipient of blows, the anvil, and Joe
does not inherit his mother's ill-health. We learn nothing more
of Biddy's relatives than that she was Mr Wopsle's great-aunt's
granddaughter; 'I confess myself quite unequal to the working
out of the problem, what relation she was to Mr. Wopsle' (74).
Additionally, we are completely ignorant of the characteristics
of Pip's own parents, knowing only their names and the fact
that they and five of their infant children are dead, and are left
to puzzle over the fact that Pip and his Rampage-ing elder sister
seem to have no family resemblance whatsoever. Moreover,
though we eventually learn Estella's parentage, she appears to
have no physical or mental connection at all with Magwitch,
her father, and only takes from her mother the outward traces
of origins visible in her eyes, hands and hair: fleeting parallels
which haunt Pip until he finally connects the couple.
Wemmick, describing Estella's mother's murderous characteristics, remarks that 'She was a very handsome young woman, and
I believe had some gipsy blood in her. Anyhow, it was hot
enough when it was up, as you may suppose' (405). But if one
presumes that the same blood must have been flowing in Estella's
veins, it seems to have chilled conspicuously. Of course, it may
be that – to quote the *All the Year Round* summary of Darwin's
argument – these variations show that 'all organised and
animated forms are in a state of passage from one stage of difference to another; all nature is moving insensibly forwards up the
slope of one vast sliding scale; the world is a never-ceasing
workshop for the process of manufacturing new species of
plants and animals' (NS, 296). But the speed with which differ-

ence is registered between one generation and the next would seem to work against such a hypothesis. So, too, would the fact that the centrally important workshop of *Great Expectations*, Joe's forge, is, so far as one can tell, a place of repair, renovation and renewal – whether of horseshoes or farm implements – rather than a pioneering, inventive industrial crucible.

The relegation of the importance of biological origins is of crucial importance to *Great Expectations*. First, it allows Dickens to indicate how one's way in the world should be dependent on one's own efforts, rather than on the status, power, even struggles of one's predecessors. Second, and more emphatically, Dickens's choice of priorities allows him to stress the importance played by culture and by upbringing. The juxtaposition of hereditary and circumstantial factors in relation to the formation of an individual's subjectivity recurs constantly. Estella forms the prime exhibit in Dickens's demonstration, in this novel, of the effect of the environment upon individual. Her cold-bloodedness and hard-heartedness are foregrounded on several occasions. When Miss Havisham berates her for being unfeeling, she replies '"I am what you have made me."' '"Who taught me to be hard?".' The fact that Miss Havisham is peeved and indignant – '"But to be proud and hard to *me*!"' (323) suggests the uncompromising nature of the lesson of upbringing which has been thoroughly learnt. When Estella calmly retorts '"I have never been unfaithful to you or your schooling. I have never shown any weakness that I can charge myself with"' (324), we are shown that she has been as model a pupil as Bitzer in *Hard Times* (1854) who, when asked by the broken, submissive Mr Gradgrind '"have you a heart?"' replies, 'smiling at the oddity of the question', '"the circulation, sir, ... couldn't be carried on without one."'[29] Estella reiterates her position a little later when Pip fully declares his love for her. She tells him once again that she had continually said that he touched nothing in her breast, but that he would not be warned:

> 'I thought and hoped you could not mean it. You, so young, untried, and beautiful, Estella! Surely it is not in Nature.'
>
> 'It is in my nature,' she returned. And then she added, with a stress upon the words, 'It is in the nature formed within me' (376).

If environment and education can mould someone; if people do not carry within them their generic, genetically predetermined nature, then there is always, optimistically, the possibility that change may come about through improved physical surroundings on the one hand, and personal influence on the other. Dickens, on this point, seems closer to Lamarck's ameliorative theories than to Darwin.

Moreover and this is where, perhaps, the novelist diverges most sharply from Darwin, Dickens emphasises the importance of co-operation rather than competition. 'As the individuals of the same species come in all respects into the closest competition with each other, the struggle will generally be most severe between them' (442), writes Darwin. Yet the most active deed performed by Dickens's singularly passive hero throughout the course of the novel is his making-over of money to Herbert, to allow him to gain a foothold in business, and to marry. For Darwin's next point, that 'With animals having separated sexes, there will in most cases be a struggle between the males for the possession of the females' (442) hardly holds true either: not only could Pip hardly be less interested in Clara, but he silently relinquishes his secret plans concerning Biddy to Joe's far superior claims. G. H. Lewes, writing in *Blackwood's Magazine* in 1861, commented that the Darwinian hypothesis 'is clamorously rejected by the conservative minds, because it is thought to be revolutionary, and not less eagerly accepted by insurgent minds, because it is thought destructive of the old doctrines.'[30] Extremely conservative in class terms, *Great Expectations* is a novel which refuses to admit the desirability of any kind of reorganisation of society.

The *All the Year Round* article on 'Natural Selection' ends suspended over uncertainty, suggesting that developmental theories have themselves been susceptible to cyclical historical processes:

> The world has seen all sorts of theories rise, have their day, and fall into neglect. Those theories only survive which are based on truth, as far as our intellectual faculties can at present ascertain; such as the Newtonian theory of universal gravitation. If Mr. Darwin's theory be true, nothing can prevent its ultimate and general reception, however much it may pain and shock those to

whom it is propounded for the first time. If it be merely a clever hypothesis, an ingenious hallucination, to which a very industrious and able man has devoted the greater and the best part of his life, its failure will be nothing new in the history of science. It will be a Penelope's web, which, though woven with great skill and art, will be ruthlessly unwoven, leaving to some more competent artist the task of putting together a more solid and enduring fabric. (NS, 299)

Nor did the periodical let the matter rest there. An article on the 'Transmutation of Species' published in March 1861, revives the seventeenth-century theories of de Maillet, and runs briefly through the ideas put forward by Lamarck, by Chambers and by Owen, as well as by Darwin, concluding that a good deal of close observation of the natural world was still necessary before one could come down in favour of one hypothesis or another. And, though its original stance of provisional assent in the matter of natural selection was a fair reflection of opinion among contemporary scientists, the magazine, like a good number of other contemporary publications, notably swung towards a far more conservative religious position on the issue in the next few years. Thus we read, in a notice of an adaptation of Louis Figuier's *The World Before the Deluge*, published by Chapman and Hall in 1866, that:

> It is according to a plan emanating from the All-powerful, that the races which have lived for a certain time upon the earth, have made way for others, and frequently for races nearer perfection, as far as complexity of organisation is concerned. We see the work of creation perfecting itself unceasingly, in the hands of Him who has said, 'Before the world was, I am.' The ever-increasing beauty of the fabric compels us to adore the Artificer.[31]

But *Great Expectations*, like *All the Year Round*'s initial line on Darwin's arguments, is a text which resists closure, and not just in the familiar sense of the existence of two endings, and the indeterminacy of the parting which may or may not shadow the final words of the printed version. The future is uncertain in other ways. For even if Pip's marriage, and thus the germination of a new generation, is envisaged, it is hard to imagine where, and how. The new Pip sits, after all, the mirror image of his predecessor, on a stool at Joe's side, his name and appearance functioning as a guarantee of repetition, of *desire for* a form of history that can recuperate the past, rather than, in Darwinian fashion, never looking back. But such repetition does not leave a space for the older Pip. Had the first ending prevailed, with him visiting London with his younger namesake, we might infer that he had at least come to terms with the urban environment and its rules of survival, and was passing them on to the next generation. Yet topographically, the conclusion of *Great Expectations* as we now read it again emphasises the desire for return, rather than a forging of new links. Returning Pip to the countryside is, in fact, very much in line with the first of *All the Year Round*'s articles on Darwin, which lamented 'the crowds who continually stream into great cities and die there childless ... the great surplus of the rural population is drawn off by the temptations of town, leaving the field clear for the occupancy of brutes in default of the occupancy of men' (S, 178). Whether 'brutes' designates cattle or those such as Orlick is unclear: what comes across in the article, as in *Great Expectations*, is a suspicion of the rootlessness and discontinuity threatened by urban life. But the very fact that Pip fails to reproduce himself during the course of the novel suggests a sterility resulting from an inability to adapt to changing conditions. To quote the summary of Darwin given in 'Natural Selection':

> Though nature grants vast periods of time for the work of natural selection, she does not grant an indefinite period; for as all organic beings are striving, it may be said, to seize on each place in the economy of nature, if any one species does not become modified and improved in a corresponding degree with its competitors, it will soon be exterminated (NS, 297).

Those who are genuinely successful in the London world - Jaggers, and, at a different level of power, Wemmick; those who are fit to thrive and evolve in these new urban conditions, do so by separating their private lives from the ruthless, compassionless efficiency of their public ones. It is as though Dickens has seen the type which will dominate future urban life: while he may be fascinated by it, he is not able to endorse it. Only Herbert provides a more optimistic model, but his career develops away from the metropolitan centre. It may well prove, as Darwin writes on his last page, and as the 'Natural Selection' article reiterates in its own conclusion, that 'from the war of nature, from famine and death, the most exalted object which we are capable of conceiving namely, the production of the higher animals, directly follows' (459). Yet, as we have seen, Dickens was far from sanguine when it came to adopting the view that competition is the way to perfection. More than that, to accept that the *process* of natural selection – something which appears to lie outside the active intervention of the individual – 'works solely by and for the good of each being' (NS, 299) seems to deny the necessity of each individual taking charge of his or her life. But then, quite what Pip is to do once *he* has recognised this necessity is uncertain, too. What one sees, in *Great Expectations*, as more broadly in *All the Year Round* during 1860–61, is the spectacle of a new, exciting, troubling hypothesis about the very nature of life being kept, explicitly and implicitly, wide open.

Notes

1 A further direct connection with Darwin's work is made by John Schad, who, in a suggestive chapter on 'The Reader, Language and Nature', notes how Dickens, in *Our Mutual Friend*, adds 'to the playfulness of nature's vocabulary by rendering the word species as "speeches". Indeed, by doing so in the very attempt to explain how the name "Harmon's Jail" became "Harmony Jail" –"Like a speeches of chaff", "Working it round like" – the gentleman's error makes an obvious allusion to the evolutionist analogy between changing words and changing species.' John Schad, *The Reader in the Dickensian Mirrors: Some New Language* (Basingstoke: Macmillan, 1992), p. 77.

2 Peter Ackroyd, *Dickens* (London: Sinclair-Stevenson, 1990), p. 663.

3 Gillian Beer, 'Origin and Oblivion in Victorian Narrative', *Arguing with the Past: Essays in Narrative from Woolf to Sidney* (London, Routledge, 1989), p. 14, quoting her own 'Anxiety and Interchange: Daniel Deronda and the implications of Darwin's Writing', *Journal of the History of the Behavioral Sciences* 19 (1983), p. 31.

4 George Levine, *Darwin and the Novelists. Patterns of Science in Victorian Fiction* (Cambridge, MA: and London: Harvard University Press, 1988), p. 153.

5 Charles Dickens, *Bleak House* (1853; Harmondsworth: Penguin, 1971), p. 49.

6 The belief that only a finite amount of solar energy existed had become increasingly firmly established during the 1840s (see ed. A. J. Meadows, *Early Solar Physics* (Oxford: Basil Blackwell, 1970) and Levine, *Darwin*

and the Novelists, pp. 153–76). The destruction which will follow from the cooling of the sun is opposed, incidentally, to the later incendiary implosion when Krook perishes from spontaneous combustion, a proleptic image of which is given by the 'soft black drizzle with flakes of soot'.

7   See Susan Shatto, 'Byron, Dickens, Tennyson, and the Monstrous Efts', *Yearbook of English Studies* 6 (1976), pp. 144–155; Philip James Wilson, 'Notice on the Megalosaurus or Great Fossil Lizard of Stonefield: Observations on the Beginning of Bleak House', *Dickensian* 78 (1982), pp. 97–104.

8   [Henry Morley], 'Our Phantom Ship on an Antediluvian Cruise', *Household Words* 3 (16 August 1851), p. 494.

9   [F. K. Hunt], 'The Hunterian Museum', *Household Words* 2 (14 December 1850), pp. 277–82.

10 'Owen's Museum', *All the Year Round* 8 (27 September 1862), pp. 62–7; 'Mary Anning, the Fossil Finder', *All the Year Round* 13 (11 February 1865), pp. 60–3.

11 Shatto, 'Byron, Dickens ...' p. 150.

12 Alvar Ellegård, *Darwin and the General Reader: The Reception of Darwin's Theory of Evolution in the British Periodical Press, 1859–1872* (Göteborg: Gothenburg Studies in English VIII, 1958), p. 26

13 'Species', *All the Year Round* 3 (2 June 1860), pp. 174–9, 179. This article, like its sequel, 'Natural Selection' (7 July 1860), pp. 293–9, is unsigned: no attribution is suggested in Ella Ann Oppenlander, *Dickens' All the Year Round: Descriptive Index and Contributor List* (Troy: Whitston Publishing Co., 1984). Subsequent references to these articles in the text will appear as 'S' and 'NS'.

14 Charles Dickens, *Great Expectations* (1861; Harmondsworth: Penguin Classics, 1985), p. 101. Subsequent page references in the text are to this edition.

15 Gillian Beer, *Darwin's Plots: Evolutionary Narrative in Darwin, George Eliot and Nineteenth-Century Fiction* (London: Routledge and Kegan Paul, 1983), p. 8.

16 Charles Dickens, *The Uncommercial Traveller*: XV: 'Nurse's Stories' (1860; London: Oxford University Press, *The Uncommercial Traveller and Reprinted Pieces Etc.*, 1988), pp. 150, 151.

17 James E. Marlow, 'English Cannibalism: Dickens After 1859', *Studies in English Literature* 23 (1983), p. 655.

17 'Life in Africa', *All the Year Round* 5 (6 July 1861), p. 355.

19 'Acclimatisation', *All the Year Round* 5 (17 August 1861), p. 492.

20 'Next Door Neighbours to the Gorilla', *All the Year Round* 5 (27 July 1861), p. 425.

21 'An Ugly Likeness', *All the Year Round* 5 (1 June 1861), p. 238. The passage occurs in Paul B. du Chaillu, *Explorations and Adventures in Equatorial Africa; with accounts of the manners and customs of the people, and of the chace of the Gorilla, Crocodile, Leopard, Hippopotamus, and other animals* (London: John Murray, 1861), p. 74. The final phrase in fact reads 'and carry thence a roast or steak'.

22 Charles Dickens, *Martin Chuzzlewit* (1844; ed. Margaret Cardwell,

Oxford: Clarendon Press, 1982), p. 6.

23 Iain Crawford, one of the surprisingly tiny number of critics who has picked up – relatively briefly – on the possible relationship between the dates of publication of the *Origin* and *Great Expectations*, also notes the animalistic language employed here. His overall conclusion about the connection between the two texts, whilst suggestive, does not move in the same direction as the present piece, since Crawford finds nostalgia and regret at what humanity loses during the evolutionary process. The novel, he claims: 'endorses Darwin's conception of the common ancestry of species and portrays the ancestry of the gentleman, and thus by implication of the bourgeoisie as a whole, in, if not the monkey, then at least the criminal classes. While this assertion might in itself be sufficiently troubling to the Victorian mind, what is perhaps even more disturbing is the novel's intimation of the price that is demanded for this evolution into a state of refinement, grace, and sophistication. For not only does Pip achieve his social mobility at the price of losing his roots in the marshes and his closest ties of affection, but also, like Herbert, he lacks the raw power of Magwitch, Orlick, and, indeed, Mary Shelley's Monster. In this sense, if *Great Expectations* revises *Frankenstein*, it does so with the implied acknowledgement that Victorian social progress may also comprise the descent of man himself, that the beast may have been worked out but that with him has also vanished the primal energy of both the ape and the tiger.' Iain Crawford, 'Pip and the Monster: The Joys of Bondage', *Studies in English Literature* 28 (1988), pp. 637–8.

24 'Sweets', *All the Year Round* 5 (8 June 1861), p. 247.

25 'Metamorphoses of Food', *All the Year Round* 5 (30 March 1861), p. 6.

26 'Kissing', *All the Year Round* 5 (25 May 1861), p. 200.

27 'Next Door Neighbours to the Gorilla', p. 240.

28 Chris Baldick pushes this point an interesting step further: 'Just as Victor and the monster [in Mary Shelley's novel] refer themselves back to Milton to define their positions but become uncertain which roles they are playing, so Pip too loses his allusive bearings and is unable honestly to confine Magwitch to the realm of monstrosity when he knows that he belongs there himself … the new Dickens monster of *Great Expectations* appears no longer as an alien to be dismissed, but as a presence beneath our skins.' Chris Baldick, *In Frankenstein's Shadow: Myth, Monstrosity, and Nineteenth-century Writing* (Oxford: Oxford University Press, 1987), pp. 119–20.

29 Charles Dickens, *Hard Times* (1854; Harmondsworth: Penguin English Library, 1969), pp. 302–3.

30 [G. H. Lewes], 'Spontaneous Generation', *Blackwood's Magazine* 89 (1861), p. 166.

31 'Before the Deluge', *All the Year Round* 15 (13 January 1866), p. 7.

7

Hinduism, Darwinism and evolution in late-nineteenth-century India

DERMOT KILLINGLEY

When we talk of the relation between Darwin and culture, whether we are thinking of the cultural assumptions underlying the *Origin of Species* or of its influence on social attitudes, political discourse, and fiction as well as on science, we are usually thinking of Western culture as found in Britain, Europe and the United States. In this chapter, we shall look at the impact of evolutionary theory in late nineteenth-century India.[1] During that time Darwin became a familiar name in India, but it was often the name on the cover of a closed book, and the ideas which Indian thinkers associated with Darwin were often not those with which the *Origin* is most closely associated. To put the matter in its Indian context will involve looking at the institutionalisation of British cultural and educational policy towards India. This cultural and educational policy was founded on certain assumptions about the kind of transformations that 'practical' empirical Western science could effect on the the Indian mind, shaped as it was by an apparently 'speculative' Hindu world-view and cosmology. However, as this chapter will argue, as Western evolutionary thought was encountered by late-nineteenth-century Hindu thinkers, whose Hinduism was inflected by emergent Indian nationalistic aspirations, the result was far more complex. Hinduism by no means simply incorporated Western evolutionary thought. Indeed, it can be argued that these Hindu thinkers elaborated a framework of interpretation which challenged those notions of evolution that were usually associated with the writings of Darwin and Spencer. Paradoxically, these thinkers invoked the authority attached to the name of Darwin to order to achieve this.

Science in nineteenth-century India

The impact of Darwin took effect among the relatively small part of the Indian population which had been profoundly affected by the British presence in India: those educated in English, and often dependent for their employment directly or indirectly on the British. This class developed in the centres in which the British presence was concentrated: chiefly the three 'Presidency towns' of Calcutta, Bombay and Madras, where the first universities of modern India were founded in 1857. The population of these towns was predominantly Hindu, and many of the thinkers we shall examine were of Hindu background. The system of education which the English-educated class received had been developed in the early nineteenth century partly by Indians responding to new opportunities and needs, and partly by missionaries. Though the government supported many such ventures, it was not until 1835 that it adopted a definite education policy, and this policy followed ideas that had already been developed by non-officials.

The education provided by the missionaries often included elementary science: missionary educators believed that a correct knowledge of such matters as the rotation of the earth, Newtonian physics, mathematics and chemistry, as well as general literacy in Indian languages or in English, would prepare the way for Christian truth by discrediting the errors, as they saw them, taught by Hindu pandits. As Laird has noted, their combination of religious zeal with the pursuit of up-to-date knowledge followed the tradition of the Dissenting academies in England.[2] The Bengali brahmin Rammohun Roy, who was the first Indian to become internationally known in his lifetime as an intellectual figure, urged in 1823 that public money should be spent on 'employing European gentlemen of talents and education to instruct the natives of India in Mathematics, Natural Philosophy, Chemistry, Anatomy and other useful sciences'.[3]

The education policy which emerged in the 1830s, however, promoted literary and historical knowledge far more than science. Applied science, particularly medicine, engineering and agriculture, received some encouragement, but it was not until the twentieth century that Indians achieved international eminence in scientific research, and scientists of any kind remained a very small minority.[4] While technical education was promoted by Indians as well as by government, scientific education lagged behind; the Indian Association for the Cultivation of Science, founded in Calcutta by Mahendralal Sircar, with government support, in 1876, was hampered in its early years by public controversy over the rival claims of technical and scientific education.[5] The universities founded in 1857 were affiliating and examining bodies, taking no initiative in teaching; until the appointment of the chemist Alexander Pedler at Presidency College in 1873, the only effective science teaching in Calcutta University was provided by a Belgian Jesuit missionary, Eugène Lafont of St Xavier's College.[6]

This does not mean that there was little public interest in science. Lafont's public lectures were popular, and scientific debate attained something of the vigour of post-1859 Britain. The Bengali social reformer Akshay Kumar Datta (1820–86), for instance, who was noted for his rationalistic approach to social and religious matters, spent his declining years surrounded by botanical and geological specimens, with portraits of Darwin and Newton.[7] But whereas in Britain those who were interested in scientific ideas because of their implications for social and political theory, or for metaphysics, interacted with a cadre of professional scientists and were open to criticism from them, in India such criticism was far rarer. Science was seen as a set of findings rather than a set of methods; and the scientific claims of Auguste Comte's Positivism, as well as of the various systems which went by the name of Darwinism, seemed to be accepted uncritically.[8] As the founder of the Indian Association for the Cultivation of Science complained,

> The Hindu mind ... has become more of a speculative than of a practical character, singularly deficient in patient industry to

observe and collect materials, too prone to hasty generalisations, depending more upon its own inspiration, than upon outward facts. Thus, though highly endowed, it has been little productive of results.[9]

Those who discussed scientific ideas were aware of an interaction between Western thought and the Hindu tradition. Hindus, many of them educated in missionary schools and colleges, looked to the West as a source of enlightenment. The aim of missionaries, and their evangelical sympathizers in official circles, to confront Hindu ideas with secular education, including natural science, was thus embodied in early-nineteenth-century school curricula in which direct Christian teaching was often either kept in the background or completely absent. As one of the most successful of the missionary educators, the Scots Presbyterian Alexander Duff, put it in 1835: '*If in India you only impart useful knowledge, you thereby demolish what by its people is regarded as sacred.* A course of instruction that professes to convey *truth of any kind* thus becomes a species of *religious education* in such a land.[10] In the following year Lord Macaulay, the evangelically inclined member of the Legislative Council whose minute on education had decided the government in favour of a Western education policy, formulated this belief more dramatically and ambitiously:

> The Hindoo religion is so extravagantly absurd that it is impossible to teach a boy astronomy, geography, natural history, without completely destroying the hold which that religion has on his mind ... It is my firm belief that, if our plans for education are followed up, there will not be a single idolator among the respectable classes in Bengal thirty years hence. And this will be effected without any efforts to proselytize, without the smallest interference with religious liberty, merely by the natural operation of knowledge and reflection.[11]

One of the ways in which Duff sought to promote modern secular knowledge as 'a species of *religious education*' was through the *Calcutta Review*. This periodical, founded in 1844, published reviews of books bearing on India, often highly critical of traditional Indian thought and society. While most of the contributors were British, some were Bengalis who accepted the view that Indian culture needed to be reformed through the

introduction of Western ideas and values. Though Duff does
not appear to have been involved in its foundation, he took
over as editor at the end of 1844, and the next three editors
were Scottish missionaries, as he was.[12] The *Review* can be taken
as representing the views of those British who aspired to
promote the intellectual improvement of India, and of those
Bengalis who saw themselves as pioneers of this improvement.
Many of the latter were educated at the General Assembly's
Institution, the school founded by Duff in Calcutta.

In 1879, the *Review* published an anonymous article in
which the writer, who was probably British like most of the
contributors, shared with Duff and Macaulay the view that
modern knowledge must supplant traditional Indian thought.
He thus welcomed the teaching of science at Calcutta University
on the grounds that it would prevent the growth of delusions
'by the substitution of, at least, relative truth' – implying that
while absolute truth is to be found only in the Christian revelation, the partial truths found by science are a preparation for
it. He urged that the progress of science invariably entails social
progress, since, for instance, those who had learnt to predict
eclipses would no longer believe that they were caused by a
demon (as they are according to Hindu mythology), and the
elimination of belief in demons is essential to the doctrine of
law. He went on to praise Herbert Spencer for his synthesis of
evolutionary science and philosophy, and the American
philosopher John Fiske for his synthesis of Spencer with
Darwin, Huxley, Lewes and Haeckel.[13]

Thus, just as James Moore has shown with regard to post-
Darwinian controversies in Britain, many Christians in India do
not seem to have seen developments in science as inimical to
Christianity.[14] They thought of science as a part of European
culture from which India would benefit, and as a form of
natural revelation which would not conflict with Christianity
but would strike a fatal blow at Hinduism. Yet the planned
collision between Hinduism and science did not happen. Some
students rebelled against Hindu norms, and some of these
became atheists or even Christians, but it was by no means
necessary. Muslims did indeed find science objectionable,
because it seemed to contradict the cosmology of the Qur'an,

and above all because the concept of laws of nature was a challenge to God's absolute power over the universe. Sayyid Ahmad Khan (1817–98) attempted to overcome these objections by arguing that modern knowledge was not incompatible with the Qur'an, and that the laws of nature were an expression of God's will. However, he rejected the view that the world was 'without a creator, as it is in the religion of Darwin (God preserve us from that)'.[15]

While Indian Muslims held aloof from modern education until around 1870,[16] Hindus flocked to missionary, government and other schools and colleges from the beginning of the century onwards – a movement which may be said to have helped reinforce the division between themselves and Muslims, and hindered them from meeting on common ground in the modern world. It was easier for a Hindu to combine modern knowledge with adherence to tradition than for a Muslim, or even, as might appear from the controversies in the West over Darwin, for a Christian. Hindus, as British observers pointed out at the time, are less concerned with doctrine than with practice. Furthermore, there is no body of scripture common to all Hindus that could be said to be contradicted by modern knowledge. There is a great variety of texts, such as the Puranas, which are used as authorities for ritual and social behaviour, or for knowledge of the fundamental nature of reality and of human personality, but not as sources of information about the external world. The ultimate scriptural authority, many Hindus would agree, is the Veda; but it is known only to relatively few. Besides, according to the traditional principles of Vedic hermeneutics, the function of the Veda is to tell us about things that would otherwise be unknown, and its main purpose is not to provide information but to give practical instruction for ritual action. A clash between the Veda and science on the subject of cosmology was therefore unlikely.

Many nineteenth-century Hindus therefore accepted the idea that India should learn from the West about the physical world, and called for more scientific education as a key to progress.[17] Modern education was welcomed not only by those who gained materially from the employment opportunities which it offered, but also by some traditional pandits; for it was generally agreed by the pandits themselves, and with good reason, that traditional learning had declined and was in need of revitalisation.

Among the English-educated, it was commonly believed that the coming of the British was providential, bringing order and learning to a country that had degenerated into lawlessness and ignorance. This view, widely held within the Indian liberal tradition which prevailed throughout the nineteenth century, justified British political and intellectual ascendancy. Indian liberals combined a respect for the rule of law and for liberal education, which justified the British presence, with belief in a benevolent God, the use of humanitarian criteria rather than traditional norms in questions of morality, and a Whiggish faith in historical progress.[18] They accepted the idea of a natural progress in English history, as marked by Magna Charta, the Reformation, the revolution of 1688, the industrial revolution, and the 1832 Reform Act; but they had also to accept that progress in India had been thwarted or even reversed, and could now only be achieved with British help. If evolution was a natural law whose operation had ensured progress in England, it was necessary to explain why its operation had been suspended in India. In his explanation of this process the liberal lawyer and social reformer Mahadev Govind Ranade (1842–1901) showed a familiarity not only with the theory of natural selection, but also with the associated discourse of degeneration which had become prevalent in Western evolutionary debate:

> The theory of evolution has, in this country, to be studied in its other aspect of what may conveniently be called devolution. When decay and corruption set in, it is not the fittest and strongest that survives in the conflict of dead with living matter, but the healthy parts give way, and their place is taken up by all that is indicative of the fact that corruption has set in, and the vital force extinguished.[19]

When Indian liberals said that British rule was providential, they meant it quite literally: the British had been guided to India by a benevolent God. As Ranade put it: 'The hand of God in history is but dimly seen by those who cannot recognise in the contact of European with Eastern thought a higher possibility for both races'.[20] Keshub Chunder Sen (1838–84), who shared some of the liberal outlook, expressed this view with characteristic extravagance:

> Do you not recognise the finger of special Providence in the progress of nations? Assuredly the record of British rule in India is not a chapter of profane history, but of ecclesiastical history. The book which treats of the moral, social, and religious advancement of our great country with the help of Western science, under the paternal rule of the British nation, is indeed a sacred book.[21]

The Indian liberals respected science as a liberator from superstition and oppressive tradition, numbering Bacon among their heroes as well as Luther. They believed that 'science in its ultimate essentials echoes the voice of the living God.[22] Science possessed, of course, in a colonial situation, the *ideological* power of appearing to be the least politically, culturally and religiously biased branch of learning which the British could offer; the processes of cultural imperialism worked fundamentally under the guise of disinterested and universal knowledge.

But while there was much discussion of science in India, and much public controversy over religion, there was surprisingly little debate on the challenge presented by natural selection to a theistic view of the universe. Two Bengali journals which regularly published material on science (*Tattvabodhini Patrika* and *Sambad Prabhakar*) showed no reference to the controversies over Darwinism between 1860 and the end of the century.[23] The explanation may lie in the context in which Western books and ideas became available in India. As we have seen, science was highly regarded by those who wished to promote Christianity in India, and also by English-educated Indians. At the same time, many of the latter upheld theism as staunchly as they opposed Christianity.[24] A leading liberal, R. G. Bhandarkar (1837–1925), saw the English language as the medium through which students in Indian universities were exposed to the twin dangers of Christianity and materialism, and proposed to meet these dangers through a presentation of theism in which evolution had a prominent part, though the notion of natural selection was overshadowed by that of divine guidance.[25] In this way, a specifically-nuanced version of 'evolution' could be integrated into already-existent traditions and language, precisely in order to sidestep the subversive potential of Darwinian natural selection.

Nevertheless, in the last three decades of the nineteenth century the name of Darwin, together with the key word 'evolution', became a familiar part of Indian discourse in English. As Peter Bowler has observed of the labelling and dissemination of evolutionary ideas in the West, 'for those who did not inquire too deeply into the technical details, Darwinism and evolution became synonymous'.[26] To look more closely at the configuration of those ideas would be for example to discover, as Jeff Wallace notes earlier in this volume, that Darwinian natural selection actually ran counter to pre-existing senses of 'evolution' in natural history. If the Indian context, and that of Hindu theology in particular, thus constitutes a pronounced model of the cultural processes of elision and assimilation which could dissolve and transform 'Darwin' and his ideas, the key to this process might lie in the notion of the 'speculative'. Earlier, we saw the 'speculative' character of the 'Hindu mind' viewed as an obstacle to the development of sound empirical-scientific habits and methodologies. Yet the speculative character of Western evolutionary theory was consistently acknowledged both by its proponents and by its critics. Normally, Herbert Spencer's synthetic philosophy would be invoked here: overarching all natural laws for Spencer was a general principle of evolution, defined as 'an integration of matter and concomitant dissipation of motion, during which the matter passes from an indefinite, incoherent homogeneity to a definite, coherent heterogeneity', creating a natural movement of progress in all human and social as well as natural life.[27] Darwin's somewhat ambivalent treatment of Spencer in his autobiography seems designed to establish a contrastive sense of his own soundly inductive methods: after expressing general admiration for Spencer's work, he declares that his 'deductive manner of treating every subject is wholly opposed to my frame of mind'.[28] Yet the inherently unprovable nature of Darwin's proposals in the *Origin*, together with the difficulties and obstacles which the text itself highlights so regularly, were consistently alluded to in the reception of the text by the scientific community; and what could be more speculative than Darwin's own projection that, 'as natural selection works solely by and for the good of each being, all corporeal and mental endowments will tend to progress towards perfection'? (*Origin*, p. 459). In the rest of this chapter we will explore the speculative assimilation of evolutionary theory, both pre-Darwinian and post-Darwinian, in nineteenth-century Hindu culture.

Evolution and English-educated attitudes to the Hindu tradition

In the model of Western intellectual hegemony envisaged by Duff and Macaulay, ideas and habits of thought inherited from the Indian past were simply to be displaced by Western ones. Many English-educated nineteenth-century Indians did not accept this wholesale displacement, but sought continuity of thought with the Indian past, particularly the traditions enshrined in Sanskrit literature, while seeking also to build systems of thought that were acceptable in Western terms. Distribution processes made key texts quickly and readily available to the Indian intelligentsia, producing what could appear to be a smooth assimilation of Western scientific discourse. For example, racial theories claiming Darwinian legitimation soon became widespread among the British in India, and were later taken up by Indians, who applied the notion of primitive races to the lower castes.[29] The work of Bankim Chandra Chatterji (1838–94), for example, extended the notion of the primitive to non-Indian races.[30] But assimilation was invariably a complex process; most concerns to which evolutionary theory might be applicable were distinctively Indian, and this distinctiveness was reflected in the selection and interpretation of Western evolutionary ideas.

One such area of concern centred on the conflict between the movements for social reform and the strictly hierarchical, hereditary and male-dominated social tradition inherited by upper-caste Hindus. In Bengal in the 1830s there was a battle between traditionalists and radicals; but by the middle of the century it had given way to a general consensus among the

English-educated in all parts of India about the kind of reform
that was needed. Society was not a mechanical structure to be
tinkered with, overhauled, redesigned, or scrapped and replaced
with a new model, but an organism which could change only
by the gradual development of its existing resources.[31] A
Spencerian, meliorative notion of evolution, directed by God,
was thus mobilised: for R. G. Bhandarkar,

> The great discovery of the nineteenth century – the law of evolu-
> tion – is receiving confirmation from every side. The law implies
> that there has been throughout the universe a progress in the
> material as well as the spiritual world from the simple to the
> complex, from the dead to the living, from good to better, from
> the irrational to the rational. This is the law of God, and if instead
> of obstinately clinging to what is bad and irrational, we move
> forwards to what is good and rational, we shall be obeying the
> law of the universe and co-operating with God.[32]

Keshub Chunder Sen, who sought to reinterpret Christian
doctrines on Hindu lines, similarly saw evolution as a metaphor
for the gradual spiritual progress of humankind: after describing evolution as 'the great idea of the day', he notes:

> Your protoplasm, your natural selection, I leave to be discussed
> by men like Huxley and Darwin ... But this, I believe, is indis-
> putably true, that in the individual there is something like evolu-
> tion going on unceasingly ... The animal lives in us still, and wars
> with incipient humanity ... If the war goes on, the ultimate result
> of this protracted series of struggles will be the evolution of pure
> humanity.[33]

The concept, or metaphor, of evolution also offered a solution to the problem of revelation in religion - a recurrent issue
for nineteenth-century Hindus who accepted Western ideas but
rejected Christianity. Traditionally the Veda was the only
source of salvific knowledge. Yet the English-educated classes
were turning away from this view of revelation. In the early
nineteenth century, Rammohun Roy had been able to find in
the Veda a theology consistent with contemporary European
rational theism.[34] But in the middle of the century the movement which he founded, the Brahmo Samaj, found that
increased access to the Vedas, combined with Christian criticism of their contents, made this position untenable. The prob-

lem which faced any Hindu who claimed to follow the authority of received texts became more acute as modern scholarship revealed the variety of textual sources within the mass of traditions which had come to be known as Hinduism, and the variety of views on theology, social practice and ritual which they encompassed. Members of the Brahmo Samaj found themselves forced to abandon textual revelation and rely instead on intuition, as did the Unitarians in the West with whom they were closely associated.[35] But intuition was unsatisfactory as a source of publicly agreed truth.

Perhaps the first explicit use of the evolutionary approach to revelation was by Friedrich Max Müller (1823–1900), the German Vedic scholar and polymath who spent most of his working life in England, and who contributed more to Indian self-understanding than any other Western indologist.[36] Rejecting the theological distinction between natural and revealed religion, Müller claimed to 'see in the history of the ancient religions ... the *Divine education of the human race*'.[37] The Veda he found a particularly instructive example of this process. The earliest part of the Veda, the hymns addressed to many gods, he suggested was the childhood of the Vedic religion; the next, the Brahmanas which discuss details of ritual, was 'the busy manhood'; and the last part, the Upanishads, a wise and highly respected old age.[38]

Müller's approach was followed by Bhandarkar, one of the first Indians to apply Western methods to Sanskrit studies, and a leading member of the Prarthana Samaj, a Hindu reform movement based in Bombay. In a passage explicitly aimed against the Christian claim to a unique revelation, Bhandarkar argues, as Müller does, that all religions have some truth in them as well as something objectionable, that the essential religious truth is the recognition of the Infinite, and that revelation has been going on from the dawn of human intelligence.[39] He then turns to the history of Indian religion. First, he portrays the early Vedic hymns, as Müller does, as records of a fairly primitive stage in which natural phenomena were spoken of as gods. Next come the later Vedic hymns which attributed all these phenomena to one power; then the Brahmanas and the Upanishads. He then goes further in history, taking in Buddhism, the

Bhagavad-Gita and the medieval devotional movements.[40] Bhandarkar combines the notion of evolution with that of divine guidance; as he explains elsewhere:

> If Lord Kelvin has recently told us that evolution in external nature is under the direction of a Higher Power, should we not consider the evolution of religion also to be under the direction of that Power? Hence then our doctrine and belief is that God has been leading men, from the times when they were in the primitive condition to the present day, towards the realization of higher and higher religious truth. The evolution of religion therefore means a continuous Revelation.[41]

In this form of revelation the ancient texts have a place. The Vedas are still a source of truth, for though religion has advanced beyond their primitive speculations to clearer views of truth, Bhandarkar still urges the Prarthana Samaj to 'learn from the Vedic hymns that the temple in which we should find God and worship him is the universe and the heart of man'; but he also urges his listeners to learn from later stages in the evolution of Indian religion.[42] Intuition has a place too, for Bhandarkar goes on to say that the utterances of Hindu devotional poets, for example, are 'flashes of religious truth' through which God guides the evolution of religion. And the Prarthana Samaj itself, which is 'the latest phase' of God's self-revelation, is in a position to learn from the mistakes as well as from the insights of its predecessors.[43]

In the next section, we shall examine more closely the ways in which Hindus seeking continuity between modern thought and the Indian tradition found ancient Indian ideas compatible with evolutionary thinking.

Evolution and ancient Indian cosmology and cosmogony

Indian culture was particularly receptive to evolutionary theory because of its perceived affinities with various systems of ancient Hindu cosmogony and cosmology. In these systems, the complexity of the world is seen as having developed, unfolded or evolved from an original substance – sometimes seen mythologically as an egg or a golden embryo, sometimes in more abstract terms as absolute being or Brahman, or as Prakriti or nature. This process, according to many accounts, has produced not only the phenomenal world, starting with the five elements of ether, air, fire, water and earth, but the five sense faculties through which we observe the world around us, the faculties such as speech and manipulation through which we act on the world, the mind through which we control these faculties, our sense of our existence as individuals, and our capacity to be aware of all these. There are many versions of this cosmogony, but they agree in holding that the world which we observe and act on, and our own personality which observes and acts on it, have arisen from an original undifferentiated substance.

As such, these systems were able to occupy a fascinating position in relation to the unstable meaning of the term 'evolution' across pre-Darwinian and post-Darwinian biological history. First, there are distinct elements of compatibility with the older use of the term which signifies the unrolling or unfolding of already pre-existent parts in the embryo.[44] Accordingly, accounts in English of the Indian systems, even before Darwin and Spencer, refer to the process outlined above as 'evolution'. Hindu ideas of the origin of the world are governed by the principle that any effect must exist already in its cause, though in a latent form.[45] The stock example in Sanskrit literature is the process of pressing oil from sesame seeds: the oil can be produced because it is present in the seeds, while no amount of pressing could produce oil from sand. Nineteenth-century Hindu thinkers equated this principle with the laws of conservation of matter and energy which governed contemporary Western theories of cosmology and cosmogony. These were not only fundamental to Herbert Spencer's thinking, but also implicit in the maxim *Natura non facit saltum*, 'Nature does not make leaps', which was central to the argument of Darwin's *Origin*.[46]

The earliest Indian cosmogony that makes explicit use of the principle that the effect exists in the cause is in one of the later Vedic texts, the Upanishads, dating perhaps from 600 BC:

> The world in the beginning was Being, one alone without a second. Some people say the world in the beginning was Not-being, one alone without a second, and Being was born from Not-being. But how could it be so? How could Being be born from Not-being?

No, the world in the beginning was Being, one alone without a
second. It wished: 'May I be many, may I reproduce myself'.[47]

The Upanishad then proceeds to describe how the world was
created by the gradual and progressive differentiation of this
original substance called Being.[48] Here, after 'evolution' became
well known in connection with theories of the origin of living
forms, the Hindu doctrine could be seen to reach towards a
Spencerian concept of increasing global complexity arising out
of original unity and following a predetermined pattern. There
are many different accounts of this process in Hindu
cosmogony, but they all agree in starting from an originally
existing unitary source. They also agree that consciousness was
present from the beginning.[49] This is implied in the creative, or
rather procreative, wish at the end of the above quotation,
which is found in some form in most ancient Indian cosmogonies. One example in an early Upanishad begins: 'The world in
the beginning was a self, alone in the form of a man'. He
divided himself into husband and wife, and begot the human
race. Since the original man had produced his wife from
himself, the myth contains the widespread motif of primal
incest. She was ashamed, and hid by turning into a cow; he
became a bull, and begot the race of cattle. She became a mare,
and the process continued until 'he thus created everything in
the world that is in pairs, right down to ants'.[50]

Another point of contact with evolutionary science centred
on concepts of time. It was clear, for example, that the vast periods of time described in Hindu cosmology were more compatible with modern geology and evolutionary theory than the
widely accepted dating of the Biblical creation at 4004 BC. The
Hindu view of the world involves a vast time-scale, to be
measured not in our years but in years of the gods, which are
360 times the length of ours, our year being only a day to them.
Time is beginningless and endless, for the world is created,
destroyed and recreated over and over again, each cycle taking
twenty-four million years of the gods. The Hindu cosmos is
cyclic and reciprocating; it alternates between the differentiated,
active state which we now observe and a state of unity and rest.[51]
It follows, on a larger scale, the same kind of natural rhythm
which we find in summer and winter, full moon and new moon,

day and night, waking and sleeping, inhalation and exhalation, systole and diastole. This cyclic view of time is formed by extrapolating from ordinary observations of time, in which each day or year is preceded and followed by other days or years. Similarly, the sequence of cause and effect is cyclic; for any cause must be the effect of a preceding cause, and, as with the chicken and the egg, or the seed and the plant (to use the stock Indian example), every known instance of the one is preceded and caused by an instance of the other. While ancient Indian thinkers were able to envisage an uncaused first cause outside time, anything within time has to follow the known pattern of cause and effect, in which the effect is already latent in the cause.

This cyclic view of time involves the periodic temporal realisation of an eternal pattern. The world passes over and over again through four ages: the first perfect, the others declining, till we come to the last, thoroughly fallen age in which we now live. This fallen age started five thousand years ago, and will continue for another four thousand centuries. In the course of thousands of repetitions of this pattern of ages, each living being is reborn many times, sometimes in human form, sometimes as an animal, a plant, or a higher being such as a god. Even the gods come and go; for in time they die and are reborn in some other form, while other beings are reborn as gods to take their place.

As Manilal Manubhai Dvivedi observed in his speech to the Parliament of Religions in Chicago in 1893, 'whereas the Indian religion claims exorbitant antiquity for its teaching, the tendency of Christian writers has been to cramp everything within the narrow period of 6,000 years'.[52] Darwin's critics did not fail to point out the 'exorbitant' nature of his own claims concerning the earth's history, for his theory required just such a time-scale as that of the Indian religion; otherwise, 'it may be objected that time will not have sufficed for so great an amount of organic change, all changes having been effected very slowly through natural selection ... He who can read Sir Charles Lyell's grand work on the Principles of Geology ... yet does not admit how incomprehensively vast have been the past periods of time, may at once close this volume'.[53] Of course, Darwin's view is not cyclic but linear: it envisages a unique series of events each of which is unprecedented and unrepeatable. Indeed, most scientific cosmologies, like the Biblical one, start from a beginning, go through various creative events, and envisage an eventual end.[54] Yet despite the complex combination of affinities and contrasts at the level of cosmological theory, Hindus could use the vast scale of evolutionary time as ammunition in their resistance against Western intellectual hegemony. Contrary to the situation earlier in the century, when Christians could claim to be bringing scientific enlightenment to a country in the grip of an irrational religious tradition, Hindus could and did now claim to be on the side of enlightenment against the Christians.

Modern claims to an ancient Indian theory of evolution

Many nineteenth-century Hindu thinkers responded to British attempts at intellectual hegemony by claiming that ancient Indian ideas were corroborated by modern science. Dayananda Sarasvati (1824–83), who was able to find steamships and the electric telegraph in the Veda, was notoriously specific in this respect.[55] Others, such as the Bengali Keshub Chunder Sen, claimed a broader affinity between evolution and Vedic cosmogony. After quoting a well-known Vedic cosmogonic hymn, and adding a commentary that seeks to assimilate it to the beginning of Genesis, Keshub here proceeds to sketch a theistic version of evolution: 'Creation means not a single act, but a continued process. It began, but has gone on unceasingly through all ages ever since it began. It is nothing but a continued evolution of creative force, a ceaseless emanation of power and wisdom from the Divine Mind.'[56] Having thus briefly synthesised Vedic, Biblical and evolutionary cosmogonies, Keshub turns to the avataras or incarnations of the god Vishnu, who in a series of myths took the form of a fish, a tortoise, a boar, a man-lion, a dwarf and a succession of fully human forms.[57] He explains these as an evolutionary series of manifestations of the divine Logos. 'Indian Avatarism is, indeed, a crude representation of the ascending scale of Divine creation. Such precisely is the modern theory of evolution'.[58] While there is here a revealing use of licence in the word 'precisely', the idea that the avataras recapitulate evolution has been repeated many times since.[59]

However, a more explicit and elaborate claim for a pre-modern, ancient Indian theory of evolution was also a politically oppositional one. Swami Vivekananda (1862–1902), the Bengali monk who caused a sensation on his first visit to the West at the Parliament of Religions in Chicago in 1893, was educated at the college founded by Duff, and was prominent among those who challenged Western intellectual hegemony. While he showed a wide knowledge of contemporary Western thought and believed that India could learn from the West in material matters, Vivekananda consistently maintained the moral and spiritual superiority of Indian ideas and culture; he frequently invoked evolution as a part of the ancient Indian heritage which was now being vindicated by modern science: 'The idea of evolution was to be found in the Vedas long before the Christian era; but until Darwin said it was true, it was regarded as a mere Hindu superstition.'[60] Vivekananda also exploited the difficulties which Christian thinkers had with Darwinism; he probably had the exchange between Wilberforce and Huxley in mind when he noted that: 'Your Darwins, your Mills, your Humes, have never received the endorsement of your prelates'.[61]

However, while Vivekananda identified modern Western with ancient Indian evolutionary theory, he rejected certain aspects of Darwinism. Like many contemporaries, he found natural selection objectionable because it seemed to deny any pre-existing order in the universe, making its present form the product of a random process: what John Herschel, to Darwin's distress, called 'the law of higgledy-piggledy'.[62] It raised the law of the jungle, or of fish as the Sanskrit tradition calls it, to a cosmic principle, as suggested in Darwin's claim that 'the most exalted object which we are capable of conceiving, namely, the production of the higher animals' resulted from 'the war of nature, from famine and death'.[63] The evolutionary cosmogony also denied any pre-existing spiritual reality; and it denied a special place to humankind. In Vivekananda's work these strands are woven into an extensive critique of the ideologies of progress implicit in Social Darwinism. Unlike the Indian liberals, he was highly critical of concepts of social reform: the notion that evolution can eliminate evil from the world, he said, 'panders to the vanity of those who have enough of this world's goods ... and are not being crushed under the wheels of this so-called evolution ... Machines are making things cheap, making for progress and evolution, but millions are crushed, that one may become rich'.[64]

In speaking of the ancient Indian view of evolution, Vivekananda was thinking partly of the idea of rebirth, in which an individual is reborn in a succession of bodies, human and non-human, and may eventually reach release from rebirth. He claims that rebirth agrees with evolutionary theory in 'explaining the tendencies of the present life by past conscious efforts'. This Lamarckian allusion might be linked to a reported conversation in which he illustrates 'the Darwinian theory' by claiming that 'the tortoise has evolved in course of time' from a python which 'by remaining in one spot for a long time, has gradually turned hardbacked'.[65] Yet Vivekananda nowhere mentions Lamarck; for him, all Western evolutionary theories are Darwinian. The traces of Lamarck perhaps functioned for Vivekananda less as a sign of 'progress' than as a way of indicating a spiritual continuity implicit in the notion of conscious effort. The difference between rebirth and evolution which Vivekananda emphasises is not that the Indian theory concerns individuals and not species, but that it is spiritual and not merely physical.[66] Later, the philosopher P. T. Raju similarly found the essential difference between Western evolution ('Darwin first formulated it scientifically and popularised it') and the ancient Indian theory of evolution to be that the former is 'outward' and the latter 'inward'.[67] Vivekananda sees rebirth as a struggle to restore a primordial spiritual perfection.[68] He finds this theory morally superior to that of 'sexual selection and survival of the fittest', where 'the result of this theory is to furnish every oppressor with an argument to calm the qualms of conscience'.[69]

In 1893, T. H. Huxley sought in 'Evolution and Ethics' to establish a distinction between the realm of nature, in which the struggle for existence operates, and the realm of human society and ethics, in which self-sacrifice and 'the fitting of as many as possible to survive' are imperative. 'The ethical progress of Society depends, not on imitating the cosmic process, still less in running away from it, but in combating it'.[70] Vivekananda's work was equally preoccupied with the place of humanity within nature, and it operated a similar distinction:'In the animal kingdom we really see such laws as struggle for existence, survival of the fittest, etc., evidently at work. Therefore Darwin's theory seems true to a certain extent. But in the human kingdom, where there is the manifestation of rationality, we find just the reverse of those laws.'[71] The 'reverse of those laws' is morality, in particular self-sacrifice in the service of others.[72] The human struggle is not for survival but for spiritual perfection. Since the spirit exists in latent form in animals, their evolution is part of the spiritual struggle too, but only man, in whom spirit is manifest, is aware of the struggle and can contribute to it purposefully. 'It is a struggle against nature, and not conformity to nature, that makes man what he is'.[73]

As we have seen, there is a difficulty in reconciling the linear Darwinian theory with the cyclic Hindu one. Another difficulty is that human consciousness is a relatively recent product of evolution in Darwin's view, while in Indian thought it is the foundation of it. Vivekananda meets both difficulties by declaring that 'every evolution is preceded by an involution'.[74] That is, the process which science calls evolution is only one half of a cycle which is eternally repeating itself: the other half is the reverse process, involution, meaning a change from complex organisms in which consciousness is fully manifest to simple ones in which it is completely hidden: 'If the Buddha is the evolved amoeba, the amoeba was the involved Buddha also'.[75] This, according to Vivekananda, follows from the law of conservation of energy; it also returns us to the ancient Indian principle that the effect exists in the cause: 'The whole meaning of evolution is simply that the nature of a thing is reproduced, that the effect is nothing but the cause in another form, that all the potentialities of the effect were present in the cause.'[76] The emergence of consciousness and reason is thus not the unprecedented result of a linear process, as it is in Western models of Darwinian evolution, but the realisation of innate possibilities which had been realised previously before becoming latent, in an infinite cycle.

In the context of ontogeny, where 'evolution' is growth in

194 Charles Darwin's *The Origin of Species*

an outward direction, as a plant from a seed or an animal from an embryo, 'involution' is growth in an inward direction, as in the formation of the ear or the eye. 'Involution' in Vivekananda's sense is no part of Darwinian evolutionary theory, or indeed of any evolutionary theory that uses a linear view of time. It becomes crucial in Vivekananda's accommodation of evolution with the Indian cyclical view, and instrumental in maintaining a sense of the moral superiority of Indian ideas over the degraded capitalist–materialist structures of Social Darwinism: higher forms are latent in lower forms, and consciousness is present, whether manifest or latent, in all living beings. There are in fact affinities here with a monistic and idealistic view of the world such as that of Herbert Spencer, in which evolution is traced back to an ultimate being which he calls the Unknowable.[77] For the German biologist Ernst Haeckel (1834–1919) too, the discovery of evolution meant that monism 'must ultimately prevail throughout philosophy'.[78] Haeckel calls his theory both monistic and mechanical, rejecting the distinction between spiritual and material. 'Spirit exists everywhere in nature, and we know of no spirit outside of nature'.[79] Vivekananda claims indeed that the Western theory of evolution supports monism: 'the doctrine of physical evolution preached in the Western world by the German and the English savants ... tells us that the bodies of the different animals are really one ... We had that idea also'.[80] But the word 'bodies' shows his need to insist on the distinction of spirit and matter which Haeckelian terms like 'psychoplasm' or 'soul substance' sought to elide.

'If all men were dead, then monkeys make men. - Men make angels'.[81] This fascinating projection from Darwin's 1837 B notebook points towards perhaps the clearest sense in which Hindu theology might exploit the speculative possibilities of Darwinian theory. The evolutionary process has given rise to humankind; have we any reason to believe that it will stop there? Keshub Chunder Sen suggests that it will not.

> But while scientific men stop at the evolution of humanity, we go further and recognise a yet higher stage of development. What is it? Godliness. Out of humanity is evolved divinity, and till that is done our destined evolution is not completed ... There are thus

four stages through which man has to pass, the inorganic, carnal, human and divine ...The highest evolution is regeneration, – the destruction of the lower type of humanity and the evolution of a new species of godly humanity – life divine instead of life human.'[82]

The context suggests that Keshub is thinking of the spiritual development of individuals, rather than the biology of the future, but the rhetoric is clearly based on evolutionary theory. Vivekananda describes a similar progression: 'In the animal the man was suppressed, but as soon as the door was opened, out rushed man. So in man there is the potential god, kept in by the locks and bars of ignorance. When knowledge breaks these bars, the god becomes manifest.'[83] Like Keshub, Vivekananda is thinking of the exceptional individual who reverses the cosmic trend; and in accordance with his own view that the higher form is involved in the lower, he thinks of the emergence of the god as the manifestation of what is already latent.

This aspect of evolutionary theory was however carried furthest by another Bengali, Aurobindo Ghose (1872–1950). Educated in England, Aurobindo returned to India in 1893 to devote himself to Indian nationalism in both the political and the cultural field. In 1910 he retired to Pondicherry and devoted himself to a bold reinterpretation of the Veda and other ancient Indian texts. His interpretation of these texts supports a programme which he called 'Integral Yoga', which is intended to further the evolution of man, who is to rise above consciousness into superconsciousness, and eventually into 'the Divine' from which the world originated. More systematically than Vivekananda, Aurobindo uses the word 'involution' to indicate the process whereby the Divine becomes the manifest world, reserving 'evolution' for the reverse process whereby the world, led by pioneering individuals, is brought back to the Divine.

This terminology makes for clarity within Aurobindo's system; but it is at odds with earlier uses of the word 'evolution'. We have seen that accounts of ancient Indian thought in English regularly use 'evolution' for the emergence of the world, and of personality, from their original source. Since this source is a unity without parts, while the world contains a multiplicity of phenomena, and personality comprises a number of faculties, this process entails increasing differentiation and complexity, just as does evolution as defined by Spencer. But, in the terminology introduced by Vivekananda and developed by Aurobindo, this is a process of 'involution'. Aurobindo insists that at each stage in evolution the previous stages are not left behind but taken up. Thus a plant, which is the result of the evolution of life from lifeless matter, is not only living but also material; an animal, which besides life has the faculty which Aurobindo calls psyche, also has life and matter as the plant does; and a human being, who in addition has mind, also has psyche, life and matter. Someone who has risen beyond mind into the overmind, as Aurobindo believed himself to have done, lives in his superconscious state without abandoning the mind, psyche, life and material body which he had before. Moreover, each of these stages is not the production of something new but the manifestation of what was hitherto latent; for matter itself, from which they have evolved, has sprung from the Divine by a process of involution.[84]

Conclusions

The foregoing history of ideas, while necessarily incomplete, has sought to establish a distinction between the power of the name of Darwin in India and the practical influence of ideas, associated with the name, which were either more tangibly Spencerian or were undergoing complex processes of transformation in their encounter with Indian religious cultures. In this context, 'evolution' held no such terrors for Hindu thinkers as it did for some Christians. Hindus were used to a vast timescale, and to a view of cosmogony as a long process rather than a single creative event; they were used to treating humankind as part of the same continuum of living beings as animals and plants. Indian thinkers such as Bhandarkar and (to a lesser extent) Keshub, who became assimilated into a Western liberal tradition, thereby accepting the notion that the West's destiny was to bring enlightenment to India, contented themselves with pointing to Western ideas as corroborating ancient Indian ones, or as legitimating their own ways of adapting traditional ideas to modern notions of theological truth or of social justice. Others, such as Vivekananda and Aurobindo, whose nationalist tendencies involved a rejection of the intellectual hegemony of the West, took evolution out of the hands of the British by identifying it with ancient Indian ideas. They claimed further that ancient Indian ideas of evolution were spiritual and therefore superior to those of the West.

All these thinkers exemplified the tendency, identified by Mahendralal Sircar and inherent in the synthetic evolutionary philosophies of, in particular, Spencer and Comte, transmitted in the educational establishments of Victorian India, to be bold and assimilative in their combination of Eastern and Western evolutionary ideas. If, however, as seems evident, the name of Darwin came to dominate Indian evolutionary discourse, the explanation may lie in the need for a source of revelation. Science, as we have seen, was looked to as a revelation from God. After the publication of the *Origin* in 1859, Darwin's name rapidly took on an iconic significance in both East and West, and could be invoked as a guarantee of certainty. But, as with the Veda or the Bible, the ideas associated with Darwin's name were often taken from an accumulated tradition of interpretation. Many of these ideas were popularly referred to as Darwinism in the West, and it is they which became influential in India.

Notes

1 The name 'India' today refers to one among the countries of South Asia or the subcontinent, but in the nineteenth century it included what are now Pakistan and Bangladesh. I am using the name in the nineteenth-century sense here, because the writers I refer to generally thought of themselves as Indian, and claimed to speak for a distinctive Indian culture. Further, the main centres of modern culture in the India of that time, Calcutta, Bombay and Madras, were all in what is now India. Much of my material is from Calcutta, which until 1911 was the capital of India.

2 M. A. Laird, *Missionaries and Education in Bengal 1793–1837* (Oxford: Clarendon Press, 1972).

3 *The English Works of Raja Rammohun Roy* (Allahabad: Panini Office, 1906; reprinted New York: AMS Press, 1978), p. 472.

4 Of the 3,311 men who graduated from Indian universities from 1871 to 1882, 38 per cent became civil servants, 21 per cent lawyers, 7 per cent medical practitioners, and 2 per cent engineers (D. M. Bose (ed.), *A*

Concise History of Science in India (New Delhi: Indian National Science Academy, 1971), p. 555). The lack of support for science in India reflected that in Britain (ibid., p. 565).

5 Arun Kumar Biswas, *Science in India* (Calcutta: KLM, 1969), pp. 55–9.

6 Biswas, *Science in India*, p. 54, p. 60.

7 Ramakanta Chakraborty, 'Aksayakumar Datta: The First Social Scientist', in *The Bengali Intellectual Tradition*, ed. Amal Kumar Mukhopadhyay (Calcutta: K. P. Bagchi, 1979), pp. 38–57, p. 41.

8 'Indian intellectuals expressed great respect for the conclusions of scientific studies without knowing much about science or questioning the extent to which the scientific method was used in the study' . G. H. Forbes, *Positivism in Bengal* (Calcutta: Minerva, 1975), p. 118.

9 *Calcutta Journal of Medicine* (August 1869), quoted in Biswas, *Science in India*, p. 53. Sircar may be partly echoing British views here, but he does not share the racial determinism of some of his Western contemporaries (which itself often claimed to be Darwinian); he believes that the deficiencies he describes are due to unsuitable education and not to lack of innate ability. The achievements of Indian scientists since his time have shown that he was right.

10 Alexander Duff, *The Church of Scotland's India Mission* (2nd edn., Edinburgh, 1836), p. 15 (italics his). On the aims and methods of missionary education, see Laird, *Missionaries and Education in Bengal 1793–1837*.

11 Thomas Babington Macaulay, letter to his father, 12 October 1836, in *The Letters of Thomas Babington Macaulay*, ed. T. Pinney (6 vols, Cambridge: Cambridge University Press, 1974–81), vol III (1976), p. 193.

12 George Smith, 'The First Twenty Years of the "Calcutta Review"', *Calcutta Review* LIX , CXVII (1874), pp. 215–33.

13 Anon., 'On the Study of Physical Science', *Calcutta Review* 69 (1879), pp. 42–67, 42; 44. Cf. John Fiske (1842–1901), *Outlines of Cosmic Philosophy*, 2 vols, Boston and New York: Houghton Mifflin, 1874.

14 James Moore, *The Post-Darwinian Controversies: A Study of the Protestant Struggle to Come to Terms with Darwin in Great Britain and America 1870–1900* (Cambridge: Cambridge University Press, 1979).

15 Sayyid Ahmad Khan, introduction to *Khuubāt-i Amadyah*, tr. in C. W. Troll, *Sayyid Ahmad Khan* (Delhi: Vikas, 1978), p. 247.

16 P. Hardy, *The Muslims of British India* (Cambridge: Cambridge University Press, 1972).

17 David Gosling, *Science and Religion in India* (Madras: Christian Literature Society, 1976), p. 16.

18 Herbert Butterfield, *The Whig Interpretation of History* (London: G. Bell, 1931).

19 Mahadeva Govind Ranade, 'The Sutra and Smriti Texts on the Age of Hindu Marriage' in his *Religious and Social Reform: A Collection of Essays and Speeches*, ed. M. B. Kolasker (Bombay: Gopal Narayen, 1902), pp. 25–52, p. 27.

20 'The Philosophy of Indian Theism', reprinted in his *Religious and Social Reform*, pp. 1–25, p. 3.

21 Keshub Chunder Sen, 'Philosophy and Madness in Religion', lecture delivered in 1877, in T. E. Slater, *Keshab Chandra Sen and the Brahma*

Samáj (Madras: Society for Promoting Christian Knowledge, 1884), pp, 84–91, p. 90.

22 Asutosh Mukherji (1864–1924, mathematician and lawyer, Vice-Chancellor of Calcutta University 1906–14, 1921–23), quoted in Gosling, *Science and Religion in India*, p. 37.

23 Gosling, *Science and Religion in India*, pp. 14f.; cf. p. 22.

24 For a study of the conflict between Christianity and Indian theism in Bengal, see S. K. Das, *The Shadow of the Cross: Christianity and Hinduism in a Colonial Situation* (Delhi: Munshiram Manoharlal, 1974).

25 R. G. Bhandarkar, presidential address to National Social Conference, 1902, in *Collected Works of Sir R. G. Bhandarkar*, vol. II (Poona: Bhandarkar Oriental Research Institute, 1928), pp. 527–37, p. 528. His evolutionary view of revelation is described below, p. 184; 185f.

26 Peter J Bowler, *The Eclipse of Darwinism: Anti-Darwinian Evolution Theories in the Decades around 1900* (Baltimore: Johns Hopkins University Press, 1983), p. 26.

27 Herbert Spencer, *First Principles* (London: Williams and Norgate, 1862), p. 396.

28 *The Autobiography of Charles Darwin*, ed. N. Barlow (London: Collins, 1958), pp. 108f.

29 To be discussed by Susan Bayly in a forthcoming volume in the New Cambridge History of India.

30 Bankim Chandra Chatterji, *Essentials of Dharma* (Dharmatattva), first published 1884/5, tr. Manmohan Ghos (Calcutta: Sribiumi, 1977), p. 15.

31 Pradip Sinha, *Nineteenth Century Bengal* (Calcutta: KLM, 1965), pp. 91–143, terms this consensus Bengal Victorianism. Similar attitudes developed in other parts of India, notably among the Prarthana Samaj in Bombay.

32 R. G. Bhandarkar, presidential address, pp. 527–37, p. 537. The printed text has 'obstinately changing'; 'obstinately clinging' is my conjectural emendation. Bhandarkar's view of evolution as revelation is further exemplified below, pp. 185f.

33 Sen, 'Philosophy and Madness in Religion', pp. 87f.

34 Dermot Killingley, *Rammohun Roy in Hindu and Christian Tradition* (Newcastle upon Tyne: Grevatt & Grevatt, 1993).

35 Das, *The Shadow of the Cross*, pp. 69–77.

36 Wilhelm Halbfass, *India and Europe: An Essay in Understanding* (Albany: State University of New York Press, 1988), p. 134. In his *Lectures on the Science of Language* (2 vols., London: Longmans, Green & Co., 1882), and in his works on religion quoted below, where he often bases analogies on the history of language, Müller shows the influence of evolutionary thinking, seeing for example a process of natural selection among words in a language through a struggle for life (*Lectures on the Science of Language*, vol I, pp. 437f.). Unlike many versions of Darwinism, however, he envisages not a continuous amelioration but an inevitable alternation of growth and decay. He describes contemporary Hinduism as 'like a half-fossilised megatherion walking about in the broad daylight of the nineteenth century' (*Lectures on the Science of Religion*, p. 279) – a case

200   Charles Darwin's *The Origin of Species*

in which for some unknown reason natural selection has not operated.
Many Hindu contemporaries thought of it similarly; cf. n. 19 above.

37 Max Müller, *Lectures on the Science of Religion*, p. 226 (italics his).
38 F. Max Müller, *Lectures on the Origin and Growth of Religion* (the Hibbert
    Lectures, 1878) (London: Longmans, Green & Co., 1880), p. 362.
39 Bhandarkar, 'Basis of Theism, and its Relation to the So-called Revealed
    Religions', in *Works*, vol. II, pp. 603–16, pp. 607–9.
40 Ibid., pp. 610–15.
41 Bhandarkar, 'The Position of the Prarthana Samaj in the Religious
    World', in *Works*, vol. II, pp. 617–23, p. 621.
42 Bhandarkar, 'Basis of Theism', pp. 615–6.
43 Bhandarkar,'Basis of Theism', pp. 609; 615f.
44 See Peter J. Bowler, 'The Changing Meaning of "Evolution"', *Journal of
    the History of Ideas*, 36 (1975), pp. 95–114.
45 This is known in Sanskrit as *sat-karya-vada*, literally 'doctrine of the
    existent effect'. It is accepted in all brahmanical systems, but is rejected
    by Buddhism, which unlike them does not regard consciousness as an
    eternal entity.
46 Darwin, *Origin*, p. 223; p. 263. The maxim occurs in several forms in the
    seventeenth and eighteenth centuries, and is apparently older; see W.
    Francis H. King, *Classical and Foreign Quotations* (New York: Frederick
    Ungar, n.d.), p. 209. Darwin's use of it supports his claim to be making
    sense of well-established theories rather than producing a totally new
    one; for him science, like nature, does not make leaps.
47 *Chandogya Upanishad*, 6, 2, 1–3.'
48 Some object to the term 'creation' in this context, on the grounds that
    creation must be from nothing. But if we do not assume this as part of
    the definition of creation (as we do not when we speak of the creative
    arts), we may legitimately speak of creation in a Hindu context.
49 In most cosmogonies, the original being is itself conscious. The Samkhya
    system, however, starts from two principles, man (*purusha*) which is
    conscious but not active, and nature (*prakriti*) which is active but not
    conscious.
50 *Brihad-Aranyaka Upanishad*, 1, 4, 1–4. The species named in the passage
    (humans, cattle, horses, asses, goats, sheep) are chosen for their impor-
    tance in Vedic economy and ritual.
51 The cyclic view of time is found in texts dating from about 500 BC or
    later, while the Vedic accounts generally describe one creative event. But
    in the Hindu tradition, older ideas are reinterpreted rather than
    discarded; so that each Vedic account of what happened in the begin-
    ning can be understood as describing what happened in one of an endless
    succession of beginnings.
52 Manilal Manubhai Dvivedi, speech to the Parliament of Religions,
    Chicago, 1893, in *The World's Parliament of Religions*, ed. John H.
    Barrows (Chicago, Parliament Publication Co., 1893), vol. I Pt 2, p. 316.
    I am grateful to Dr Indira Chowdhury-Sengupta of Jadavpur University,
    Calcutta, for this reference.
53 Darwin, *Origin*, p. 293. Sir Charles Lyell's *Principles of Geology* (1830–

33) was Darwin's textbook on the subject; he had taken the first volume with him on the *Beagle*.

54 Some scientists have considered cyclic cosmologies. Sir Charles Lyell's *Principles of Geology* (1830–33) attempts to account for fossil evidence of successive changes in animals by means of a theory of cycles, and T. H. Huxley hints at a cycle by speaking of a downward course after evolution has reached its summit, and of 'the procession of the great year' ('Evolution and Ethics', in T. H. Huxley, *Evolution and Ethics and other Essays* (London: Macmillan, 1903), pp. 44–116, p. 85).

55 J. T. F. Jordens, *Dayananda Sarasvati: His Life and Ideas* (Delhi, Oxford University Press, 1978), p. 272.

56 Keshub Chunder Sen, 'That Marvellous Mystery – the Trinity' (lecture given in 1882), in *Keshub Chunder Sen: A Selection*, ed. David C. Scott (Madras: Christian Literature Society, 1979), pp. 219–47, p. 225. The passage is based on *Rig-Veda*, 10, 129.

57 A. L. Basham, *The Wonder that was India* (London: Sidgwick & Jackson, 1953), pp. 302–7.

58 *Keshub Chunder Sen: A Selection*, p. 226. For a passage in which Keshub briefly mentions Darwin, see note 33.

59 Aurobindo Ghose, *Essays on the Gita* (Pondicherry: Sri Aurobindo Ashram, 1959), chapter XVI, pp. 223f.; Aurobindo Ghose, *Letters on Yoga*, Part One (Sri Aurobindo Birth Centenary Library, vol. 22, Pondicherry, Sri Aurobindo Ashram, 1970), pp. 401–4; Ayodhya Chandra Dass, 'Vaiṣṇava incarnations and Biological Evolution', *Bharatiya Vidya*, 41 (1981), pp. 48–55; Ramakanta Chakravarti, *Vaiṣṇavism in Bengal* (Calcutta: Sanskrit Pustak Bhandar, 1985), p. 399, citing Kedarnath Datt, also called Bhaktivinode (1838–1914).

60 *The Complete Works of Swami Vivekananda* (8 vols, Calcutta: Advaita Ashrama, 1972–78), vol. VIII, p. 25; cf. vol. V, p. 519.

61 Vivekananda, talk in Memphis, 1894, *Complete Works*, vol. VII, p. 283.

62 Francis Darwin (ed.), *The Life and Letters of Charles Darwin* (3 vols, London: John Murray, 1887), vol. II, p. 240.

63 Darwin, *Origin*, p. 459.

64 Vivekananda, *Complete Works*, vol. II, pp. 95f.

65 Vivekananda, *Complete Works*, vol. VII, p. 151.

66 Vivekananda, *Complete Works*, vol IV, p. 271.

67 P. T. Raju, 'The Inward Absolute and the Activism of the Finite Self', in *Contemporary Indian Philosophy*, ed. S. Radhakrishnan and J. H. Muirhead, 2nd edn (London: Allen & Unwin, 1952), pp. 509–34, p. 511). In speaking of evolution, Raju is referring specifically to the parinama of the Indian Samkhya school, which Vivekananda also has in mind.

68 Vivekananda, *Complete Works*, vol. VI, p. 45.

69 Vivekananda, *Complete Works*, vol. I, p. 292. Cf. vol. V, pp. 278f.

70 T. H. Huxley, 'Evolution and Ethics', pp. 82f.

71 Vivekananda, *Complete Works*, vol. VII, p. 152.

72 Vivekananda, *Complete Works*, vol. VII, p. 154.

73 Vivekananda, *Complete Works*, vol. VI, pp. 35f.; cf. vol. VII, p. 153.

74 Vivekananda, *Complete Works*, vol. V, p. 255; cf. vol. II, p. 174.

75 Vivekananda, *Complete Works*, vol. III, p. 407. Cf. vol. V, p. 255, where he describes a recurrent transformation from 'a nebulous form' to the earth as we know it, and back again, as an example of the alternation of involution and evolution.

76 Vivekananda, *Complete Works*, vol. I, p. 372.

77 Since Spencer's theory shows some affinity with Indian thought, we might expect Vivekananda to cite him in corroboration on this point. But he does not wish to treat Spencer as an authority; he describes him as indebted to Indian thought without wishing to admit it (*Complete Works*, vol. VII, p. 376), and identifies Spencer's Unknowable not with Brahman, the ultimate reality, but with *maya*, the principle of falsehood which pervades phenomena (*Complete Works*, vol. VI, p. 104).

78 Ernst Haeckel, *The Evolution of Man: A Popular Exposition of the Principal Points of Human Ontogeny and Phylogeny* (2 vols, London: Kegan Paul, Trench & Co., 1883), vol. I, p. 17.

79 Haeckel, *The Evolution of Man*, vol. II, pp. 455f.

80 Vivekananda, *Complete Works*, vol. III, p. 406. Vivekananda never mentions Haeckel by name, but the mention of Germans here is probably an oblique reference to him.

81 Charles Darwin, *B notebook*, p. 169, November 1837; quoted as epigraph to Howard E. Gruber and Paul H. Barrett, *Darwin on Man: A Psychological Study of Scientific Creativity* (London: Wildwood House, 1974).

82 Sen, 'Philosophy and Madness in Religion' (above, no. 21), p. 88. The last six words especially anticipate Aurobindo Ghose; see below.

83 Vivekananda, *Complete Works*, vol. III, p. 407.

84 Sri Aurobindo (Aurobindo Ghose), *The Life Divine*, 2 vols (Pondicherry: Sri Aurobindo Ashram, 1939–40).

Select bibliography

Alaya, Flavia, 'Victorian Science and the Genius of Woman', *Journal of the History of Ideas* (1977), pp. 261–280

Barrish, Phillip, 'Accumulating Variation: Darwin's 'On the Origin of Species' and Contemporary Literary and Cultural Theory', *Victorian Studies* 34:4 (Summer 1991), pp. 431–53

Bartley, Mary M. , 'Darwin and Domestication: Studies on Inheritance', *Journal of the History of Biology* 25 (1992), pp. 307–33

Black, Joel, 'The Hermeneutics of Extinction: Denial and Discovery in Scientific Literature', in *Comparative Criticism Volume 13: Literature and Science*, ed. E. S. Shaffer (Cambridge: Cambridge University Press, 1991)

Burrow, John, *Evolution and Society: A Study in Victorian Social Theory* (Cambridge: Cambridge University Press, 1966)

Beer, Gillian, *Darwin's Plots: Evolutionary Narrative in Darwin, George Eliot and Nineteenth-Century Fiction* (London: Routledge & Kegan Paul, 1983; London: Ark, 1985)

——, 'Darwin and the Growth of Language Theory', in *Nature Transfigured: Science and literature, 1700–1900*, eds John Christie and Sally Shuttleworth (Manchester: Manchester University Press, 1989)

——, '"The Face of Nature": Anthropomorphic Elements in the Language of *The Origin of Species*', in *Languages of Nature: Critical Essays on Science and Literature*, ed. Ludmilla Jordanova (London: Free Association Books, 1986)

——, 'Darwin's Reading and the Fictions of Development', in *The Darwinian Heritage*, ed. David Kohn (Princeton: Princeton University Press, 1985)

Bowler, Peter J., 'The Changing Meaning of "Evolution"', *Journal of the History of Ideas* 36 (1975), pp. 95–114

Cannon, Walter F., 'Darwin's Vision in *The Origin of Species*', in *The Art of Victorian Prose*, eds George Levine and William Madden (London, New York and Toronto: Oxford University Press, 1968)

——, 'The Bases of Darwin's Achievement: A Revaluation', in *Victorian Studies* 5:2 (December 1961), pp. 109–34

Cornell, John F., 'Analogy and Technology in Darwin's Vision of Nature', *Journal of the History of Biology* 17 (1984), pp. 303–44

Crook, D.P., 'Darwinism – The Political Implications', *History of European Ideas* 2 (1981), pp. 19–34

Dear, Peter , *The Literary Structure of Scientific Argument* (Philadelphia: University of Pennsylvania, 1991)

Desmond, Adrian, *The Politics of Evolution: Morphology, Medicine, and Reform in Radical London* (Chicago: University of Chicago Press, 1989)

Desmon, Adrian, and James Moore, *Darwin* (London: Michael Joseph, 1991; Harmondsworth: Penguin, 1992)

Duffin, Lorna, 'Prisoners of Progress: Women and Evolution', in *The Nineteenth-Century Woman: Her Cultural and Physical World*, eds Sarah Delamont and Lorna Duffin (Beckenham: Croom Helm, 1978)

Ellegård, Alvar, *Darwin and the General Reader: The Reception of Darwin's Theory of Evolution in the British Periodical Press, 1859–1872* (Gothenburg: Elanders Boktryckeri Aktiebolag, 1958)

Evans, L. T., 'Darwin's Use of the Analogy between Artificial and Natural Selection' , *Journal of the History of Biology* 17 (1984), pp. 113–40

Fausto-Sterling, Anne, *Myths of Gender: Biological Theories about Women and Men* (New York: Basic Books, 1985)

Fee, Elizabeth, 'The Sexual Politics of Victorian Social Anthropology', in *Clio's Consciousness Raised: New Perspectives on the History of Women*, eds Mary S. Hartman and Lois Banner (New York: Harper & Row, 1974)

——, 'Women's Nature and Scientific Objectivity', in *Women's Nature: Rationalisations of Inequality*, eds Marion Lowe and Ruth Hubbard (Oxford: Pergamon, 1983)

Fleming, Donald, 'Charles Darwin, The Anaesthetic Man', *Victorian Studies* 4:3 (March 1961), pp. 219–36

Gerratana, V., 'Marx and Darwin', *New Left Review* 82 (Nov./Dec. 1973), pp. 60–82

Ghiselin, Michael T., 'The Individual in the Darwinian Revolution', *New Literary History* 3 (1972), pp. 113–34

Glick, T. F., *The Comparative Reception of Darwinism* (Austin: University of Texas Press, 1974)

Goff, Barbara Munson, 'Between Natural Theology and Natural Selection: Breeding the Human Animal in *Wuthering Heights*', *Victorian Studies* 27:4 (1984), pp. 477–508

Gould, Stephen Jay, *Ever Since Darwin: Reflections in Natural History* (New York and London: Norton, 1977)

Greene, John C., *The Death of Adam: Evolution and its Impact on Western Thought* (Ames: The Iowa State University Press, 1959)

——, 'Darwin as a Social Evolutionist', *Journal of the History of Biology*, 10:1 (spring 1977), pp. 1–27

Gruber, Howard E., and Paul H. Barrett, *Darwin on Man: A Psychological Study of Scientific Creativity, together with Darwin's Early and Unpublished Notebooks* (London: Wildwood House, 1974)

Hoenigswald, Henry M., and Linda F. Wiener, eds, *Biological Metaphor and Cladistic Classification: An Interdisciplinary Perspective* (Philadelphia: University of Pennsylvania Press, 1987)

Hubbard, Ruth , 'Have Only Men Evolved?' in *Discovering Reality*, eds Sandra Harding and Merrill B. Hintikka (Dordrecht: Reidel, 1983)

Hull, David, *Science as Process: An Evolutionary Account of the Social and Conceptual Development of Science* (Chicago: University of Chicago Press, 1988)

——, *Darwin and His Critics: The Reception of Darwin's Theory of Evolution by the Scientific Community* (Cambridge, MA: Harvard University Press, 1973)

Jones, Greta, *Social Darwinism and English Thought: The Interaction Between Biological and Social Theory* (Brighton: Harvester Press, 1980)

Jordanova, Ludmilla, ed., *Languages of Nature: Critical Essays on Science and Literature* (London: Free Association Books, 1986)

Keefe, Robert, 'Literati, Language, and Darwinism', *Language and Style* 19:2 (Spring 1986) , pp. 123–37

Knight, David, *Ordering the World: A History of Classifying Man* (London: Burnett Books, 1981)

Kohn, David, ed., *The Darwinian Heritage* (Princeton: Princeton University Press, 1985)

Krasner, James, 'A Chaos of Delight: Perception and Illusion in Darwin's Scientific Writing', *Representations* 31 (1990), pp. 118–41

Levine, George, *Darwin and the Novelists: Patterns of Science in Victorian Fiction* (Cambridge, MA: Harvard University Press, 1988)

Livingstone, David N., 'The Darwinian Diffusion: Darwin and Darwinism, Divinity and Design' *Christian Scholar's Review* 19:2 (1989) pp. 186–99

Mayr, Ernst, *The Growth of Biological Thought: Diversity, Evolution, and Inheritance* (Cambridge, MA: Harvard University Press, 1982)

James R. Moore, *The Post-Darwinian Controversies: A study of the Protestant struggle to come to terms with Darwin in Great Britain and America 1870–1900* (Cambridge: Cambridge University Press, 1979)

——, 'Darwin of Down: The Evolutionist as Squarson-Naturalist', in *The Darwinian Heritage*, ed. David Kohn (Princeton: Princeton University Press, 1985)

—— (Jim), 'Socializing Darwinism: Historiography and the Fortunes of a Phrase', in *Science as Politics*, ed. Les Levidow (London: Free Association Books, 1986)

Morton, Peter, *The Vital Science: Biology and the Literary Imagination, 1860–1900* (London: George Allen & Unwin, 1984)

Oldroyd, D., and I. Langham, eds, *The Wider Domain of Evolutionary Thought* (Dordrecht: Reidel, 1983)

Paradis, James, 'Darwin and Landscape', in *Victorian Science and Victorian Values: Literary Perspectives*, eds James Paradis and Thomas Postlewait (1981; New Brunswick: Rutgers University Press, 1985)

Panchen, Alec L. , *Classification, Evolution, and the Nature of Biology* (Cambridge: Cambridge University Press, 1992)

Pick, Daniel, *Faces of Degeneration: A European Disorder, c. 1848–c. 1918* (Cambridge: Cambridge University Press, 1989)

Rachels, J., 'Darwinism, Species, and Morality', *Monist* 10 (January 1987), pp. 98–113

Richards, Evelleen, 'Darwin and the Descent of Woman', in *The Wider Domain of Evolutionary Thought*, eds D. Oldroyd and I. Langham (Dordrecht: Reidel, 1983)

——, 'Huxley and Woman's Place in Science: The "Woman Question" and the Control of Victorian Anthropology' in *History, Humanity and Evolution: Essays for John C. Greene*, ed. James R. Moore (New York:

Cambridge University Press, 1989)

Ridley, Mark, *Evolution and Classification: The Reformation of Cladism* (London: Longman, 1986)

Ritvo, Harriet, *The Animal Estate: The English and Other Creatures in the Victorian Age* (Cambridge, MA: Harvard University Press, 1987)

——, 'The Power of the Word: Scientific Nomenclature and the Spread of Empire', *Victorian Newsletter* (spring 1990), pp. 5–8.

Russett, Cynthia Eagle, *Sexual Science: The Victorian Construction of Womanhood* (Cambridge MA: Harvard University Press, 1989)

Sayers, Janet, *Biological Politics: Feminist and Anti-Feminist Perspectives* (London and New York: Tavistock, 1982)

Secord, James A. , 'Nature's Fancy: Charles Darwin and the Breeding of Pigeons', *Isis* 72 (1985), pp. 163–186

Shapin, Steven, and Barry Barnes, 'Darwin and Social Darwinism: Purity and History', in *Natural Order: Historical Studies of Scientific Culture*, eds Barry Barnes and Steven Shapin (Beverly Hills and London: Sage Publications, 1979)

Smith, Charles K. , 'Logical and Persuasive Structures in Charles Darwin's Prose Style', *Language and Style* III:4 (1970), pp. 243–73

Stevens, L. Robert , 'Darwin's Humane Reading: The Anaesthetic Man Reconsidered', *Victorian Studies* 26:1 (Autumn 1982), pp. 51–63

Ulin, Donald , 'A Clerisy of Worms in Darwin's Inverted World', *Victorian Studies* 35:3 (spring 1992), pp. 294–308

Vorzimmer, Peter J., *Charles Darwin: The Years of Controversy: The Origin of Species and its Critics 1859–1882* (Philadelphia: Temple University Press, 1970)

Williams, Raymond , 'Social Darwinism', in *Problems in Materialism and Culture: Selected Essays* (London: Verso, 1980)

Winsor, Mary P. , *Starfish, Jellyfish and the Order of Life: Issues in Nineteenth-Century Science* (New Haven: Yale University Press, 1976)

Young, Robert M. , *Darwin's Metaphor: Nature's Place in Victorian Culture* (Cambridge: Cambridge University Press, 1985)

——, 'Darwin and the Genre of Biography', in *One Culture: Essays in Science and Literature*, ed. George Levine (Madison: University of Wisconsin Press, 1987)

Notes on contributors

DAVID AMIGONI   teaches English at the University of Sunderland. He has published essays on Matthew Arnold, the *Dictionary of National Biography*, and his book *Victorian Biography: Intellectuals and the Ordering of Discourse*, appeared in 1993.

TED BENTON   is Professor of Sociology at the University of Essex. His publications include *The Philosophical Foundations of the Three Sociologies* (1977), *The Rise and Fall of Structural Marxism* (1984), and his latest book, *Natural Relations: Ecology, Animal Rights and Social Justice*, was published in 1993. His current interests are in Green and Socialist social theory.

FIONA ERSKINE   lectures in modern British and American History at the University of Greenwich. She is the author of *Darwin in Context: the London Years 1837–42* (unpublished Pd.D. thesis, Open University, 1987).

KATE FLINT   is University Lecturer in Victorian and Modern English Language and Literature and Fellow of Linacre College, Oxford University. Her publications include *The Woman Reader, 1837–1914* (1993) and *Dickens* (1986), as well as numerous articles on nineteenth- and early twentieth-century fiction, painting and cultural history. She is currently working on a study of contemporary disruptions to Victorian systems of representation.

DERMOT KILLINGLEY   is Senior Lecturer in Religious Studies at the University of Newcastle upon Tyne, where he organises an annual seminar on 'The Sanskrit Tradition in the Modern World'. His publications include *Rammohun Roy in Hindu and Christian Tradition* (1993) and, with Robert Jackson, *Approaches to Hinduism* (1988).

HARRIET RITVO   is Professor in the History Faculty, Massachusetts Institute of Technology. She has been editor of the *Bulletin of the American Academy of Arts and Sciences* and book review editor of *Science, Technology and Human Values*. She is the author of *The Animal Estate: The English and Other Creatures in the Victorian Age* (1987) and editor, with Jonathan Arac, of *Macropolitics of Nineteenth-Century Literature: Nationalism, Exoticism, Imperialism* (1991).

JEFF WALLACE   is Senior Lecturer in Literary Studies at the University of Glamorgan. He has published essays on D. H. Lawrence, the relations between history of science and literary studies, Raymond Williams and Italo Calvino. He is currently working on a study of science in D. H. Lawrence's philosophical writing.

Index